Reading Public Romanticism

Reading Public Romanticism

Paul Magnuson

PRINCETON UNIVERSITY PRESS

PRINCETON, NEW JERSEY

Copyright © 1998 by Princeton University Press
Published by Princeton University Press, 41 William Street,
Princeton, New Jersey 08540
In the United Kingdom: Princeton University Press, Chichester, West Sussex

Library of Congress Cataloging-in-Publication Data

Magnuson, Paul.
Reading public Romanticism / Paul Magnuson.
p.   cm.
Includes bibliographical references and index.
ISBN 0-691-05794-X (cl : alk paper)
1. English poetry—19th century—History and criticism.   2. Literature
and society—Great Britain—History—19th century.   3. Authors and
readers—Great Britain—History—19th century.   4. English poetry—
18th century—History and criticism.   5. Public opinion—Great
Britain—History—19th century.   6. Public opinion— Great Britain—
History—18th century.   7. Public opinion in literature.   8. Romanticism—
Great Britain.   9. Speech acts (Linguistics)   10. Literary form.   I. Title.
PR590.M22   1998   821'.709145—dc21   97-33387

Publication of this book has been aided by the Abraham and Rebecca Stein
Faculty Publication Fund of New York University, Department of English

This book has been composed in Janson

Princeton University Press books are printed on acid-free paper,
and meet the guidelines for permanence and durability of the
Committee on Production Guidelines for Book Longevity
of the Council on Library Resources

http://pup.princeton.edu

Printed in the United States of America
1 3 5 7 9 10 8 6 4 2

In Memory of

Fannie Campbell Magnuson

CONTENTS

Acknowledgments	ix
Abbreviations and Key Words	xi
INTRODUCTION	3
CHAPTER ONE The Corresponding Society: The Public Discourse	11
CHAPTER TWO The Corresponding Society: Reading the Correspondence	37
CHAPTER THREE The Politics of "Frost at Midnight"	67
CHAPTER FOUR The Mariner's Extravagance and the Tempests of *Lyrical Ballads*	95
CHAPTER FIVE The Dedication of *Don Juan*	122
CHAPTER SIX Keats's "Leaf-Fringed Legend"	167
Index	211

ACKNOWLEDGMENTS

IN A BOOK that argues that works of literature are created and read in a dialogic and discursive exchange among many voices, it is a particular pleasure to acknowledge those who have contributed to its argument and documentation. I owe particular debts to those who have read early versions and made valuable suggestions: Jonathan Bate, Paul Elledge, Alice Fasano, Doucet Fischer, Kathleen Fowler, Dustin Griffin, Timothy Morton, and Aileen Ward. I would also like to thank those who have offered identifications and valuable bibliographical information, found obscure references, seen good jokes where others have seen none, explained references that I would have missed, assisted with the subtleties of translation and philological transmission, speculated on the dates of composition of manuscripts, challenged my readings and expanded the horizons of the tropes I discuss, and patiently answered my persistent queries: James Butler, Mary Carruthers, Chad Edgar, Angela Esterhammer, Lauren Fitzgerald, Bruce Graver, Lauren Henry, Geoffrey Hartman, John Kandl, Heather Masri, Raimonda Modiano, Robert Raymo, Nicholas Roe, Michael Scrivener, Mary Seabey, Daniel Senes, Jack Stillinger, George Thompson, Mike Wiley, Jonathan Wordsworth, and Duncan Wu.

Sections of all of the following chapters have been presented as conference papers, and I would like to thank those who made it possible for me to present works in progress: Stephen Parrish, Peter Manning, Tilottama Rajan and James McKucisk of the North American Society for the Study of Romanticism, Alice Levine of the Byron Society, Robert Ryan of the Keats-Shelley Association, Alan Richardson of the Center for Literary and Cultural Studies at Harvard, David Miall of the Coleridge Conference, and the late Richard Wordsworth of the Wordsworth Summer Conference at Grasmere. The audiences at these presentations were invariably helpful and generous in their responses. I owe particular gratitude to the scholars of Romanticism who gathered over a period of years at New York University to share our queries, conference papers, professional chat, and enthusiasm for a period of literature that is constantly being reconfigured and constantly providing pleasure and astonishment to us all.

For kind efficiency, helpful inquiries, and thoughtful readings, I thank my editors, Mary Murrell and Marta Steele. My gratitude also goes to my Chair, Josephine Hendin, who generously provided support for publication. Finally, I would like to thank Marilyn Gaull for permission to reprint my article "The Politics of 'Frost at Midnight'" from the *Wordsworth Circle* (Winter 1991) copyright © Marilyn Gaull.

ABBREVIATIONS AND KEY WORDS

AFA   *Annals of the Fine Arts* (1816–1820)

BL   *Biographia Literaria.* 2 vols. Ed. James Engell and W. Jackson Bate. Vol. 7 of *The Collected Works of Samuel Taylor Coleridge*, ed. Kathleen Coburn. Princeton: Princeton University Press, 1983.

BLJ   *Byron's Letters and Journals.* 12 vols. Ed. Leslie A. Marchand. Cambridge, Mass.: Harvard University Press, 1973–82.

BP   *Lord Byron: The Complete Poetical Works.* 7 vols. Ed. Jerome J. McGann. Oxford: The Clarendon Press, 1980–93.

CL   *Collected Letters of Samuel Taylor Coleridge.* 6 vols. Ed. Earl Leslie Griggs. Oxford: Clarendon Press, 1956–71.

CN   *The Notebooks of Samuel Taylor Coleridge.* 5 vols. Ed. Kathleen Coburn. Princeton: Princeton University Press, 1957–.

CP   *Complete Poetical Works of Samuel Taylor Coleridge.* 2 vols. Ed. Ernest Hartley Coleridge. Oxford: Clarendon Press, 1912.

EOT   *Essays on His Times in* The Morning Post *and* The Courier. 3 vols. Ed. David V. Erdman. Vol. 3 of *The Collected Works of Samuel Taylor Coleridge*, ed. Kathleen Coburn. Princeton: Princeton University Press, 1978.

Friend   *The Friend.* 2 vols. Ed. Barbara E. Rooke. Vol. 4 of *The Collected Works of Samuel Taylor Coleridge*, ed. Kathleen Coburn. Princeton: Princeton University Press, 1969.

FS   Samuel Taylor Coleridge, *Fears in Solitude.* 1798. Reprint edited by Jonathan Wordsworth, Oxford: Woodstock, 1989.

Haydon   *The Autobiography of Benjamin Robert Haydon.* Ed. Malcolm Elwin. London: Macdonald, 1853, 1950.

Howe   *The Complete Works of William Hazlitt.* 21 vols. Ed. P. P. Howe. London: M. M. Dent, 1930–34.

KC   *The Keats Circle.* 2d ed. 2 vols. Ed. Hyder Edward Rollins. Cambridge, Mass.: Harvard University Press, 1965.

KP   *John Keats: Complete Poems.* Ed. Jack Stillinger. Cambridge, Mass.: Harvard University Press, 1982.

Lect.   *Lectures 1795 On Politics and Religion.* Ed. Lewis Patton and Peter Mann. Vol. 1 of *The Collected Works of Samuel Taylor Coleridge*, ed. Kathleen Coburn. Princeton: Princeton University Press, 1971.

Margin.   *Marginalia.* 5 vols. Ed. H. J. Jackson and George Whalley. Vol. 12 of *The Collected Works of Samuel Taylor Coleridge*, ed.

             Kathleen Coburn. Princeton: Princeton University Press, 1980–.

OED   *Oxford English Dictionary.*

PAJ   *Poetry of the Anti-Jacobin.* 1799. Reprint edited by Jonathan Wordsworth, Oxford: Woodstock, 1991.

PJ   William Godwin, *Political Justice.* 1973. Reprint edited by Jonathan Wordsworth, Oxford: Woodstock, 1992.

PL   *Paradise Lost. John Milton: Complete Poems and Major Prose.* Ed. Merritt Y. Hughes. New York: Odyssey, 1957.

RR   *The Romantics Reviewed. Contemporary Reviews of British Romantic Writers.* Ed. Donald H. Reiman. New York: Garland, 1972. Unless otherwise noted, quotations from reviews are from this edition.

RRF   *Reflections on the Revolution in France. The French Revolution.* Ed. L. G. Mitchell. Vol. 8 of *The Writings and Speeches of Edmund Burke*, ed. Paul Langford. Oxford: Clarendon Press, 1989.

SIR   *Studies in Romanticism.*

SP   *Poems of Robert Southey.* Ed. Maurice H. Fitzgerald. London: Oxford University Press, 1909.

TT   *Table Talk.* 2 vols. Ed. Carl Woodring. Vol. 14 of *The Collected Works of Samuel Taylor Coleridge*, ed. Kathleen Coburn. Princeton: Princeton University Press, 1990.

Watchman *The Watchman.* Ed. Lewis Patton. Vol. 2 of *The Collected Works of Samuel Taylor Coleridge*, ed. Kathleen Coburn. Princeton: Princeton University Press, 1970.

WP   *The Poetical Works of William Wordsworth.* 5 vols. Ed. Ernest de Selincourt and Helen Darbishire. Oxford: Clarendon Press, 1940–49.

Reading Public Romanticism

INTRODUCTION

My FUNDAMENTAL argument is that much of the poetry published between 1789 and 1830 is public poetry, but that one cannot discover its public nature by reading individual works of literature apart from the public discourse that literature enters when it is published. Justice cannot be done to a work's literary and cultural significance by disregarding its various locations in collections of the author's own poetry, collaborative publications with several authors, reviews, newspapers, or anthologies. In their original publication with their verbal boundaries or frames, which are the crossroads of the discursive forms of cultural significance, their complex allusive figures, and their answerability, they appear as very different kinds of public utterances than those familiar to us in the late twentieth century. The public significance of a literary work rests, not in itself, not within its own generic boundaries, but in its locations for the simple reason that without precise location, there is no cultural significance.

I propose to read the locations of canonical Romantic poems in the public discourse. In recent years such poems have been contextualized by detailed examination of the history of their writing and publication as social and collaborative acts involving authors, editors, and publishers. They have also been contextualized by materialist analyses of the economic and social conditions of their production and of their ideology. While these methods contribute to my readings of locations, I am primarily interested in publication as an illocutionary and discursive speech act that responds to public debates and takes a stand on those issues. I locate the poems in the public discourse of politics, nationalism and domesticity, morality and sexuality as well as esthetics and will argue that the poems are neither isolated, integral reflections of imagination presented in a purely esthetic reading, nor tendentious denials and evasions of social issues, nor even unknowing repetitions of a suspect ideology presented by some historicist readings. Borrowing the strategies of conventional reading, I explore a methodology of historical close reading, of reading the public discourse that constitutes the discursive field in which literary works are located.

The immediate constraints on the public discourse from 1789 to 1830 are found in the law, which defined what could be published and circulated, and which is the material embodiment of ideology. Within the public discourse, the historical questions of cultural significance become questions of the laws of free speech. Thomas Erskine's point of law in his defense of Thomas Paine's publication of the second part of the *Rights of Man* may serve as a starting point and a caution for criticism: "A writing may undoubtedly proceed from a motive, and be directed to a purpose, not to be decyphered by the mere construction of the thing written" and that to prove libel, the primary charge against seditious writing in the late eighteenth century, requires "extrinsic facts and circumstances, *dehors the writing* ... that the defendant may know what crime he is called upon to answer, and how to stand upon his defense."[1] A defense offered in an eighteenth-century court or in the court of cultural criticism in the late twentieth century must go beyond the writing, beyond the individual poem to the works to which it responds. To read those connections, it is necessary to be precise as to a particular version of a work and its location. Many Romantic poems were first published in newspapers, reviews, anthologies, magazines, and collaborative volumes with several authors, each with its unique editorial policy, its own political views, and its class of readers. Many poems were also reprinted in different contexts and revised, sometimes radically, each time they were republished. The first step in reading a public Romanticism is to determine a work's location and relevant version.

I will explore a philological criticism that hears the nuances of individual words, common to literary and nonliterary writing, which form the linguistic connections from work to work. I will read a public rhetoric of Romanticism in allusion and quotation, rather than in symbol or allegory, in address rather than apostrophe, and in innuendo, primarily a legal term for a rhetoric that was defined in libel cases. Allusion is the most belated of rhetorical strategies and has been little explored in its reference to the nonliterary. In tracing the allusive complexity of a poetic utterance, the tactic of tracing a dialogue or dialectic is insufficient for a discursive reading because it supposes only two voices, echoing and responding, a binary opposition adequate to a more limited field of discourse, but inadequate to a complex circulation or flow in an environment of a multiplicity of voices. Simple dichotomies or oppositions do not adequately describe the complexity of utterances in the public discourse. To replace the model of a dialogue or dialectic with a freer form of circulation, however, is not to replace the fiercely oppositional nature of the public discourse or the class and gender interests involved. For any given word or figure, many voices and interests contribute to its public shades of meaning, no one of which is determining, no one of which can stand for the full meaning of a word. One major purpose of this book is to trace these manifold nuances and to read them in individual poems.

In this somewhat uncharted territory, I will regard paratext as an esthetic border constantly crossed and re-crossed, so that reading regularly moves across the paratext from poem to a previous public utterance. Gérard

---

[1] *The Whole Proceedings of the Trial of Thomas Paine*, in *The Prosecution of Thomas Paine: Seven Tracts, 1793–1798*, ed. Stephen Parks (New York: Garland, 1974) 110–11.

Genette has defined the paratext, generally the writing that surrounds a work, titles, prefaces, mottoes, and the like, as the means by which a book presents itself to a public; it makes the private writing a public *topos*, a public topic,[2] but I regard paratext as more than an entryway or threshold by which the reader enters the work. The pun on "entrance" suggests that it may be read as the boundary of the esthetic, and the paratext, merely as the archway to enchantment, in which case it would simply reinforce an esthetic reading. Yet paratext as used in the Romantic period is much more than an entrance. It is also an exit, the road of allusion to other works; it points to and responds to a public discourse that indicates subjects of social and political concern. For a historical reading of the public discourse, the problem of esthetics is not idealism or representation but the problem of the frame. My purpose is not to erase that frame or to submerge literature in the chatter and clatter of the public discourse. Rather, it is to restore the frames and read them as forms of mediation, as gestures of address, and as paths of allusion. Similarly, my purpose is not to read literature as ordinary language, but to read ordinary language as highly figurative.

Esthetics is thus a question not of literary form, but of locations. *Reading Public Romanticism* examines the generic structures of private poems in public places, particularly the genre of the letter, under the assumption that the genre is changed with a change of location and paratext. The public space of Romanticism is the book and the periodical. I study the mediation of the public press, in which the literary is transformed when its rhetoric is echoed in the public discourse. I read authors by reading their signatures as those supplementary signatures are read and caricatured in the public space of the book and the periodical. Such readings constitute an attempt at a historical close reading. A significant irony in twentieth-century criticism of subjective, first-person lyric poetry is that the very reason that it appears to be utterly self-involved is that its public utterance is always under the personal sign of the author, and yet in publication that personal sign is a mark of a public standing. Public authorship is a location in the discourse defined by its intertextual connections. So defined, publicness does not efface subjectivity; it augments it.

Reading locations and paratexts is a method of reading the gaps, the blank spaces, that appear between text and context in twentieth-century historical orderings of Romantic literature. Alan Liu has pointedly remarked that "a New Historicist paradigm holds up to view a historical context on one side, a literary text on the other, and, in between, a connection of pure nothing."[3]

[2] Gérard Genette, "Introduction to the Paratext," trans. Marie Maclean, *New Literary History* 22 (1991): 261–72. See also Genette, *Paratexts: Thresholds of Interpretation*, trans. Jane E. Lewin (Cambridge: Cambridge University Press, 1997).

[3] Alan Liu, "The Power of Formalism: The New Historicism," *English Literary History* 56 (1989): 743.

Reading the writing around a poem, reading the location, requires reading a particular version of a poem in the unique details of its publication, the material specificity of its utterance. The more precise one is about that particular utterance, the clearer the connections between text and context become. Liu has justifiably complained that the gaps are too often bridged by the vague notion of metaphorical connection or resemblance; reading locations, reading the paratext, fills those gaps with transcribed transitions. If the writing around a poem is read as a narrow, isolating frame or rigid boundary, then it merely confirms a formalism that separates it from other writing. If, on the other hand, one reads paratext as a located frame without boundaries either in the interior or exterior of a work, it forges connections to other writings and begins to trace the public discourse.

The frame, in other words, points to the mediation of the work that makes it public. A criticism that would escape the confinements of formalism must read the frame. Trying to determine the public and historical significance of a poem or novel by reading only the interior is a procedure limited from the start and inevitably confined to a late-twentieth-century presentness, from which it cannot exit because its artifacts have been arranged to suit its unexamined esthetic assumptions. The persistent incompatibility of esthetic readings with historical readings where public concerns are construed within the boundaries of the esthetic lead to readings that are merely an allegory of the method used to produce the reading. History becomes bound to the present moment by an esthetic of isolating boundaries. Regarding the esthetic as either a negation of social conditions or a utopian vision of what does not exist is unfortunately of little help in practical criticism. One ends up by decoding what one has previously and silently encoded in a work. One must begin, not with the purely esthetic, but with its boundaries, with the particular versions and instances. To begin with the particular and the local utterance is not to remain confined to the local as though it were an isolated artifact. On the contrary, I begin with the local version and its paratext because there a poem's connections to other utterances are to be found, often in abundance.

The local, in this study, is what is located, not what is isolated by determinate negation or exclusion. To read literature we must have esthetic boundaries and, at the same time, we must transgress them by reading them closely. I present examples of this method of reading from the canonical male poets for several reasons, the most immediate of which is that those are the ones that I know best. They are also the poems most written about in criticism, and for many one can identify a standard or received opinion, even considering the differences among interpreters. It is my conviction that reading public Romanticism changes these traditional readings and questions historicists and cultural critics who have accused the Romantic poets of selfish inhumanity and irresponsible evasions of social issues. Such evasions are possible in private writing, but not in publication, because to publish is to become public, to enter a mediated discourse that resonates with public issues. Shifting focus from private manuscripts to published works is a preliminary step in reading the locations and the paratexts and in generalizing about the cultural significance either in the Romantic period or our own time. I offer these essays as practical historical criticism and as close reading of the literature itself. The canonical literature may appear new and strange, and although I concentrate on commonly read texts, I am confident that this method of reading the public nature of literature will be useful for works that we are now reading, especially those of the laboring and uneducated poor, radical dissenters, unjustly neglected women writers, and slave narratives of the large community of freed African slaves in Britain in the late eighteenth century.

As a brief example of the paratext's significance in the public discourse, I offer *Poems on Various Subjects* (1773) by "Phillis Wheatley, Negro Servant to Mr. John Wheatley, of Boston, in New England," as announced on the title page, first published in London.[4] The volume begins with a Preface, a letter from John Wheatley giving a one-page biography of Phillis, and an "Attestation" addressed "To the Publick." The attestation was not published with the first edition but was included in subsequent editions in 1773. It was circulated, however, before publication as an advertisement in several newspapers. In Britain in 1773 "the Publick" was, as I shall discuss in Chapter 1, not synonymous with the entire population, but composed of a limited number of educated and enfranchised property owners, who would believe that a slave could not read, let alone write. The attestation states that although many "would be ready to suspect that they were not really the Writings of Phillis. . . . She has been examined by some of the best Judges, and is thought qualified to write them." The attestation is then signed by "His Excellency Thomas Hutchinson, Governor" and "The Hon. Andrew Oliver, Lieutenant-Governor" along with five gentlemen bearing the title "The Hon.," three dignified by "Esq.," seven titled "The Rev.," and Wheatley at the end of the list signified only by "Mr." They can attest to the "Publick" because they constitute the public. Without being public, one cannot easily publish, enter into the public discourse, or speak in public without the sponsorship or patronage of someone in the public, preferably someone who possesses some title above the rank of mere "Mr." A personal name alone does not constitute the authority to enter the public discourse, and, as a result, public signatures must include signs of nobility, professional standing, university degree, or similar signs of rank. The word *attestation* is

---

[4] *The Collected Works of Phillis C. Wheatley*, ed. John C. Shields (New York: Oxford University Press, 1988). vii. Henry Louis Gates, Jr., discusses the attestation in *Loose Canons: Notes on the Culture Wars* (New York: Oxford University Press, 1992) 51–55.

specifically legal. The *OED* cites Blackstone: "The last requisite to the validity of a deed is the attestation, or execution of it in the presence of witnesses." Obviously without the attestation, the poems as deeds are invalid. Since the word *attestation* embodies an "oath," or "test" as it was called in the eighteenth century, the poem's legal validity rests on Scripture. With the attestation, the poetry and the author are valid and legal. The certification of their validity and authenticity comprises their legitimacy. The implicit assumption made by public figures is that they form a legally constituted circle, an assumption enforced later in the eighteenth century by treason and libel trials and attempts to suppress the freedom of speech.

There are dangers in reading public Romanticism that must, in the economics of criticism, concentrate upon the differences between received readings and those available for select versions in historical close readings. The obvious problems, those of the unfamiliarity of the texts and locations, the destabilizations of idealized readings, the dispersal of a text through the public discourse, and the apparent capriciousness of the connections between text and context that prompt one to ask why one or another context is more appropriate than any other, are of minor significance. The original publications are now being reprinted in photographic reproduction, and newer means of computer publication will, I hope, make it possible to present many versions of one work. The play between located texts and received readings will generate fuller readings of poems while at the same time they unmask many of our assumptions about what, for these many years, we have been reading. Dispersion of a text in such ways is not destruction; on the contrary, one should always return to the text to read its figures with a richer understanding of their nuances and innuendoes. If one reads through or across the paratextual boundaries, the transcribed transitions of a work to its exterior, the associations of text and context are neither capricious nor arbitrary. The more serious problem is the danger of paratextual memorializing, a changing of a text to a rigid historical artifact. Such a memorialization, such representation of a particular textual moment, binds the work to the public discourse. While memorialization remembers what the lapses of history have effaced, memorialization locates a version as a distant, unchanging, and unspeaking monument, silent about its prefiguring of our own intelligence. The frame should not be the prison or crypt in which the enigma code is only partially read. Such location, in our times, is not enough, since a poem as a bound memorial will almost inevitably be lost in the burdensome bounty of other such representations. Perhaps in the play among such memorials, we can generate a possible knowledge and revitalize a private and a public imagination. One "On a Grecian Urn" will not do, whether it is a modern esthetic object or a bound historical memorial.

The first section of this book describes a method of reading literature in the public discourse. Chapter 1 begins with Jürgen Habermas's definition of the "public sphere" and his inadequate historical description and proceeds to substitute and define a "public discourse," constituted by all published or privately circulated writing. The immediate constraints on the public discourse were legal limits on the freedom of speech, so the public discourse, as the literature that was located in it, was highly figurative. Unlike the discontinuous discourses defined by exclusion, as Michel Foucault described, the public discourse was composed of topics that were highly figurative of public issues. Reading public Romanticism in such circumstances is a reading of the claims of the esthetic that rest in the connections between text and context and are inscribed on the borders of poems. One must read the frame that, as Derrida suggests, is both inside and outside the poem, and essential meaning mere extrinsic decoration. My readings do not separate background and foreground in which the literary work is explained in terms of a set of ideas or material conditions; rather, the poem speaks in and to the public discourse. The poem is not only an incarnation of an idea or consciousness, but a temporally located performance or recitation. The problem of esthetics is not, in this method, a problem of mere surfaces, nor of purposeless commodities. Nor is it a problem of idealism. Esthetics is the problem of the frame and its location. To explore the inscribed frame or transition between poems within a volume, I offer a reading of the title page and allusive motto, *paulò majora canamus*, that precedes Wordsworth's "Ode" in *Poems in Two Volumes*.

Chapter 2 explores the genres and rhetoric of the public discourse. When literary genres are placed in the public press, they assimilate the conventions of public discursive writing and cannot be fully read only in their literary genres. The discursive genre closest to Romantic lyric poetry is the public letter that is located, addressed, signed, allusive, and mediated. As an example of a lyric that changes its genre when located in the public discourse, I offer a reading of Coleridge's "This Lime-Tree Bower My Prison," which in its first publication in Southey's *Annual Anthology* is framed as a public letter to Charles Lamb signed by Coleridge as "ESTEESI," a signature that re-sites the poem on the trope of standing.

Subsequent chapters locate and read canonical poems through their allusive and apostrophic paratexts. Chapter 3 explores Coleridge's "Frost at Midnight" in *Fears in Solitude* (1798) as a public defense of accusations that he is seditious and unpatriotic. The entire volume is a public speech act in the court of public opinion. Chapter 4 reads "The Ancient Mariner" in *Lyrical Ballads* (1798) defined by its reviewers as a German poem. The word *German* in the public discourse meant "Jacobin" in the 1790s. If "The Ancient Mariner" was read as a Jacobin poem, then the trope of tempest throughout *Lyrical Ballads* may be read as the volume's major trope signifying social turmoil. The final two chapters explore the issue of poetic and political legitimacy. Chapter 5 reads the paratextual Dedication to *Don Juan* as an address to Southey composed from many of the reviews and parodies of Southey's laureate verse and the satire on him in the public press. Finally, Chapter 6 reads the "leaf-fringed legend" in "On a Grecian Urn" in the *Annals of the Fine Arts*, where it supports the esthetics of Haydon, Hazlitt, and Richard Payne Knight—an esthetics that opposed not only the ideal art of Sir Joshua Reynolds, but the system of patronage that supported the Royal Academy and what Hazlitt called legitimacy.

My purpose in these readings is not to argue that they should substitute for received opinion, or even that they are more historically accurate than readings in which the poems are differently located. Substitution of one reading for another is the exchange of one form of blindness for another. For literary and cultural self-knowledge, both traditional and historical, discursive readings are necessary. They mark a difference in which our knowledge may be consciousness of itself. The exchange between readings is not, or need not be, random play. The particular version that one reads is not, nor should be, a matter of some indifference. With the exception of the Dedication to *Don Juan*, I have not discussed explicitly political poems for the simple reason that for the canonical writers, these poems have been adequately explicated. I have focused on lyric poems commonly considered nonpolitical because their public significance has been lost in the late twentieth century, and because that significance is uncovered through reading their allusive paratexts. If these readings destabilize the ideal objects that these poems are often taken to be, the loss is compensated, I hope, with a richer consciousness of their horizons of allusion. If this method's esthetic assumptions provide a recompense, it is in understanding. Location is all. To read a poem in different locations, to read the frame, to read public Romanticism is not only to read a more complex poem, but also to become aware of the critical assumptions that have made reading the frame difficult in the past. It makes us ask questions about our own locations and those of the poems that we read. Historical discourse in general and literature in particular are clothed and cloaked by our own unquestioned assumptions.

Chapter One

THE CORRESPONDING SOCIETY: THE PUBLIC DISCOURSE

IN THESE TWO opening chapters, I offer a preliminary sketch of the public discourse from 1789 to 1830, a survey of paratextual conventions, and readings of poems to illustrate their significance within the field of discourse. We commonly read Romantic poetry in anthologies or editions of an author's works that illustrate the author's poetic development, or else read it in anthologies that sample Romantic literature, where the context of literature is literature itself. With such editions, scholars such as David Erdman, Carl Woodring, and Kenneth Cameron have mapped the explicit political and social themes in Romantic literature, the allusions to contemporary events, the terms of political debate, and the evolution of a writer's political thought. More needs to be done with the politics of writers relatively neglected in the twentieth century, particularly women and the laboring poor, but it should be done with an awareness of the discursive field in which their works are published. My method is to locate a work in the discourse and then to read its significance. Although this procedure places a priority on discursive networks rather than on the individual work, it does not reduce authorial intention to a historical illusion or minimize it as mere agency. To center a discussion of political and social thought exclusively within the individual expressive acts of single authors is to ignore writing's inevitable public nature. To define that public nature, it is necessary to explore a public discourse.

In *The Structural Transformation of the Public Sphere*, Jürgen Habermas described a public sphere as it developed in eighteenth-century England from merchants' associations and coffee-house discussions, a bourgeois society that gathered to create and sustain a market for private individuals separate from the intrusions of church and state. In a century of emerging capitalism, private individuals came "together as a public" for the purposes of "commodity exchange and social labor": "The fully developed bourgeois public sphere was based on the fictitious identity of the two roles assumed by the privatized individuals who came together to form a public: the role of property owners and the role of human beings pure and simple."[1] Their

---

[1] Jürgen Habermas, *The Structural Transformation of the Public Sphere: An Inquiry into a Category of Bourgeois Society*, trans. Thomas Burger and Frederick Lawrence (Cambridge, Mass.: MIT Press, 1991) 27, 56. See also "Romanticism and Its Publics," a special number of *SIR* (Winter 1994), ed. Jon Klancher.

humanity was expressed by the publication of private letters of feeling, the great epistolary novels of the eighteenth century; and their private interests as owners of capital motivated a rational inquiry into the general good. The public discussion, conducted in the increasing number of journals and magazines, transformed a social sphere based on the arbitrary display of courtly power into a "public competition of private arguments" that led to a "consensus about what was practically necessary in the interest of all" (83). This consensus, he argued, formed the basis of the modern constitutional state, that is, individual rights of free speech and assembly.

Habermas dated the decline of the English public sphere to about 1832 with the Chartist movement, which he claimed so divided public opinion that no consensus was possible, and to a time later in the nineteenth century when the state began to regulate the marketplace and control public opinion. Up to that point, he argues, "a certain rationality admittedly expressed itself in the reasonable forms of public discussion as well as in the convergence of opinions regarding the standards of criticism and the goal of polemics" (131), a rationality that he implies is fundamentally a calculation of an independent individual's economic self-interest. Habermas's account agrees with the assumptions of Edmund Burke and William Godwin that rational discourse on public matters should be restricted to a limited circle of educated, enfranchised men. Terry Eagleton has pointed out in *The Function of Criticism*, however, that there was a "counter-public sphere" in the corresponding societies, political associations, dissenting churches, and in the radical press represented by such journalists as Daniel Isaac Eaton, Thomas Spence, and William Cobbett. To Eagleton, the "'public sphere' is a notion difficult to rid of nostalgic, idealizing connotations; like the 'organic society,' it sometimes seems to have been disintegrating since its inception." The exchange among free and autonomous individuals is an idealization of "real bourgeois social relations."[2] In the view of those within the public sphere in the 1790s, a clear boundary existed between the public and the private, but if one changes perspective with Eagleton and looks outside the public sphere, one hears diverse individuals speaking out. For those within the public sphere, its boundaries should be preserved; for those

---

[2] Terry Eagleton, *The Function of Criticism: From* The Spectator *to Post-Structuralism* (London: Verso, 1984) 36, 8, 26. See other criticisms of Habermas in Oskar Negt and Alexander Kluge, *The Public Sphere and Experience: Toward an Analysis of the Bourgeois and Proletarian Public Sphere*, trans. Peter Labanyi et al. (Minneapolis: University of Minnesota Press, 1993); *Habermas and the Public Sphere*, ed. Craig Calhoun (Cambridge, Mass.: MIT Press, 1992); and *The Phantom Public Sphere*, ed. Bruce Robbins (Minneapolis: University of Minnesota Press, 1993). For a survey of the idea of a "republic of letters," see Dustin Griffin, "Fictions of Eighteenth Century Authorship," *Essays in Criticism* 43 (1993): 181–94. For samples of the debate, see *Burke, Paine, Godwin, and the Revolution Controversy*, ed. Marilyn Butler (Cambridge: Cambridge University Press, 1984).

outside the public sphere, the boundaries exist only to be crossed, violated, or ignored.

In place of Habermas's public sphere, I offer a description of a public discourse that is far more inclusive. By "public" I mean works that are published and thus exist in a public space, available to any reader who can afford to buy them, or who receives them through free distribution by either reformist or conservative societies, or who hears magazines or newspapers read in public houses and meetings. A published and circulated work is both a material object and the site of public debates. The public discourse includes the pamphlet warfare on the principles and events of the French Revolution beginning in 1789 with Dr. Richard Price's *Discourse on the Love of our Country*, answered by Burke's *Reflections on the Revolution in France* and the flood of pamphlets answering Burke.[3] The public discourse also includes the publications of the periodical press, the newspapers, reviews, and magazines, whose number and circulation were expanding rapidly during these years. It includes as well records of parliamentary debates and trials, published versions of lectures and sermons, and printed texts of dramatic performances. Some of these sources are reasonably reliable records of what was actually said. Others, such as printed texts of addresses or dramatic performances, may be intentionally inaccurate records and must be used with caution. Coleridge's 1795 Bristol lectures, for instance, may have been published in a form less likely to be judged seditious in order to avoid accusations of sedition from those who heard them. Also dramatic texts were changed in performance. Sheridan deleted speeches in his adaptation of Kotzebue's *Pizarro* and inserted his own from Parliament.[4] It is not possible to recover the spoken word, with all the nuances of oral expression, so a tracing of the public discourse must rely on the written word, which was available to a wide audience and capable of being reviewed and reread.

There was, in addition, the practice of the private circulation of literary works, which, although not frequently a factor in the debates on public issues, offers an opportunity to trace the circulation of a work and its audience. Legally, circulation of any kind constituted publication. William Wickwar explains that publication "included the wholesale selling which we call publishing; but it also included retailing, and booksellers and newsvenders were therefore publishers at law. Furthermore, to let what one had

---

[3] For an analysis of this debate, see James T. Boulton, *The Language of Politics in the Age of Wilkes and Burke* (London: Routledge & Kegan Paul, 1963) and Olivia Smith, *The Politics of Language, 1791–1819* (Oxford: Clarendon Press, 1984). For samples of the controversy, see Butler (above, n. 2). Boulton includes a "Chronological Survey of the Controversy Concerning Burke's *Reflections*, 1790–93." A similar list is in Appendix C of *RRF*.

[4] *The London Stage: 1660–1800. Part 5, 1776–1800*, ed. Charles Beecher Hogan (Carbondale: Southern Illinois University Press, 1968) 2097.

written come into the hands of another person, even without any publicity, was an act of publication." In the eyes of the law, "publishing is a popular term and it is a legal term; legally speaking every seller of printed matter is a publisher."[5] Coleridge's "Christabel" is an obvious example of a work that before its publication circulated in manuscript, was read at social gatherings, was imitated, and was well known to the Wordsworths, Scott, Hazlitt, and Byron. Tracing the circulation of unprinted manuscripts forms an important element in the history of the poem, its publication with Coleridge's apologetic preface, its reviews, and Coleridge's subsequent revisions and annotations in presentation copies. Some works were privately printed. The most notorious instance was Byron's private printing of fifty copies of two poems on his separation, "Fare Thee Well" and "A Sketch from Private Life." Within a week, John Scott published them in *The Champion* with severe criticism of Byron, causing a scandal.[6] Byron seemed determined to repeat the mistake when Murray's advisors insisted that the Dedication to *Don Juan* be omitted, and he insisted that fifty copies be printed for private circulation. Even without that private printing, the Dedication was well known, since detailed word of it reached Southey in the Lake District. The tracing of circulation of manuscripts defines a writer's first audience, an audience that is in a position to comment, to respond, to imitate, and to criticize. This answerability, whether it takes place in the privacy of a drawing room or in the public press, constitutes one form of the discourse that surrounds a work. As James T. Boulton remarked, once a "pamphlet is published it becomes part of a highly fluid situation; its words may be pillaged and distorted or, owing to some new factor, it may be necessary to redirect the pamphlet to an audience for which it was not originally intended," (259) such as happened to abridgments of Burke's *Reflections on the Revolution in France*.

The larger audience may be defined in a number of ways. Literary production was a social act, and some recent critics, following Jerome McGann's suggestions, have insisted that the history of its printing and sale form part of its significance.[7] Some works such as Southey's *Joan of Arc* were printed in expensive quarto format intended for a wealthy audience. A public may therefore be defined by its economic status. But as Jon Klancher has so ably shown, it is possible to segment readers into various interest groups in the same way that individual journals and reviews took political positions: a middle-class audience, a mass audience, a polemical and radical audience, and an institutional audience, all of which are defined not as much by their

[5] William H. Wickwar, *The Struggle for the Freedom of the Press, 1819–32* (London: George Allen & Unwin, 1928) 19, 96.

[6] See David V. Erdman's article on Byron's poems in *Shelley and His Circle*, ed. Kenneth Neill Cameron (Cambridge, Mass.: Harvard University Press, 1970) 4: 638–53.

[7] Jerome J. McGann, *Beauty of Inflections: Literary Investigations in Historical Method and Theory* (Oxford: Clarendon Press, 1985) 69–89.

economic class as by their ability to read semiotically, to read the signs and the theatricality of public significance.[8] Since I am interested in the forms of literature's discursive responsiveness, I am less concerned with anonymous readers as consumers and construers of a material product, or with theories of exchange value in an age when the much radical as well as the most conservative literature for the lower classes was freely distributed. I will not attempt to document the reactions of silent readers, either individually or collectively, by inferring their readings from evidence within the text itself, always a highly speculative procedure. I will emphasize the responsive nature of reading, the significance of a work's answerability, the ways in which it is shaped both by what has previously been uttered and by potential responses.

In his *First Letter on a Regicide Peace* (1796), Burke calculated the numbers of the British public:

> We are a divided people. . . . I have often endeavoured to compute and to class those who, in any political view, are to be called the people. . . . In England and Scotland, I compute that those of adult age, not declining in life, of tolerable leisure for [political] discussions, and of some means of information, more or less, and who are above menial dependence . . . may amount to about four hundred thousand. . . . This is the British publick; and it is a publick very numerous. The rest, when feeble, are the objects of protection; when strong, the means of force.

Of this number, Burke calculates that one-fifth are "pure Jacobins; utterly incapable of amendment; objects of eternal vigilance; and when they break out, of legal constraint. On these, no reason, no argument, no example, no venerable authority, can have the slightest influence."[9] In 1796 Burke defined a Jacobin as one who opposed the war with France and claimed that the Jacobins hoped that if the war were ended, the rest of their political program would succeed. Burke's definition of a British public, separate from the institutions of government yet still a legitimate voice of the people and a natural expression of a public opinion, includes the two elements commonly assumed as qualifications for entering what Habermas calls the public sphere: education and enfranchisement based on some form of property. Burke's "numerous" public includes not only those whose opinions are published but all those who are able to engage in some form of public discussion. If we think of all who expressed opinions, Burke's numbers may be far too small. Surely thinking of Paine's *Rights of Man* and Thelwall's lectures, Burke recognizes that those who oppose the war will not be per-

---

[8] Jon P. Klancher, *The Making of English Reading Audiences, 1790–1832* (Madison: University of Wisconsin Press, 1987).

[9] *The Writings and Speeches of Edmund Burke*, ed. R. B. McDowell and William B. Todd (Oxford: Clarendon Press, 1991) 9: 223–24.

suaded by others. Thus, while he includes Jacobins in his calculations, he leaves them out of his dialogue and recognizes that the British public is so sharply divided that no fruitful or reasonable debates can occur. The goal of Habermas's idealized public sphere is to reach a consensus, which Burke knew was impossible.

Burke's fear of Jacobin intransigence—the clamorous meetings of the London Corresponding Society for example—and his admission that they were unconvinced by his rhetoric was shared on the opposite end of the political spectrum by William Godwin, who in *Political Justice* (1793) expressed wariness of public meetings designed to arouse the populace. In a section titled "Of Political Associations," Godwin defined associations as "voluntary confederacies of certain members of the society with each other, the tendency of which is to give weight to the opinions of the persons so associated." With a fear similar to Burke's, he warned that "associations must be formed with great caution not to be allied to tumult. The conviviality of a feast may lead to the depredations of a riot. . . . There is nothing more barbarous, cruel and bloodthirsty, than the triumph of a mob." Further agreeing with Burke, he was certain that political discussion must originate in "the conceptions of persons of some degree of study and reflection. . . . Society, as it at present exists in the world, will long be divided into two classes, those who have leisure for study, and those whose importunate necessities perpetually urge them to temporary industry." Leisure and some means of education were necessary for the few to deliberate and to disseminate their policies. These few individuals are "prepared by mutual intercourse, to go forth to the world, to explain with succinctness and simplicity, and in a manner well calculated to arrest attention, the true principles of society. . . . Reason will spread itself, and not a brute and unintelligent sympathy" (*PJ* 1: 205–14).

Coleridge's notion of a clerisy, focused on a national church but including the learned professions[10] as the legitimating deliberative body in the nation, differs from Burke's and Godwin's notion of a popular voice, of a Socratic and rational debate, only in that Coleridge saw it institutionalized in the Church, where it was located later in the nineteenth century alongside the clerisy of the academy. Hazlitt disagrees. In an essay titled "What is the People?" he seems to agree with Habermas that "the people" is the opposite of hereditary government but extends membership in "the people" much more widely than does Habermas. For Hazlitt, the voice of the people is public opinion and universal suffrage (Howe 7: 259–81). Yet for Burke, Godwin, and Coleridge, the public debates, the rancorous and passionate uproar, was less than rational and polite conversation. Coleridge

---

[10] *On the Constitution of the Church and State*, ed. John Colmer (Princeton: Princeton University Press, 1976) 46. See also *TT* 1: 285.

complained in the first of his *Lectures on Shakespeare and Milton* (1811) when he enumerated the impediments to a just criticism: "the enormous multiplication of Authors & Books—At first Oracles, then preceptors, then agreeable Companions, but now Culprits by anticipation—& they act accordingly flattering basely the imaginary Word, *Public*—which is yet of pernicious effect by habituating every Reader to consider himself as the Judge & therefore the Superior of the Writer who yet if he has any justifiable claim to write ought to be his Superior."[11] Authors had lost the aura of their authority. The public, in the individual voices of tendentious reviewers, assumes the role of audience and legitimating jury.

The fractious debates in the public press were not confined to political topics. Morality, politics, esthetics, religion, and philosophy were so intricately combined that one commonly implied the others. Jacobins were portrayed as not only democrats or republicans, but also as immoral materialists, atheists, and theophilanthropists, who wanted to replace Christianity with a form of deism. In an age that debated Burke's principles of inherited monarchy and established church, of primogeniture, and of the nationalistic value of domestic affections, even domesticity and the intimate spheres of private affections and sensibility had political and social implications.[12] When Coleridge eulogizes an ass, or when Southey apostrophizes a frog, mammals and amphibians are not the issue. Mary Wollstonecraft's *Vindication of the Rights of Women* and Helen Maria Williams's *Letters from France* with tales of domestic tyranny, no less than Wordsworth's "Vaudracour and Julia" and Shelley's *Cenci*, parallel domestic tyranny with political tyranny, a comparison common in English political controversies since at least the time of the Puritan revolution in the seventeenth century. Distinctions between disciplines or subjects were not recognized. For example, literature is cited in the law. Thomas Erskine defended Thomas Paine by invoking a precedent in English Law that "extracts from authors of high reputation" could be cited in courts and quoted extensively from Paley, Locke, Milton, Harrington, and Doctor Johnson to defend the liberty of the press. Poems in the public discourse are not exclusively about their manifest subject. The public discourse is highly rhetorical, rather than literal and rational. Reading highly figurative literature within a complexly duplicitous public discourse, further complicates the rhetoric of the literature that we have read in the twentieth century removed from that context or, as Erskine said, removed from what is "*dehors the writing*."[13] We have seen political signifi-

---

[11] *Lectures 1808–1819 On Literature*, ed. R. A. Foakes (Princeton: Princeton University Press, 1987) 1: 186–87. See also *BL* 1: 57 and *Friend* 2: 86.

[12] For the role of feeling, see Seamus Deane, *The French Revolution and Enlightenment in England, 1789–1832* (Cambridge, Mass.: Harvard University Press, 1988).

[13] *The Whole Proceedings on the Trial . . . Thomas Paine* (1793) in *The Prosecution of Thomas Paine: Seven Tracts, 1793–98*, ed. Stephen Parks (New York: Garland, 1974) 118, 111.

cance in Romantic literature only when it is explicit or when it appears to be conspicuously absent.

Law circumscribed the public debates. What one could say publicly was determined by a series of court decisions, proclamations, and acts of Parliament that dealt with the problems of prosecuting treason and seditious libel and determining who was authorized to judge whether a figurative statement constituted a criminal act. Dissidents were often tried in cases of seditious or blasphemous libel. Before 1790 the government defined both the meaning, or the *innuendo*, of writing and the criminal intention, usually the intention to stir up popular resentment against the monarch. The word *innuendo* in the eighteenth century was a legal term for words not in themselves actionable but intended to be injurious by implication. The only decision that a jury could make was whether the accused actually published or sold a work that the government had previously decided was a seditious libel. In 1791 Charles James Fox introduced a bill in the House of Commons, which passed the following year, that gave to juries, not to the government, the power to judge whether a publication was libelous and whether there was criminal intent to cause general disaffection, although in many instances the government could easily pack juries. The major issue was the freedom of the press.[14] Michael Scrivener has astutely analyzed the trial of Daniel Isaac Eaton for publishing Thelwall's allegory of "King Chaunticlere; or, The Fate of Tyranny," in *Politics for the People, or Hog's Wash* in 1793. Thelwall's fable introduced a "game cock" as a barnyard tyrant, which the indictment claimed intended to "denote and represent our said Lord the King." Thelwall's fable recounts his exasperation at the bird's tyranny and his solution of decapitating him. The defense asked the jury to determine whether this was or was not the appropriate innuendo, arguing that the British monarch was represented by a lion and the French, by a cock, since the Latin word for "rooster" was *gallus*. Eaton was acquitted by a clever reading of innuendo.[15] Consequently, Thomas Spence printed "Examples of Safe Printing" in *Pig's Meat* (1794), in which the italicized passages parody the innuendo included in indictments against seditious writing:

> To prevent misrepresentation in these prosecuting times, it seems necessary to publish every thing relating to Tyranny and Oppression, though only among brutes, in the most guarded manner.

[14] A. Aspinall, *Politics and the Press, c. 1780–1850* (1949; rept. London: Home & Van Thal, 1973), 37. See also *Five Tracts on Libel Addressed to Charles James Fox 1791–92*, ed. Stephen Parks (New York: Garland, 1974).

[15] See Michael Scrivener's forthcoming *Literary Jacobinism and British Romanticism*. See also *The Trial of Daniel Isaac Eaton for Publishing a Supposed Libel* (1794), in *Daniel Issac Eaton and Thomas Paine: Five tracts 1793–1812*, ed. Stephen Parks (New York: Garland, 1974). Thelwall's allegory is reprinted in Butler (above, n. 2) 186–88.

The following are meant as Specimens:—

That tyger, or that other salvage wight
Is so exceeding furious and fell,
   As WRONG,
                   [*Not meaning our most gracious sovereign Lord*
                     the King, or the Government of this country]
                when it hath arm'd himself with might;
Not fit 'mong men that do with reason mell,
But 'mong wild beasts and salvage woods to dwell;
   Where still the stronger
              [*Not meaning the great men of this country*]
              doth the weak devour,
And they that most in boldness doe excell,
   And draded most, and feared by their powre.
                  E. Spencer[16]

As an incident in literary history, Spence's trial is trivial, but it does indicate, first, a shift in determining what one can say publicly from the government to the jury, the representatives of the people, and, second, the problems in prosecuting seditious writing that relied on innuendo or any other form of figurative writing. The trial indicates, as well, the complex relationships between discourses and between public disputes and literature.

Fable, allegory, prophecy, and parody were the genres of dissent that the legal system tried to control, not always with success. They were at the same time the genres that supporters of the government used against dissent. With such pressure on dissent, the language of political involvement became indirect, figurative, and allusive, a rhetoric obscure to twentieth-century readers who do not read "*dehors the writing*." This intertextual discourse influenced literature in ways that twentieth-century readers find difficult to trace. John Barrell has called attention to the presentation by the defense in the 1794 treason trials, in which the accused were charged with "compassing and imagining the death of the king." The prosecution tried to limit the meaning of "imagining" the king's death, while the defense relied on "the interdiscursive play of the language of law" and invoked "a wide range of discourses" to confound the law's clarity.[17] The public discourse in these years cannot be read without attention to the "innuendo," Thelwall's and Spence's "game cock" and "tyger" for examples. Part of the rhetoric of the public disputes takes its definition from the law, not from

[16] *Poetry and Reform: Periodical Verse from the English Democratic Press 1792–1824*, ed. Michael Scrivener (Detroit: Wayne State University Press, 1992) 68.

[17] John Barrell, "Imaginary Treason, Imaginary Law: The State Trials of 1794," *The Birth of Pandora and the Division of Knowledge* (Philadephia: University of Pennsylvania Press, 1992) 134.

the rhetorical traditions following Cicero and Quintilian. One may read Blake's tyger as a Spencean innuendo.

The government's fear was not primarily of the content of seditious writing but of its dissemination among the lower classes, particularly in public meetings. Paine was prosecuted for writing the Second Part of the *Rights of Man*, not only because it was seditious, but also because it was being freely distributed to the public. Mr. Perceval, the prosecutor, was shocked to find that

> it was either totally or partially thrust into the hands of all persons in this country, of subjects of every description; when I found that even children's sweetmeats were wrapped up with parts of this, and delivered into their hands, in the hope that they would read it, when all industry was used, such as I describe to you, in order to obtrude and force this upon that part of the public whose minds cannot be supposed to be conversant with subjects of this sort, and who cannot therefore correct as they go along, I thought it behoved me upon the earliest occasion . . .to put a charge upon record against its author.[18]

In May 1820 Richard Carlile, who had been jailed in 1819 for republishing Paine's works, wrote in the *Republican* that "we have pretty good proof . . . that the Attorney-General does not altogether want the authors; he knows that the authors remain authors after committed to prison; but the vender who has a large family is sure to be ruined and reduced to misery by the prosecution. It is here only, that the Attorney-General can act with effect."[19] From the perspective of the government, the lower classes were simply incompetent readers, unable to judge what they read. At the trial of Sir Francis Burdett for seditious libel after the Peterloo Massacre, the judge instructed the jury that the liberty of the press permits one to "communicate any information that you think proper to communicate by print: that you may point out *to the Government* their errors, and endeavour to convince them their system of policy is wrong and attended with disadvantage to the country, and that another system of politics would be attended with benefit." The jury was told that if they find the work "begins with a statement which the writer cannot know to be true or false, if you find it states many things not correct, *if you find it an appeal to the passions of the lower orders of the people, and not having a tendency to inform those who can correct abuses, it is a libel*."[20] In other words, the intended or implied audiences, like the problems of "innuendo," were as much legal concerns as they were literary. Legal actions and public rhetoric defined each other. William Godwin parodied the government's position: "You may write against the system we patronize, provided you will write in an imbecil and ineffectual manner; you

---

[18] *Trial of Thomas Paine* (above, n. 13) 47.
[19] Wickwar (above, n. 5) 101.
[20] Ibid., 118–19.

may enquire and investigate as much as you please, provided, when you undertake to communicate the result, you carefully check your ardour, and be upon your guard that you do not convey any of your own feelings to your readers" (*PJ* 2: 638).

To regard poetry's intense figuration as distinct from a literalism of the public press and public assembly is to miss the intertextual exchange and the rhetorical similarities between the two, which neither de-idealizes the first nor renders the second an aimless art. A literalist reading of discourse, especially one done from the perspective of the social sciences, commonly misreads by acknowledging only a literalism empty of figurative power and illocutionary force. An unhistorical and idealized reading, whether done to praise poets or to criticize them, is blind to the local, to the particular innuendo, to the moment that gives the utterance its uniqueness. Viewed from outside the public sphere defined by Habermas and exemplified by Burke and Godwin, the public discourse admits participation of all who wish to speak their mind. Significant reading is an act of speaking out, not of silent and passive consumption. It is possible to begin a reading of the public discourse with local instances and precise texts, and to read across a text's boundaries to the rich web of connections provided by local instances of publication. One may begin with any published text. Habermas's limited public sphere severely restricts our understanding of the period and of individual works written by those with legitimate claims to be heard, dissenters, women writers, the laboring poor, and freed slaves. If one defines a public discourse, in contrast to a public sphere, to include all public voices, all published works, tracing the connections among them is a daunting task yet gives both the individual works a historical close reading and the culture a clearer definition through an elaboration of its communicative practices. Members of a society who hear and read cannot choose but speak their minds, if only to their neighbors, and they become, as Blake would have wished, their own prophets.

In England the public discourse, in contrast to Habermas's "public sphere," was far more rhetorical than rational, although it was passionately interested and motivated, far less restricted to material or economic calculation, far more inclusive of the political opinions of private individuals, far more contentious than consensual, far more of a legal battle than a legitimating myth of public policy, far more tolerant of dissenting voices than restricted to the propertied class as Burke wished, and far more involved with the system of patronage than purely capitalistic. The value of the public sphere, to those who spoke within it, was not, as Habermas argued, that it was a center of power separate from the court. Its value to Burke and Godwin was that it was a stable order separate from the agitation of the Jacobins and popular societies. The public discourse was less independent of government influence than Habermas suggests, not only because of legal restraints, but also because the government itself entered the debates both through Pitt's supervision of the *Anti-Jacobin* and support for John Reeves's Association for Preserving Liberty and Property, established in 1792, to distribute loyalist tracts. It may be impossible finally to calculate the amount of financial support the government gave to its supporters in the public press, but it gave financial support to a large number of newspapers. Aspinall reports that "the Government's expenditure on the Press during the early years of the French Revolution was not far short of £5,000 a year."[21] The public discourse contains all that is published or publicly spoken; it is open and available, rather than silent or secluded in the privacy of a library or domestic circle; it is answerable, both in the sense that it responds to the public issues, no matter what its ostensible subject matter, and in the sense that it anticipates the response of private readers and public courts; it is visible and reviewed rather than isolated. The public discourse does not distinguish between the special privilege of the literary to rest in unanswerable retirement and the ordinary language of the commercial press, not because literature is merely a material object or commodity, but because the public discourse is in many instances as rhetorical and artful, allusive, theatrical, and densely packed with implication and innuendo.

The Discourse

The field of discourse in which public utterances are located is a complicated fabric of other utterances. Such a public discourse is the field of cultural significance. As Michel Foucault argues, discursive analysis does not rely on the traditional unities of author, *oeuvre*, or the unity of a particular book or publication. For a reading of public Romanticism, such traditional unities slight the differences between public and private statements and often rely exclusively on the author's unpublished and private statements to explicate public questions. In determining the public cultural consciousness, the private comments of authors in diaries, journals, and conversations are of secondary importance. While they may help to define an author's intention in published writings, they do not fully account for the responsiveness of a particular utterance.

A discursive analysis, on the other hand, locates a utterance, not only in relationship to the author, but also to the field of public debates. Foucault offers a definition of discourse that must be modified to fit actual publication practices during the years of the French Revolution.

> We must grasp the statement in the exact specificity of its occurrence; determine its conditions of existence, fix at least its limits, establish its correlations with other statements that may be connected with it, and show what other

[21] Aspinall (above, n. 14) 68.

forms of statements it excludes. We do not seek below what is manifest the half silent murmur of another discourse; we must show why it could not be other than it was, in what respect it is exclusive of any other, how it assumes, in the midst of others and in relation to them, a place that no other could occupy. The question proper to such an analysis might be formulated in this way: what is this specific existence that emerges from what is said and nowhere else?[22]

Since my purpose is to describe Romantic literature "in the exact specificity of its occurrence" in its public location, I do not attempt to speculate on comprehensive accounts of Romantic discourse.[23] It is a vast arena of contention that defies a unifying theory. It cannot be circumscribed; it cannot be totalized, but its connections can be traced. Foucault admits his varying meanings of the word *discourse*: he treats it "sometimes as the general domain of all statements, sometimes as an individualizable group of statements, and sometimes as a regulated practice that accounts for a certain number of statements" (80). I use the word *discourse* in Foucault's first sense, but not in his second and third. It is not a matter of placing Romantic literature in a unique field of discourse that defines a particular field of study, such as literature, linguistics, economics, or sexuality. Foucault's individual or regulated discourses are defined on the basis of exclusion; each discourse is defined by "other forms of statements it excludes."

I use the word *discourse* to indicate the possible connections of all statements because both the literary and the nonliterary context in which literature appears is rhetorical. Beginning with the specificity of a poem's location, one can trace within the public discourse a network of echoes, allusions, repetitions, innuendoes, signatures, and apostrophes that mediate the work's public significance. From 1789 to 1830, one crucial meeting place between two discourses usually considered to be distinct, literature and the law, is the libel law where rhetoric is the issue. The public discourse is an extended commentary on, among other subjects, both the law and literature. Literature confounds any attempt to restrict an utterance to one or another distinct discourse, to categorize a poem in the public press as exclusively literary, or to define its subject as excluding all other subjects. The connections in the public discourse cross the boundaries of individual discourses defined on the basis of exclusion, whether that exclusion defines a public sphere, as in the case of Habermas, or in the practice of discursive analysis in the social sciences, as in the case of Foucault's early writing. A discursive reading of public Romanticism, since it cannot be parsed into separate fields or disciplines of human knowledge, must read the connec-

[22] Michel Foucault, *The Archeology of Knowledge*, trans. A. M. Sheridan Smith (New York: Pantheon, 1972) 28.

[23] Clifford Siskin describes a "Romantic discourse" defined primarily by the age's literature (*The Historicity of Romantic Discourse* [New York: Oxford, 1988]).

tions between those fields, between domesticity and public policy, between esthetics and morality, between economics and sexuality.

A statement in the public discourse is significant only if it is precisely located. Discursive analysis cannot account for the atomistic and unresponsive utterance, that which is never finally answerable or answered. Foucault defines the statement in a discourse by its connections. The statement "always belongs to a series or a whole, always plays a role among other statements, deriving support from them and distinguishing itself from them: it is always part of a network of statements, in which it has a role, however minimal it may be, to play" (99). As he remarks, "the frontiers of a book are never clear-cut: beyond the title, the first lines, and the last full stop, beyond its internal configuration and its autonomous form, it is caught up in a system of references to other books, other texts, other sentences: it is a node within a network" (23).

The questions for a practical criticism of Romantic literature are thus how to trace the connections among statements, how to locate a work in the discourse, how to characterize the rhetoric of connections, how to define the work as a node in the network, and how to describe the differences between the interior of a work and its exterior, its context. Foucault considers and rejects a traditional mode of analysis that works from the exterior "towards the essential nucleus of interiority. . ., to go back from statements preserved through time and dispersed in space, towards that interior secret that preceded them" which "can be given a philosophical status in the recollection of the Logos or the teleology of reason." For literature such a process implies reading the rhetoric of symbolism. Foucault turns from the "teleology of reason" and "a transcendental subjectivity": "Statements should no longer be situated in relation to a sovereign subjectivity, but recognize in the different forms of the speaking subjectivity effects proper to the enunciative field" (121–22). His procedure is to follow the statement's "*repeatable materiality*" as it "enters various networks and various fields of use, is subjected to transferences or modifications, is integrated into operations and strategies in which its identity is maintained or effaced" (102–5). While Foucault concentrates on repetition and transformation of the statement, I am concerned with the rhetoric of connections among statements. The significance of an utterance is dispersed through the field of public discourse by allusion and address, and the act of reading is an act of tracing its extensions and dispersions. Significance is traced in the horizontal sequence of specific enunciations. The horizon of circulation, repetition, and transformation defines significance, and the "transcendental subjectivity" is not, in a reading of public Romanticism, effaced, but relocated within contentious debates.

To locate a work and to trace its connections with other statements, I will modify and extend Foucault's "speaking subject," not merely as a function or agent of discourse, but as the site of purposeful speech acts. The connections among statements are formed by a statement's responsiveness. As Bakhtin says, "Discourse . . . has a twofold direction—it is directed both toward the referential object of speech, as in ordinary discourse, and toward *another's discourse*, toward *someone else's speech*."[24] Works published in the Romantic period, whether as individual volumes or in collections, newspapers, or journals, are often addressed to another's utterance directly by dedication or apostrophe or indirectly by quotation or allusion. The condition of their utterance is that they speak through their paratexts to other individual speakers, classes of readers, or other works. Insofar as utterances speak directly to other utterances, they convey more than just their referential meanings.

Following J. L. Austin, Quentin Skinner has argued that "in the case of a writer's illocutionary intentions (what he may have been intending to do simply *in* writing a certain way) their recovery does require a separate form of study, which will in fact be essential to undertake if the critic's aim is to understand 'the meaning' of the writer's corresponding works."[25] In other words, Austin insists that speaking out is a particular form of action, a particular form of doing things with words in saying, writing, and publishing, that cannot be accounted for by the simple referential meanings of the words. Skinner futher remarks "that an agent's motives . . . will usually be mixed and complicated, and it is arguable that the need to attain an appropriate self-image by legitimating his behavior to himself and his sympathizers may often be of paramount importance" (111). Exactly so. In many literary publications from 1789 to 1830, the author's public character or legitimacy is at stake. As I shall argue at the end of this chapter, Coleridge's "This Lime-Tree Bower" is not only a poem about vision and imagination, but it also defines his political stance. In Chapter 2 I argue that his *Fears in Solitude* volume is a defense in the court of public opinion. In Chapter 5 I argue that the Dedication and canto I of *Don Juan* are not only topical Regency parody but also Byron's offering his "claim to praise," his claim for legitimacy. While these works vary widely in their tone and content, they are speech acts that argue public issues and claim a legitimacy for poet and work.

Foucault's tendency to define discourses by exclusion has other limitations. As Pierre Bourdieu, mapping the fields of culture, has remarked, Foucault "refuses to look outside the 'field of discourse' for the principle which would cast light on each of the discourses within it." Bourdieu comments that

[24] Mikhail Bakhtin, *Problems of Dostoevsky's Poetics*, trans. Caryl Emerson (Minneapolis: University of Minnesota Press, 1984) 185.

[25] *Meaning and Context: Quentin Skinner and His Critics*, ed. James Tully (Princeton: Princeton University Press, 1988) 75. See also J. L. Austin, *How to Do Things with Words*, 2d ed. (New York: Oxford University Press, 1975).

Foucault transfers into the "paradise of ideas," if I may put it this way, the oppositions and antagonisms which are rooted in the relations between the producers and the consumers of cultural works. Obviously, it is not a question of
denying the specific determination which the space of possibles exerts, since
one of the functions of the notion of the relatively autonomous field, endowed
with its own history, is to account for that determination. Nevertheless, it is
not possible to treat cultural order, the *épistème*, as an autonomous and transcendent system.

In other words, Foucault excludes "the social space" of expression. One can
write a history of literature as an autonomous field, but Bourdieu is uneasy
with Foucault's early definitions of discourse that exclude reference to social and economic interests, and we may share his discomfort. Bourdieu
shifts the focus from Foucault's "orthodox structuralism" to a "genetic
structuralism"[26] that maps the field of culture in relation to the field of
power, but by shifting to a sociological mapping, he repeats Foucault's tendency to separate fields or discourses, to read difference in a social space.
His solution is to diagram a relationship of homologies between fields that
preserves both autonomy and structural similarity. While homologies may
map a sociology of literature, they are of little help in a practical criticism
that seeks to reread the traditional unities of author and work across the
boundaries of a public space. Rather than turning from those unities, as
Foucault suggests, I reread the book and the author in the public discourse,
in the complex network of public utterances connected by allusion and mediation. The reading places or locates authors and works in a social space,
as Bourdieu would wish, but is not bound by the ghost of autonomy. The
boundaries that I will read are not those of a field or the production of culture, but the boundaries of individual works. Those boundaries are, at the
very least, complex intersections between the utterance and its discursive
field.

If the public significance of a poem resonates within the public discourse,
then reading of that discourse must account not only for the work itself, but
also the outside, the exterior, the sequences of other statements, whether
they be other poems or periodical prose. One must cross boundaries that
isolate the work. The crossing, however, is not a denial of interiority, of the
animating consciousness or of the poem itself, but a liberation of interiority from the burden of its boundaries. The transgressions of reading public
Romanticism relocate interiority from its absolute ascendancy to a presence
in the contextual horizons, from a monologic finality to the dialogic reso-
nance within the sequence of utterances, from an authoritative voice to an
illocutionary speech act, from an unchanging intention to an object of ex-

---

[26] Pierre Bourdieu, *The Field of Cultural Production*, ed. Randal Johnson (New York: Columbia University Press, 1993) 33, 179, 182.

change. Subjectivity becomes communicative, and exteriority may be, but is not always nor necessarily, oppositional, critical, or antithetical.

A reading of poetry in the public discourse requires a theory of exteriority, of what is not the text, or of what is outside. At what point does the poem become another utterance? Where are its borders? What are its defining limits, without which it could not be an individual utterance? Who is responsible for placing the work in its location and providing the paratext? Where is the boundary that, as Stephen Dedalus insists in his example of the basket in *Portrait of the Artist*, is fundamental to the act of esthetic apprehension: "In order to see that basket, said Stephen, your mind first of all separates the basket from the rest of the visible universe which is not the basket. The first phase of apprehension is a bounding line drawn about the object to be apprehended."[27] Any contextual reading shifts the center of a work from its deep interior to its borders, to the possible connections and filiations to other works, to that mediating space between utterances, to that foundational, yet unbounded, circle that defines the work itself. Gérard Genette describes these inscribed boundaries as the paratext, which publicly mediates between the text and what lies outside it, a "zone not just of transition, but of *transaction*."[28] The paratext that surrounds a poem is the essential trivia, the crossroads of meaning. In *The Truth in Painting*, Jacques Derrida has circled these territories, because

> This permanent requirement—to distinguish between the internal or proper sense and the circumstance of the object being talked about—organizes all philosophical discourses on art, the meaning of art and meaning as such, from Plato to Hegel, Husserl and Heidegger. This requirement presupposes a discourse on the limit between the inside and the outside of the art object, here a *discourse on the frame*. Where is it to be found?[29]

The *it* in Derrida's final sentence literally refers to the "discourse," although *it* implies both *discourse* and *frame*. With more practical purposes, I will read the frame and the discourse to inquire about the site and composition of the boundaries of Romantic poems. Derrida explores the discourse of Kant's *Critique of Judgement* to find

> We are thus *already* at the unlocatable center of the problem. And when Kant replies to our question "What is a frame?" by saying: it's a *parergon*, a hybrid of outside and inside, but a hybrid which is not a mixture or a half-measure,

[27] Joyce, *Portrait of the Artist*, ed. Hans Walter Gabler (New York: Random House, 1993) 204.

[28] Gérard Genette, "Introduction to the Paratext," trans. Marie Maclean, *New Literary History* 22 (1991): 261. See also Genette, *Paratexts: Thresholds of Interpretation*, trans. Jane E. Lewin (Cambridge: Cambridge University Press, 1997).

[29] Jacques Derrida, *The Truth in Painting*, trans. Geoff Bennington and Ian McLeod (Chicago, University of Chicago Press, 1987) 45.

an outside which is called to the inside of the inside in order to constitute it as an inside; and when he gives as examples of the *parergon*, alongside the frame, clothing and column, we ask to see, we say to ourselves that there are "great difficulties" here, and that the choice of examples, and their association, is not self-evident.[30]

In Derrida's tracing, the parergon is and is not part of the painting, is neither inside nor outside the work of art, is neither and both interior and exterior, and from these crossings and circlings there is no exit: "Deconstruction must neither reframe nor dream of the pure and simple absence of the frame" (73).

For a practical criticism of Romantic poetry, it is possible to circle these borders, these boundaries, these frontiers in the instances of their material specificity, or, as Foucault says, the specificity of their enunciation. It is possible to question the boundaries of individual works. What, after all, is a poem? Where does it begin and end? Is the title part of the poem? Is it an essential part, or is it part of the frame that surrounds and defines the poem? Derrida asks:

> What happens when one entitles a "work of art"? What is the *topos* of the title? Does it take place [and where?] in relation to the work? On the edge? Over the edge? On the internal border? In an overboard that is re-marked and reapplied, by invagination, within, between the presumed center and the circumference? Or between that which is framed and that which is framing in the frame? (24)

Keats asks the same question in "Ode on a Grecian Urn": "What leaf-fringed legend haunts about thy shape . . . ?" The frame, the paratext, and the legend is about the poem and what the poem is about, what it is and what it does.

The questions can easily be multiplied beyond merely those of the title in reading an enunciation, or specific utterance. One could continue the questions with reference to specific Romantic works. What do we read when we wish to read a poem? If we insist on a historical reading, what elements of a work are relevant or irrelevant? What, after all, is Byron's *Childe Harold*? Is it four separate works? Or three? Are the prefaces to the later cantos to be read as prefaces to the earlier? Are the historical notes part of the poem? Many modern editions present only the poetry without the notes. The poem is thus a record of the voyage of Byron's consciousness, his psychological pilgrimage. If, however, the historical notes are read as part of the work as Byron originally insisted, in the same size type with the same size margins, the political, social, and historical material contained in

---

[30] Derrida 63–64 (above, n. 29). See Kant, *Critique of Judgement*, trans. Jamed Creed Meredith (Oxford: Clarendon Press, 1928) 68.

them changes the poem. The notes were reduced in size, then reduced in number, and finally omitted in most editions after Byron's death.[31] It is difficult to read *Childe Harold* as it was originally published, because it has never been reprinted entirely in the same form. The prevailing twentieth-century esthetic has determined that a work that is poetry be only verse.

What of titles? What happens to a poem when the title changes, as in the case of Coleridge's "The Eolian Harp," which first appeared in his 1796 volume as "Effusion XXXV"? In a collection of poems, what is the significance of the title, if it appears both on the contents page and with the poem itself? What if they are different, as is the case with Coleridge's "Reflections on Having Left a Place of Retirement," the title on the first page of the text in 1797, which is listed on the contents page as "On Leaving a Place of Residence"? The trope of reflection is absent on the contents page. Leaving a residence is not the same as leaving retirement; the first suggests a casual journey; the second, an active quest. Titles may identify a central figure, a genre, a major character, an event, a date of composition and thus identify the center or interior by repeating the poem's words, but they are not that interior. Does a title echo or repeat the interior, or does it export the interior from the poem? Does a title include epigrams or prefaces, if they come between the title and the first lines of verse? What is the case when individual poems with their titles were first published in a volume that itself had a title, and which divided the volume into individual sections, each with its own title? A poem may then have three titles, that of the volume, that of the section, and that of the individual poem, and each of the three titles may include an epigram or preface. Which, if any, is the essential title, and which title signals a poem's interior? What is changed if these titles are changed in the course of republication?[32]

Poems that appear in collections are located within the structure of that volume, in a sequence of poems, prefaces, titles, epigrams that frame what we consider to be the individual poem. If we read the poem in a modern edition, it almost certainly has been removed from that context. To illustrate I would like to look at Wordsworth's sonnet "Milton! thou should'st be living at this hour," first published in *Poems in Two Volumes* (1807). In 1807 its title is "14. London, 1802" and appears in a sequence of sonnets numbered as though each were an individual stanza in a long poem titled "Part the Second. Sonnets Dedicated to Liberty," which follows the first part, "Miscellaneous Sonnets." The larger section entitled "Sonnets" includes a "Prefatory Sonnet," "Nuns fret not at their Convent's narrow room," which introduces the limited scope of the genre but which also de-

---

[31] Doucet Fischer, *"The Grand Napoleon of the Realms of Rhyme": Byron and History* (Ph.D. diss., New York University, 1989), 115–209.

[32] For a survey of the relationship of titles to authors and works, see Anne Ferry, *The Title to the Poem* (Stanford: Stanford University Press, 1996).

fines liberty within that narrow scope: "some Souls . . . / Who have felt the weight of too much liberty, / Should find short solace there, as I have found." Most likely, Wordsworth intends to say that he has had too much liberty and finds solace in restriction, but the final clause is syntactically unclear. "Short solace" could mean that he has found a deep repose or merely brief comfort. Is the "liberty" of this prefatory sonnet the same as in the title of the second section, "Sonnets Dedicated to Liberty"? Is the "liberty" of a nun's convent the same as the liberty of London when the republican Milton, always a political figure in this period, is invoked?

Where in 1807 are the borders of "Milton! thou shouldst be living . . ."? It is framed by four titles: that of the volume; that of the section with its prefatory sonnet; that of the part, or subsection, which consists of twenty-six sonnets in all; and that of the individual sonnet. Stephen Dedalus's "bounding line" blurs, and the frames multiply. The fourteen lines of the sonnet, like all poems, have both location and boundaries, but the paratext has location and no boundaries. Do these surrounding contexts define an essential poem? As David Erdman has emphasized, sonnet 15 in the sequence invokes Sydney, Marvel, Harrington, and "Young Vane, and others who call'd Milton Friend," all stern republicans. Does this determine Milton's significance in the previous sonnet? What happens, historically, when the category's title changes from "Sonnets Dedicated to Liberty" to "Political Sonnets," in *Sonnets* (1838) and finally to "Poems Dedicated to National Independence and Liberty" in 1845?[33] The change marks a turn from the liberty of the commonwealth, invoked by those sympathetic to the French Revolution in the 1790s, to an opposite meaning indicated by Coleridge's "Letters on the Spaniards," printed in the *Courier* of 1809. He introduced them with the promise that they would contain observations "on the grounds of hope and fear, which the history of past ages suggests to us, respecting the war of a people against armies—of an injured and insulted People struggling for Religion, national independence, and *self-originating* Improvements, against the numerous hosts and celebrated Commanders of a remorseless Invader, Usurper, and Tyrant" (*EOT* 2: 39). The phrase "national independence" could not have been a neutral one, or one easily forgotten by Coleridge, for in a short-lived attempt in 1814 to revise his contributions to Southey's *Joan of Arc*, he drafted a new title, "The National Independence or the Vision of the Maid of Orleans" (*CN* 3: 4202). The significance of Wordsworth's shift of title can only be read through tracing the public discourse. Thus read, the change marks a shift from a liberty sympathetic to republican causes to one indicating nationalism and patriotism prompted by resistance to Napoleon.

---

[33] *"Poems, in Two Volumes," and other Poems, 1800–1807 by William Wordsworth*, ed. Jared Curtis, in *The Cornell Wordsworth* (Ithaca: Cornell University Press, 1983) 153. Quotations to the poems in this volume are from Curtis's edition.

If titles with their surrounding context designate a poetic interior, which liberty is at the center of Wordsworth's sonnet? A nun's liberty of devotion, Milton's republicanism, or a nationalism defined by resistance to imperial conquest? Without the burden of the paratext, the poem presents a political liberty based on freedom from sensuality and greed, but at its borders, the comforting singleness is dispersed through the differences in its various locations. At the borders of this sonnet there is not a single, well defined bounding line that divides it from other poems; there is, rather, a field of the entire volume, which by allusion points from the private space of the nun's convent to London and the public struggles for liberty. The titles point not only inward to the poem and the rest of the volume, but also to a public context, one that can be traced in the public press. Even in the most material specificity of particular versions, titles indicate both interiors elusive in the field of their depictions and exteriors multiple in the contentions of the public discourse.

"Terras Astraea Reliquit"

Any collection of poems constructs a set of frames or borders for an individual work that may significantly alter a received reading of a poem and point at the same time to another set of utterances outside of the volume by which the public word and public world enter the interior. The trivia of the volume's frames become the network of innumerable associations. Wordsworth's *Poems in Two Volumes* (1807) will serve as an example here as well. The "Immortality Ode" was first published as the final poem in the second volume, immediately preceded by "Elegiac Stanzas, Suggested by a Picture of Peele Castle, in a Storm, Painted by Sir George Beaumont." The 1807 "Immortality Ode" is unfamiliar to most readers. Its only title was "Ode," and there is no hint of the longer title added later. In addition, the later epigraph beginning "The Child is father of the Man," printed between the title and the first line, was absent. The "Ode" was separated by its own title page from "Peele Castle," which concluded a miscellaneous collection called "The Blind Highland Boy; With Other Poems." If the "Ode" is read as a separate poem, its major figure, the trope of light, takes its significance within the "Ode" itself. It opens with a recollection of the "celestial light" that gems "meadow, grove, and stream," and the fourth stanza concludes with the question "Whither is fled the visionary gleam? / Where is it now, the glory and the dream?" Whatever its precise meaning, the "celestial light" that is lost is associated with vision, the "glory and the dream." The image of the glory as radiating light is lucid, particularly since the later lines introduce the child "trailing clouds of glory."

The trope of light has a wider range of significance if the "Ode" is read as the concluding poem of a sequence of the 1807 volume. "Peele Castle" also uses the trope, but with an entirely different significance and moves from the light to a stormy twilight. Wordsworth begins with childhood recollections near the castle in a summer without tempests:

> Ah! THEN, if mine had been the Painter's hand,
> To express what then I saw; and add the gleam
> The light that never was, on sea or land,
> The consecration, and the Poet's dream;
>
> I would have painted thee, thou hoary Pile!
> Amid a world how different from this!
> Beside a sea that could not cease to smile;
> On tranquil land, beneath a sky of bliss:
>
> . . . .
>
> Such, in the fond delusion of my heart,
> Such Picture would I at that time have made:
> And seen the soul of truth in every part;
> A faith, a trust, that could not be betray'd.

Light, which in the "Ode" is objective but departed, is in "Peele Castle" the light that "never was, on sea or land," and it is seen in the "fond delusion of my heart," a youthful blindness. Both poems lament the loss of light, but the complexities of signification are difficult to ignore for the simple reason that the "Ode" uses the very same rhymes, "gleam" and "dream." Not only is the light in "Peele Castle" a projection on nature, it is an illusion, a youthful error. Is the light in the "Ode" a trope of the light in "Peele Castle"? Does the positioning of the "Ode" as the final poem elevate its myth of origins and recollection over the more somber conclusion of "Peele Castle"? With the precise echoes of "Peele Castle" in the "Ode," it is difficult to erase from consciousness the elegy's reality principle. It remains a doubting counter-statement to the consolations of the "Ode" and denies what the "Ode" affirms, that there is a connection between the visionary insight of childhood and maturity.

The title page that precedes the "Ode" constitutes a transition between the two poems. What in a modern poetic sequence would normally be a blank space, the margin of an individual poem, is here an inscribed transition. The title page sets the "Ode" apart from the preceding elegies, and the title of "Ode" suggests that the volume is making an abrupt turn toward a higher genre. On the verso of the title page, Wordsworth added a phrase from the first line of Virgil's fourth *Eclogue*, "paulò majora canamus" (let us sing a somewhat loftier song). The Latin epigraph seems to set the "Ode" apart from the other poems by indicating that its subject is of greater importance, but the phrase is comparative, and while it announces a new voice of the "Ode," it remembers what has come before. The epigraph preserves what the abrupt transition of the title page would efface and preserves the traces of the earlier elegiac mood for the opening stanzas of the "Ode," where the speaker recognizes that the light has been lost and that in the springtime of communal rejoicing the loss is "to me alone."

The Latin phrase is not a part of the "Ode" itself in 1807, in the same sense that the later epigraph, "The Child is father of the Man," is a part of the poem in later editions, where it appears between the title and the first line of the poem. It was not in any manuscript including the printer's copy for the 1807 edition. In that manuscript there were instructions for a separate title page, but no mention of the Latin phrase. Jared Curtis notes in his edition of *Poems in Two Volumes* that Wordsworth added the Latin phrase when the volume was in proof (269). Most likely he added it as the transition between the two poems and not as an integral part of the "Ode." The phrase is not as much a part of the "Ode" as it is a part of the structure of the volume itself, and it is inaccurately noted as the precursor of "The Child is father of the Man." Since the phrase is comparative, its reference must be both to the poem that precedes it and to the one that follows it, and it should be regarded as similar to other written markers that establish the structure of a volume. It remains a separate text and is not exclusively incorporated into the "Ode" by any revisionary alteration. The space or gap between poems is filled with Virgil's words, and the movement from elegy to ode is filled with Virgil's prophetic pastoral.

Wordsworth's transition cites Virgil's phrase at the beginning of the fourth *Eclogue*, which signals an abrupt turn from the preceding eclogues. Virgil turns from the common topics of pastoral, the lover's lament in the second *Eclogue*, and the singing contest of the third, to the myth of the birth of the miraculous child who will usher in a return of the golden age, or the peaceable kingdom in the fourth *Eclogue*. Its idealism is such a sharp break from the earlier poems that it was taken to foreshadow the birth of Christ. Virgil's phrase would be appropriate for the transition between Wordsworth's very different poems. It would resolve the contradictory use of the trope of light and establish a hierarchy of genre by elevating the ode over the elegy. What is gained by the elevation? How closely are we to read Virgil's transition into Wordsworth's? Is the "Ode" an exercise in the wish fulfillment that Virgil presents, a life in nature so idealized that its fictional nature is unmistakable? It may be loftier, but it is also a figure of desire, a presentation of what does not exist. Wordsworth's transition from a poem that displays the hardships of nature to the "loftier" or "grander" themes of nature's echoing joy may be merely a prefiguration of what is absent.

Wordsworth's use of Virgil raises the question of whose Virgil he quoted and the transition's allusion, of the implied context of the transition itself. Wordsworth was certainly aware of the earlier eighteenth-century view of pastoral as idealized nature defined by French Neoclassicism and Pope, and he knew the Dryden and Ogilby translations, but, as Duncan Wu has pointed out, he also knew and used the mid-century edition and translation of John Martyn in his own translations of the *Georgics* as early as 1788.[34] Martyn's edition of the *Eclogues* (London, 1749) is so extensively annotated that most pages contain only a few lines of Virgil and two columns of tightly printed commentary that extends over thirty or forty pages for the fourth *Eclogue* alone. Martyn was a botanist who delighted in describing each plant and tree that appeared in Virgil's poem. Nevertheless, his edition is rich in the traditions of annotation and sources and in the controversies of historical commentary. He accepts the earlier tradition that the miraculous child is Christ and tries to explain Virgil's knowledge of a prophetic tradition. Martyn assumes that Virgil's knowledge must have come from the *Sibylline Fragments*, which in his day were probably spurious or forgeries of the originals guarded at Rome. As Martyn says, "In the verses of the Sibyls there were some prophecies, which foretold, that a king should be born into the world about this time, under whom the happiness of the Golden Age should be restored" (146–47). He further explains that the *Sibylline Fragments* must have been influenced by Isaiah: "we may reasonably conclude, that those truly inspired writings had been seen, by the Sibyls themselves, or at least by Virgil" (148). When he annotates Virgil's lines describing the ideal word, he cites four sections of Isaiah, all of which detail the change from a desolate to a bountiful land. Isaiah contains the messianic prophecy of the coming of a child and of a great light. The literary range of allusions in Martyn's edition includes Virgil's *Eclogue*, the *Sibylline Fragments*, and Isaiah, but excludes later traditions of the myth of the miraculous child, such as Milton's anti-pastoral "On the Morning of Christ's Nativity." The margin of the "Ode," inscribed with Virgil's phrase, is a field of various texts, an excess, a convergence of fragments.

The range of allusion framed by Martyn's notes is not restricted to the sources of its prophetic myth or literature. Many of his notes speculate on the historical situation of the *Eclogues* and the history that they reflect, a tradition of commentary widely used at the end of the eighteenth century. Late in 1802 Coleridge copied in his notebook Jeremy Taylor's citation of the first *Eclogue*, which is, like Wordsworth's "Michael," a poem of dispossession. Coleridge applied Taylor's reading of Virgil's line "to the present state of England": "such unrest there is on all sides of the land" (*CN* 1: 1286 and note). The use of the fourth *Eclogue* as the transition from an essentially private elegy to the public genre of the "Ode" accentuates the public voice of the "Ode." The fourth *Eclogue* is addressed to C. Asinius Pollio, a friend

---

[34] Wu, Duncan, *Wordsworth's Reading 1770–99* (Cambridge: Cambridge University Press, 1993), 141 and "Three Translations of Virgil Read by Wordsworth in 1788," *Notes & Queries*, NS 37 (1990): 407–9. I quote from Martyn's second edition of 1749.

of Virgil, who became consul in 40 B.C. As Martyn says, after the Battle of Philippi, in 42 B.C., property, including Virgil's patrimonial lands, was confiscated and given to the soldiers of Antony and Octavian. Pollio warned Virgil of the impending confiscation, so that Virgil was able to apply successfully to Octavian for restoration of his lands. In addition, Pollio arranged the Peace of Brundisium in 40 B.C. between Antony and Octavian, who had fallen out after the defeat of Brutus. Thus the "loftier song" of the fourth *Eclogue* has a precise historical reference to the civil wars following the death of Caesar in 44 B.C. and looks forward to years of prosperity.

Wordsworth's transition from the private elegy to the public ode through the complex allusions of Virgil's transition evokes a historical reality of civil war and dispossession. Hazlitt's identification of the time of the presence of the "celestial light" as the dawn of the French Revolution is justified by the range of allusion in Martyn's notes.[35] Virgil's pastoral was not only an idealized world of an imagination that viewed a peaceable kingdom; it was the world of civil conflict. In the fourth *Eclogue*, the coming of the miraculous child will bring the descent of Astraea, the "Starry Maid," the Goddess of Justice, who fled to the heavens and became the constellation Virgo after the golden age. She will reign with Apollo and bring the ideal bounty and peaceable kingdom of Isaiah. With the inscribed transition from private elegy to public ode, one could read the "celestial light" and the "visionary gleam" in the beginning of the "Ode" not only as a lost personal vision, a failure of memory, but as Astraea, lost Justice. Martyn's notes support such a reading of the "celestial light" as justice by commenting that Virgil's "Virgo" was not, as Constantine said, "the blessed Virgin": "Virgil certainly meant Astraea or Justice, who is said by the Poets to have been driven from earth to heaven by the wickedness of mankind" (152n). As Titus Andronicus remarks to his brother, *"Terras Astraea reliquit /* Be you remembered, Marcus, she's gone, she's fled."[36] Twentieth-century readers of "Ode" have been not able to see Astraea within Urania or Apollo, the purely literary muses, not been able to see justice within imagination. The transition in the frame between poems, the Latin on the verso of the title page, is a determining center of both poems, an unbounded frame that alludes to a long literary tradition used as commentary on public issues. The lament over the loss of celestial light laments the loss of Astraea and justice and a hope that one can be sustained by recollection that Astraea once lived on earth.

[35] Marjorie Levinson quotes Hazlitt's remarks (Howe 1: 119, 12: 236) (*Wordsworth's Great Period Poems: Four Essays* [Cambridge: Cambridge University Press, 1986] 83–84). She reads the "paulò majora canamus" as an analogy to Wordsworth's own life in 1802, the Peace of Amiens, and "Wordsworth's recent betrothal to Mary Hutchinson" and reads the " 'golden hours' of the Revolution" "as a psychic and metaphysical postulate" (92). Elsewhere she notes without much elaboration the political emphasis in the quotation from Virgil (154 n 20 and 158 n 36).

[36] *Titus Andronicus* IV, iii, 4–5.

Shelley reminds us, in the *Defense of Poetry*, that the job of the poet is to "trace the footsteps of Astraea."[37] The public discourse is neither circumscribed nor limited. Speaking out is not restricted to class, economic status, gender, or education. Utterances cannot be bound by rigid theories of genre and do not constitute a plot or an argument that reaches a conclusion or finality. The public discourse is open and free. The time of the discourse is always present and tempestuous. Much to the frustration of the Tory government from 1789–1830 and to many twentieth-century critics, it is always unruly. The individual utterances that compose the discourse, particularly those usually considered literary, are precise in their locations but not clearly marked by their boundaries, because those material boundaries, those frames, those contexts are a large part of the rhetoric that connects them with other utterances, both those that are literary and those that are not. Inevitably our reading of that discourse in the late twentieth century is hindered and aided by our distance from it. Theories of what a public discourse is or should be must always be tested against the historical and textual evidence; historical evidence, in turn, must be located by a methodology that avoids history's potential randomness and that recognizes Astraea.

[37] Donald H. Reiman and Sharon B. Powers, *Shelley's Poetry and Prose* (New York: Norton, 1977) 493. For the Astraea myth, see Frances Yeats, *Astraea: The Imperial Theme in the Sixteenth Century* (London: Routledge and Kegan Paul, 1975).

Chapter Two

THE CORRESPONDING SOCIETY:
READING THE CORRESPONDENCE

ALTHOUGH the public discourse cannot have a clearly mapped horizon, its networks can be traced, and although there are not clearly defined genres in the public discourse, as there are for literary works, there are conventions, recurrent gestures that connect one work with another. The relevant forms of public utterance for a reading of Romanticism are the letter, the review, and the address or lecture. English society in the early nineteenth century was literally a corresponding society.[1] *The Nineteenth Century Short Title Catalogue* lists over one thousand publications whose titles begin "A Letter . . ." issued between 1801 and 1815. Any attempt to read all of the public discourse or to take account of all of its forms is far beyond the scope of this or any one book. Historical readings should map the genres of public utterance, categorize their conventions, and specify their locations. Their most important convention is that they speak to another text, are almost always addressed to another work, and implicitly or explicitly specify their audience. Like the public letter, they speak directly to other works in many ways: titles announce themselves as letters to specific individuals, dedications and apostrophes respond to previous writing and to individuals located in a social space, citations and allusions locate one work within another, and complex titled signatures mark the writers' public stance. The public discourse is an intertextual fabric of response and correspondence, of intricate allusive connections and circulation that are neither contingent nor arbitrary. If there is a limitation to this method, it arises from the plenitude of possible connections that one could trace, not from an absence of connections, those that are effaced as a preliminary act of reading when one decides to read a single work isolated by its own boundaries. Reading the public discourse is not a matter of reading an implied audience within the work or constructing an ideal reader who remains silent. Such a method may be helpful in understanding the esthetic structure of a work, but it is practically useless in discovering an actual reader's response. Only by reading the surrounding context of a work can one see the public mediation of its central tropes, the nuances of the individual words, and the resonances

---

[1] Mary A. Favret's *Romantic Correspondence: Women, Politics, and the Fiction of Letters* (Cambridge: Cambridge University Press, 1993) details the shift in the use of letters from sentimental fiction to subversive politics (33–34).

of its commonality. A work has public significance only if it is responsive and answerable; the public discourse is significant only if it is traceable; and the rhetoric of individual works is significant only if it receives a response.

As commonly read, individual form separates and isolates. A primary law of literary genre is that completed form divides; it declares what it is not, and that division is the sad law of genre. As dividing form, genre, particularly the lyric, tends toward elegy and melancholy because it exists by itself and accentuates its own absences. If genre is mere form, then it is without location since its universality claims a detachment from its context. Without location, genre possesses no public or historical meaning, since it has no relation to the public discourse in which it was originally published. Thus, finally, it has no determinable ideology. Further, the presence of the paratext changes a literary genre into a public genre. For example, when subjective Romantic lyrics are addressed as letters, they become public documents. Public significance is not primarily a matter of content, but of location, which is prior to significance. To change location is to change significance. When a work is placed in the public discourse, when its connections to other works can be traced, when its boundaries are transgressed, little is left of individual form. Genre, then, is of secondary importance. If form is without location, then it has no ideology; if a work is sited, it has no significant literary genre. The boundaries of form, the paratext, are not definite; the frame enters the work as a determinant and expands by allusion outward to the exterior discourse. In locating a work, paratext is one important element, but it is not the only way. The allusions within the work merge with paratext and cross its boundaries. If paratext is used only to read the text and not the public discourse, then it functions as a boundary or limit that isolates the work. Reading the public discourse is a process of reading the exterior, of reading outward, of transgressing boundaries.

Precise location within the discourse is essential for any reading of the connections. No single version of a poem will be appropriate for all its possible locations. The first act of reading literature in the public discourse is to locate a particular version. Location does not imply the isolation of the local or particular, a merely local knowledge, a condition of an utterance that defines its uniqueness by exclusion or negation.[2] An utterance is located by its connections to other utterances. If a work is local because it possesses inviolate form, then it is merely esthetic; if it is located, if its allusive and paratextual connections are clearly traced, it preserves its boundaries as permeable layers for the circulation of public significance. The genre that provides the clearest example of the paratext's function is the letter, a genre defined by its boundaries, location, address, and signature. As a primary

[2] See Clifford Geertz, *Local Knowledge: Further Essays in Interpretive Anthropology* (New York: Harper Collins, 1983) and his essay "Thick Description" in *The Interpretation of Cultures* (New York: Harper Collins, 1973) 3–30.

form of the public discourse, the letter is the underlying public form of the Romantic lyric as it is commonly defined as spoken at a particular place and time, addressed to a specific individual, and uttered by a poet whose signature is implied within the poem and often inscribed in the paratext.[3] The private, meditative lyric poem is fundamentally a public form, one in which the private and the public meet in a complex interrelationship. Unlike other literary genres that proclaim their isolation, many letters announce their precise location and should be read in their particular versions and locations. In this chapter I explore the paratextual conventions, emphasizing those of the public letter, and conclude with a discussion of "This Lime-Tree Bower" in its first publication in the *Annual Anthology* as a letter to Charles Lamb.

Locating Versions

One's mapping of the discursive field depends on what critical questions one wants to ask. If a poet's opinions in 1797 or 1798 are at issue, or if one is interested in a dialogic, discursive, or historical reading, it will not do to quote poems revised by the author much later in life, especially if they have been revised, as is often the case with poems of Coleridge and Wordsworth, and even with Blake, whose coloring of illuminated plates changes over the years. Not only did Coleridge revise poems radically ("The Ancient Mariner" is an obvious example), but in their republication he changed their context, titles, and classification within a volume. Whether a poem is published in a newspaper, review, anthology, or by itself or in a collection of a single author's poems is significant. "The Eolian Harp" in the category of "Meditative Poems in Blank Verse" in *Sibylline Leaves* (1817) is not the same poem that was published under the title of "Effusion XXXV" in 1796, for the obvious reason that an effusion is not a meditation.[4] For many Romantic lyrics there are no single definitive texts, only versions. No ideal text, no pristine original version, no final form representing an author's final intentions will satisfy all critical questions. Jack Stillinger has suggested that "we drop the concept of an ideal single text fulfilling an author's intentions and put our money instead on some theory of versions."[5] He has challenged

[3] Abrams, M. H., "Structure and Style in the Greater Romantic Lyric," in *From Sensibility to Romanticism*, ed. Frederick W. Hilles and Harold Bloom (New York: Oxford University Press, 1965) 527–60, rept. in M. H. Abrams, *The Correspondent Breeze* (New York: W. W. Norton, 1984) 76–108.

[4] See my " 'The Eolian Harp' in Context," *SIR* 24 (1985): 3–20.

[5] Jack Stillinger, *Multiple Authorship and the Myth of Solitary Genius* (New York: Oxford University Press, 1991) 200. Similar observations by Romantic editors include Jerome J. McGann's *The Beauty of Inflections* (Oxford: Clarendon Press, 1985), *A Critique of Modern Textual Criticism* (Chicago: University of Chicago Press, 1983), and *The Textual Condition* (Princeton: Princeton University Press, 1991) and Donald H. Reiman's "Romantic Bards and Historical Editors," in *Romantic Texts and Contexts* (Columbia: University of Missouri Press, 1987).

the idea that there is a "single 'best' or 'most authoritative' text for each of Coleridge's poems" and has briefly detailed the several versions of some of Coleridge's major poems: "sixteen or more manuscript and printed texts of *The Eolian Harp*, twelve distinct texts of *This Lime-Tree Bower My Prison*, eighteen or more texts of *The Rime of the Ancient Mariner*, and similar numbers for *Frost at Midnight*, *Kubla Khan*, *Christabel*, and the *Dejection* ode."[6] Stillinger defines version in such a rigorous way that even a verbal variant within a single line quoted in a letter or a word changed by pen and ink in a presentation copy constitutes a different version. Yet even allowing for these trivial instances, many of Coleridge's poems exist in various versions, all authorized at one time or another, under the pressure of different circumstances. He revised some poems simply to improve the verse or the logic of the figures, but other revisions changed the poem's significance. "Christabel," for instance, is a different poem in 1798 and 1800, when, in private manuscript and public recitation, it was a psychological portrait of dreams and the supernatural, than it was in 1816, when Coleridge presented it as a case study in failed creativity along with "Kubla Khan" and the "Pains of Sleep." The first published version of 1816, which inspired hostile reviews from Hazlitt, the *Edinburgh Review*, and a pamphlet that called it "the most obscene Poem in the English Language" (*CL* 4: 919), is different from the versions in presentation copies that Coleridge supplied with annotations similar to those for *The Ancient Mariner* and different from the final revised version.[7] A theory of versions, such as that suggested by James Thorpe and Hans Zeller, and endorsed by Stillinger and McGann, should take account, not only of the various versions of a work, but also of the work's location.[8] For a poem as for an individual consciousness, to be is to be somewhere.

The first act of reading the public discourse, that of identifying a precise version, is not sufficient for reading location. One must read beyond the frame, beyond the paratext, to the immediate exterior in which the boundaries merge into other writing. In many instances, major Romantic poems were first published in periodicals that had their own announced and vig-

[6] Jack Stillinger, "The Multiple Versions of Coleridge's Poems: How Many *Mariners* Did Coleridge Write?" *SIR* 31 (1992): 127, expanded to *Coleridge and Textual Instability* (New York: Oxford University Press, 1994). For a contrary view that "a poem is only one's poem . . . when it appears in a book with one's name on it," see Zachary Leader, *Revision and Romantic Authorship* (Oxford: Clarendon Press, 1996) 159. See also Joseph Grigely, *Textualterity: Art, Theory, and Textual Criticism* (Ann Arbor: University of Michigan Press, 1995).

[7] Stillinger, *Coleridge and Textual Instability* 89–90, reprints Coleridge's annotations to "Christabel," previously published by Barbara Rooke, in "An Annotated Copy of Coleridge's 'Christabel,' " *Studia Germanica Gandensia* 15 (1974): 179–92.

[8] James Thorpe, *Principles of Textual Criticism* (San Marino: Huntington Library, 1972) 37–47; Hans Zeller, "A New Approach to the Critical Constitution of Literary Texts," *Studies in Bibliography* 28 (1975): 231–64.

orously argued political views. Noting simply that a review was "reformist" or "Tory" is inadequate, for the simple reason that some journals, particularly those with sectarian affiliations, may be reformist on the issues of the slave trade or repeal of the Test Acts, yet rigidly conventional on religious issues. Also, the articles and reviews that surround a poem or collection of poems may address the same issues as the poem. A full reading of Romantic poetry must take into account the poems that were first published in the periodic press. Coleridge first published "Reflections on Having Left a Place of Retirement" in the *Monthly Magazine*, and "Dejection" in the *Morning Post*, and one should read these poems in those contexts. Coleridge's "The Visions of the Maid of Orleans," an extension of his contribution to Southey's *Joan of Arc*, was published in the *Morning Post*, December 26, 1797, with his signature, yet it has never been reprinted except as a part of "The Destiny of Nations," where its earlier radical context is modified. Keats's sonnet on Chapman's Homer has a different significance in Hunt's *Examiner* on December 1, 1816, where it is preceded by Hunt's attack on the school of Pope, than in *Poems* (1817), where it was revised and published as the eleventh in a sequence of seventeen sonnets and followed "To one who has been long in city pent."[9] Keats's "Ode to a Nightingale" and "Ode on a Grecian Urn" were first published in the *Annals of the Fine Arts*, which contained satires on the Royal Academy and Hazlitt's attacks on Sir Joshua Reynolds's advocacy of ideal art, which I explore below in Chapter 6. As a poem about human vanity, Shelley's "Ozymandias" takes on a more precise political application to British monarchy in the *Examiner* of January 18, 1818, and in the discussion about the relative values of Greek and Egyptian art. What is the meaning of Shelley's "Hymn to Intellectual Beauty" in its *Examiner* context? Byron's "The Vision of Judgment" was first printed in the *Liberal* and was surrounded by controversy even before its first number was issued.[10]

Some important Romantic poems were first published in collections or anthologies. Some collections, like *Lyrical Ballads*, contained poems by more than one author. Some appear to be little more than random collections of miscellaneous poems, yet others had a clear purpose. *The Poetry of the Anti-Jacobin* (1799) and a second anthology, *The Beauties of the Anti-Jacobin* (1799), perpetuated political satires, as did the reprinting of the *Anti-Jacobin, or Weekly Examiner* in smaller volumes.[11] The connection of

[9] See John Kandl, "Private Lyrics in the Public Sphere: Leigh Hunt's *Examiner* and the Construction of a Public 'John Keats,' " *Keats-Shelley Journal* 44 (1995): 84–101.

[10] William H. Marshall, *Byron, Shelley, Hunt, and* The Liberal (Philadelphia: University of Pennsylvania Press, 1960).

[11] The importance of *The Anti-Jacobin, or Weekly Examiner* is difficult to overestimate. Although it ran for less than a year, it was reprinted in at least four editions—the fourth, a resetting of the entire run. See a brief but comprehensive description in *British Literary Maga-*

Lyrical Ballads with the periodical press is even more important. Coleridge's "Lewti; or, The Circassian's Love Chant" was canceled from the first edition of *Lyrical Ballads*, because it might have been recognized as Coleridge's since it had been published in the *Morning Post* on April 13, 1798. Wordsworth's "The Convict," which immediately preceded "Tintern Abbey" in *Lyrical Ballads* (1798), was printed in the *Morning Post* on December 14, 1797, and "The Mad Mother" was reprinted in the same newspaper on April 2, 1800, with a note praising *Lyrical Ballads*. No matter how ephemeral, how miscellaneous, and how literary some collections may be, nevertheless, properly located, they occupy a space in the public discourse, which although unfamiliar to most readers in the late twentieth century, involves the public within the private.

Public Signature

Like public letters, most publications are signed in one way or another, with either or both of the author's or publisher's names. Pseudonymous or anonymous publications were motivated by simple modesty, the shame of appearing before the public, or more serious reasons: to avoid legal responsibility, personal attack, or some form of prejudice such as that against class, race, or gender. The reference of many pseudonyms is obvious and can be deciphered without difficulty. Signature, commonly taken as a sign of the author's intention and ownership, is in publication practices in the Romantic period often far more than a name; it is a sign of the author's public position, legal standing, and legitimacy. As such it rarely appears as simply a proper name; it is accompanied by personal titles, mottoes, prefaces, and biographical sketches that define an author. Additionally, the publisher may be a collaborator in the volume's construction. The Advertisement to Keats's *Lamia* (1820) states, "If any apology be thought necessary for the appearance of the unfinished poem of Hyperion, the publishers beg to state that they alone are responsible, as it was printed at their particular request, and contrary to the wish of the author."[12] This is simply one of many instances of joint or collaborative authorship that Jack Stillinger analyzes in *Multiple Authorship and the Myth of Solitary Genius*. As well as indicating a legal responsibility and financial ownership, the joint listing of the writer's and the publisher's names on the page as the signature of the volume suggests a cooperative or collaborative production.

---

zines. The Romantic Age 1789–1836, ed. Alvin Sullivan (Westport, Ct.: Greenwood Press, 1983). It was the source of two anthologies, *The Beauties of the Anti-Jacobin*, which contained both poetry and prose and was published for the "middle classes," and *The Poetry of the Anti-Jacobin*, which by 1828 had reached a sixth edition.

[12] Keats, *Lamia*, ed. Jonathan Wordsworth (1820; rept. Oxford: Woodstock, 1990).

Pierre Bourdieu has commented that "the recognition of artistic legiti-macy . . . is inseparable from the production of the artist or the writer as artist or writer, in other words, as a creator of value. A reflection on the meaning of the artist's signature would thus be in order."[13] A reading of the public discourse is more concerned with the public significance of the signature and its titles than it is with the signature as the mark of the author's conscious-ness or intention, of individual authority or possession, more concerned with the signature as a connection that links the text to its context. A title page includes not only the title of the work but the title of the author, especially if it is the author's first publication and the author is otherwise unknown. Male writers often present titles, such as "M.P.," "M.A.," "Doctor of The-ology," "The Reverend," "Patriot," or in the case of Coleridge's first publi-cation, *The Fall of Robespierre*, simply "Of Jesus College, Cambridge"; women writers were commonly identified by their marital identity, "Miss" or "Mrs." Jerome Christensen describes the instance of the signature of Byron's *Hours of Idleness*: "Lord Byron Minor." Henry Brougham's notice in the *Edinburgh Review* of the poetry of the "noble minor" reads the signature as "a defense, the recourse of a marginal aristocrat or a weak poet," and, as Christensen remarks, Brougham "reads every page as a title page," in which Byron's title is in question.[14] Southey proudly included the title Poet-Lau-reate on the title pages of his laureate verse, along with Member Royal Span-ish Academy and Member Royal Spanish Academy of History, which made him even more of a target for Whig and reformist satire, as I argue in Chap-ter 5. Occasionally individuals created their own titles, as did Thomas Tay-lor, who presented himself as "Mr. Taylor, the Platonist," as he signed his bi-ographical sketch in Richard Phillips's *Public Characters*.[15] Coleridge quickly parodied his signature by calling him the "the English Pagan" (*CL* 1: 260).

As Jerome Christensen suggests, reviewers read the author's title, the title page, and prefaces as closely as the work itself. Coleridge's preface to *Christabel*, explaining the fragmentary nature of the work, his own inability to complete it, and his claims for originality of the meter, and Keats's pref-ace to *Endymion*, apologizing for his immaturity and expressing his love of Grecian subjects, are two clear examples of prefatory material that was read by reviewers as carefully as the poetry itself. Such prefaces usually deter-

[13] Pierre Bourdieu, *The Field of Cultural Production*, ed. Randal Johnson (New York: Co-lumbia University Press, 1993) 164.

[14] Jerome Christensen, *Lord Byron's Strength* (Baltimore: The Johns Hopkins University Press, 1993) 21–22.

[15] Richard Phillips, the editor of *The Monthly Magazine*, began an annual publication of bi-ographical sketches in 1798–99. Each volume contained from thirty to seventy biographical sketches. The first volume contained articles on "Mr. Taylor, the Platonist," "Dr. Priestley," "George Dyer," and "Miss Seward"; the second, Southey; and the third, Charlotte Smith, Thelwall, and Mrs. Robinson. The sketches were written by the subject or a close friend. Ten volumes were printed through 1810.

mined the tenor of reviews. Matthew Gregory Lewis's *The Monk* was published March 12, 1796, without the author's name on the title page, but with his initials at the end of the Preface. It was issued in another edition in the middle of September with "M. G. Lewis, Esq. M. P." on the title page. Lewis had been elected to Parliament in July. The reviews of the anonymous novel were favorable. Louis Peck records that the *Monthly Mirror* (June 1796) approved: "We really do not remember to have read a more interesting production. The stronger passions are finely delineated and exemplified in the progress of the artful temptation working on self-sufficient pride, superstition, and lasciviousness. . . . The whole is very skillfully managed, and reflects the highest credit on the judgment of the writer." A similarly impressed reviewer in the *Analytical Review* (Oct. 1796) remarked that "the whole temptation is so artfully contrived, that a man, it should seem, were he made as other men are, would deserve to be d——ned who could resist even devilish spells, conducted with such address." When, however, Lewis added his name to the title page along with his new title "M.P.," the reviewers were shocked. The *European Magazine* proclaimed that it "has neither *originality*, *morals*, nor *probability* to recommend it." Coleridge in the *Critical Review* (Feb. 1797) said of it, "If a parent saw [it] in the hands of a son or daughter, he might reasonably turn pale" because it provides a "poison for youth, and a provocative for the debauchee." Coleridge's outrage concluded: "Yes! the author of the Monk signs himself a *Legislator*!— We stare and tremble."[16] Coleridge's moral pose is excessively dramatic, the public stance of a figure associated with radical causes who wishes to defend himself, but Coleridge's point is important. The significance of authorship is not in a name, but in a public title. "M.P." claims a legitimacy to rule and a franking privilege that Lewis took as license of his literary enfranchisement.

Introductory biographical and autobiographical sketches in Lewis's day are fictions designed to construct a public signature. We can learn to read Coleridge's *Biographia Literaria* as a public document only when we learn who or what "Coleridge" signified in the public mind in the years in which Coleridge wrote it. The *Biographia*'s first sentence, commonly ignored in criticism, indicates that it originated in Coleridge's attempt to re-site his own signature in the public discourse: "It has been my lot to have had my name introduced both in conversation, and in print, more frequently than I find it easy to explain, whether I consider the fewness, unimportance, and limited circulation of my writings, or the retirement and distance, in which I have lived, both from the literary and political world" (*BL* 1: 5). The *Biographia* begins not with his private life, as in his autobiographical letters to

---

[16] Coleridge's review of *The Monk* in the *Critical Review* (Feb. 1797) is in *Shorter Works and Fragments*, ed. H. J. Jackson and J. R. de J. Jackson (Princeton: Princeton University Press, 1995) 1: 57–65.

Thomas Poole or as in Wordsworth's *Prelude*, but with his first publication of poems in 1796. This beginning cannot be dismissed as excessive self-pity or evasive self-reconstruction. He understood what our distance from his age has enabled us to forget: Romantic authorship is a public matter. Any full account of a life must be an account of a public life. Any full understanding of the *Biographia* must read Coleridge's attempt to locate himself in the public discourse.

Prefaces frequently define or redefine a public character, a political position, or a social stance. Michael Scrivener has detailed the rhetorical problem facing John Thelwall while he was publishing his *Poems Chiefly Written in Retirement* (1801). Thelwall included a long autobiographical preface to present himself as a man of letters, not as the most notorious Jacobin of the 1790s, and to appeal to readers of poetry who had not constituted his earlier political audience: "It is The Man, and not The Politician, that is here delineated. The disciple of the Muses; not The Lecturer and Leader of Popular Societies now no more."[17] The sketch itself was revised and greatly extended from an earlier version published in Phillips's *Public Characters*. Francis Jeffrey responded predictably in the *Edinburgh Review* for April 1803 that he saw "traces of that impatience of honest industry, that presumptuous vanity, and precarious principle, that have thrown so many adventurers upon the world, and drawn so many females from their plain work and embroidery, to delight the public by their beauty in the streets, and their novels in the circulating library."[18] The Preface to Joseph Cottle's anonymously published volume of *Poems* (1795), which included "War A Fragment," is signed "The Author." The volume was anti-war enough to receive a reference in "New Morality" in the *Anti-Jacobin* as "Co," who along with Coleridge, Southey, Lloyd, and Lamb tune their "mystic harps to praise Lepaux" (*PAJ* 235), the French theophilanthropist. Cottle's volume opens with an explanation of "War A Fragment" but quickly turns a diatribe against war itself and takes a public stance about the duties of all to oppose it: "This small volume is presented to the Public, not from a fond persuasion of its merit, but from a belief, that it is the duty of every man to raise his feeble voice in support of sinking humanity, and not to be content with thanking God, that he feels indignant at the enormities of war, without labouring to inspire the same abhorrence in the breasts of others."[19]

Title pages also frequently include a quotation or motto to supplement the author's signature and title. The *OED* defines a "motto" as originally an inscription or legend on a personal emblem, shield, or crest, which inter-

---

[17] John Thelwall, *Poems Chiefly Written in Retirement* (1801) i.

[18] Michael Scrivener, "The Rhetoric and Context of John Thelwall's 'Memoir,' " in *Spirits of Fire: English Romantic Writers and Contemporary Historical Methods*, ed. G. A. Russo and Daniel P. Watkins (Rutherford, N.J.: Fairleigh Dickenson University Press, 1990) 125.

[19] Joseph Cottle, *Poems*, intro. Donald H. Reiman (1795; rept. New York: Garland, 1978) ii.

prets the emblem and identifies the owner of the emblem. Anne Ferry has remarked that "a motto was also useful to a poet as a coded signature added at the end of a poem printed anonymously, where it served as an actual or pretended way of disguising his identity from the uninitiated,"[20] precisely Coleridge's strategy when he added his signature or motto, ESTEESI, to the first publication of "This Lime-Tree Bower" in *The Annual Anthology*. The motto thus becomes a personal sign. Coleridge was alert to precisely this use of *motto*, when, referring to his "Ode on the Departing Year," he described himself in a letter to John Prior Estlin as "a *mottophilist*, and almost a motto-*manist*" (*CL* 1: 293). Sometimes quotations are taken from literature; in other instances, the mottoes are created as personal signatures. Sometimes those quotations speak to other works or individuals. The second volume of *Lyrical Ballads* (1800) included Wordsworth's motto "Quam nihil ad genium, Papiniane, tuum!" "Something not at all to your taste, Papinianus," a private joke on Sir James Mackintosh.[21] Like other elements of paratext, a motto or quotation may lead from the work itself to a public significance.

APOSTROPHE AS ADDRESS

A work's signature is oriented toward the public and is commonly accompanied by some form of address such as dedications, mottoes, prefaces, prefatory poems, or verse epistles in a volume of poetry, all public forms of the conventions of signing and addressing private presentation copies. The social or political relationship of author to patron, opponent, or friend is implied. Forms of address establish political and social allegiances and thus extend the range of signature. Some writing continued to be the product of a patronage system, in which dedications preserved the tone of religious devotion and the formal traces of religious apostrophe as in hymns, odes, and prayers. The secularized dedications of an earlier age are continued, for instance, in the dedication of Southey's *A Vision of Judgment* to the Prince Regent:

> We owe much to the House of Brunswick; but to none of that illustrious House more than to Your Majesty, under whose government the military renown of Great Britain has been carried to the highest point of glory. From that pure glory there has been nothing to detract; the success was not more splendid than the cause was good; and the event was deserved by the generosity, the justice, the wisdom, and the magnanimity of the counsels which prepared it. The same perfect integrity has been manifested in the whole administration of public affairs. More has been done than was ever before attempted, for mitigating the

[20] Anne Ferry, *The Title to the Poem* (Stanford: Stanford University Press, 1996) 232.
[21] *Lyrical Ballads*, ed. R. L. Brett and A. R. Jones (London: Methuen, 1963) 124–25.

evils incident to our stage of society; for imbuing the rising race with those sound principles of religion on which the welfare of states has its only secure foundation; and for opening new regions to the redundant enterprize and industry of the people.[22]

Many dedications lost much of the flattery common in earlier ages, and frequently the dedication or address is to an equal or ally. The first poem in Southey's *Poems* (1797) was "To Mary Wollstonecraft" and compares her to Joan of Arc, Mme Roland, and Charlotte Corday. The poem was preceded by a title page containing the title of the poem following "To Mary Wollstonecraft": "The Triumph of Woman." The person addressed was often invoked, not as authority figure or social superior, but as an equal. Thomas Paine dedicated *The Rights of Man* to George Washington: "I present you with a small treatise in defense of those principles of freedom which your exemplary virtue hath so eminently contributed to establish."[23] The dedication may extend the boundaries of the work but is rarely a cause for a public response by either the person who receives the gift or the reviewers. One notable exception is Lockhart's reading of Leigh Hunt's dedication of *The Story of Rimini* to "My dear Byron." Offended by Hunt's familiarity and his lack of respect for rank, Lockhart noted "The insult which he offered to Lord Byron in the dedication of Rimini,—in which he, a paltry cockney newspaper scribbler, had the assurance to address one of the most nobly-born of English Patricians, and one of the first geniuses whom the world ever produced, as 'My dear Byron,' although it may have been forgotten and despised by the illustrious person whom it most nearly concerned,—excited a feeling of utter loathing and disgust in the public mind. . . ."[24]

When one writes in opposition, the form is usually that of a letter rather than that of a worshipful dedication, as in Burke's *Letter to a Noble Lord* (1796), or Hazlitt's *Letter to William Gifford* (1819), which began, "You have an ugly trick of saying what is not true of any one you do not like; and it will be the object of this letter to cure you of it" (Howe 9: 13). Similarly, Southey's *Letter to William Smith* opens with the accusation that "you deliberately stood up for the purpose of reviling an individual who was not present to vindicate himself, and in a place which afforded you protection,"[25] a reference to Smith's accusations in Parliament over the publication of *Wat Tyler* in 1817. Perhaps the most acid address is Cobbett's to Malthus in his letter "*To Parson Malthus, on the Rights of the Poor; and on the*

[22] *A Vision of Judgment* (London, 1821) vi–vii.

[23] *The Complete Writings of Thomas Paine*, ed. Philip Foner (New York: Citadel Press, 1969) 1: 244.

[24] "On the Cockney School of Poetry," *Blackwood's* 1 (Oct. 1817): 41.

[25] *Life & Correspondence of Robert Southey*, ed. Rev. Charles Cuthbert Southey (New York, 1850) 4: 370.

Cruelty Recommended by Him To Be Exercised towards the Poor, in the *Political Register* May 1819: "I have, during my life, detested many men; but never any one so much as you." These addresses parody the signatures of the person addressed: Malthus is the "boroughmongering parson," and Gifford is the "Government Critic."

The mocking tone of these caricatures suggests the popularity of Gillray's cartoons and the satirical attacks of the *Anti-Jacobin*. As Carmela Perri points out, the word *allusion* originates in the Latin *alludere*, "to imitate and mock,"[26] and the parodies in the *Anti-Jacobin* offer a curious combination of signature, address, and allusion in the parodies of Erasmus Darwin's *Loves of the Plants* as *The Loves of the Triangles*, Richard Payne Knight's *The Progress of Civil Society* as *The Progress of Man*, and Schiller's *The Robbers*, as *The Rovers*. The author of these parodies was identified as "Mr. Higgins, of St. Mary Axe," a composite caricature of Darwin, Knight, and Coleridge, who was born at Ottery St. Mary and who published satirical sonnets under the name of Nehemiah Higginbottom (*CP* 1: 209–11), all in the eyes of the *Anti-Jacobin* equally guilty of subversive writing. The parodic address assigns authorship to Mr. Higgins, the composite of the Jacobin poet, and complicates the satire by combining address and signature. The Jacobins are addressed with much the same contempt that William Smith, William Gifford, and Thomas Malthus are addressed by Southey, Hazlitt, and Cobbett, yet by assigning authorship to Mr. Higgins, the *Anti-Jacobin* perpetrates a forgery. Not only is Mr. Higgins assigned authorship, he is assigned prefatory letters that explain his principles. His prefatory letter to the editors, which accompanies their publication of *The Loves of the Triangles*, which is actually a letter from the editors to the Jacobins, explains his principles:

> Our first principle is, then—the reverse of the trite and dull maxim of Pope—"*Whatever is, is right*." We contend that "*Whatever is, is wrong*:" —that Institutions civil and religious, that Social Order, (as it is called in *your* cant) and regular Government, and Law, and I know not what other fantastic inventions, are but so many cramps and fetters on the free agency of man's *natural intellect* and *moral sensibility*; so many badges of his degradation from the primal purity and excellence of his nature. (*PAJ* 109–10)

The parody, addressed to the Jacobins and signed by their caricature of a Jacobin, is a forgery, thus arguing that Jacobin principles are worthless coinage. Although attributed to an author, there is no author, no original but a mere fiction; the work gleefully refuses the claims of its signature. In an age fascinated with the forgeries of Macpherson and Chatterton, parody that is forgery indicates an illegitimacy associated with claims for the original purity of human nature and unrestrained freedom. Signature and ad-

[26] Carmela Perri, "On Alluding," *Poetics* 7 (1978): 301.

dress merge into a tangled web of duplicity, disguise, and forgery. Neither can be read as a simple sign of authority or intention without exploring the discourse that it enters.

Paratextual address and parody are only two of the ways in which one work speaks to another. Frequently a work quotes, echoes, or alludes to a contemporary work that it opposes, and to quote is to address. A word or phrase re-sited from one work to another locates a work within a network of recitations. Burke's lament over the mob's invasion of the Queen's bedchamber at Versailles, "The age of chivalry is gone.— That of sophisters, oeconomists, and calculators, has succeeded; and the glory of Europe is extinguished for ever" (*RRF* 127), was answered by Thomas Paine in *The Rights of Man*:

> When we see a man dramatically lamenting in a publication intended to be believed, that, "*The age of chivalry is gone!* that *The glory of Europe is extinguished forever!* that *The unbought grace of life* (if any one knows what it is), *the cheap defense of nations, the nurse of manly sentiment and heroic enterprise, is gone!*" and all this because the Quixotic age of chivalric nonsense is gone, what opinion can we form of his judgment, or what regard can we pay to his facts. (Paine 1: 259)

The innumerable answers to Burke's *Reflections on the Revolution in France* return to these phrases, through quotation or allusion, and constitute an answer to Burke.[27] Byron, having debunked the ideals of chivalry in his 1812 Addition to the Preface of *Childe Harold*, concluded that "Burke need not have regretted that its days are over, though Maria Antoinette was quite as chaste as most of those in whose honours lances were shivered, and knights unhorsed . . . I fear a little investigation will teach us not to regret those monstrous mummeries of the middle ages" (*BP* 2: 6). An age that we have agreed to call Romantic, an age we have defined by the genre of romance, writes the genre of romance between Burke's and Paine's versions of chivalry and quest, between idealizations in the name of legitimacy and skepticism in the name of reform.

The intricate repetitions of Burke's phrase and allusions to it suggest that at a fundamental level the literature that we read as romance is deeply implicated in the public discourse, in the debates over the constitution of the state and a subject's rights and liberties. Allusion and quotation assume the function of public address, since the genres of the public discourse, the lecture, the letter, and the review, all incorporate precise address. If one reads for the text's connections with its exterior, the rhetoric of public poetry is allusion that is mediated and discursive, not metaphor that troubles the is-

---

[27] See "Chronological Survey of the Controversy Concerning Burke's Reflections, 1790–1793," in James T. Boulton, *The Language of Politics* (London: Routledge & Kegan Paul, 1963) 265–71 and a similar list in *RRF* 533–37.

sues of representation. If one reads only the text, its borders, and a rhetoric based on the binary oppositions of Coleridge's distinction between allegory and symbol, or New Criticism's irony and paradox, or deconstruction's chiasmus, or even dialogics' heteroglossia, then rhetoric is bound by the assumptions of those methodologies. If, however, one wishes to read a work in the discursive field of its historical location, then one must trace the allusions that connect it with its exterior in the discourse. And if Habermas is right and a public is constructed of private individuals acting in their own self-interest, then it is possible to define a network of public discourse in which individual utterances are addressed to other individual utterances, although it may be difficult to find examples of reasonable discourse. Allusion in such a network is not dispersed in an impersonal intertextuality, where the specific references of allusion are lost in the network of language, so that mapping the figure of allusion is an impossibility. With such an intertextuality, allusion is impossible to trace, because it has no identifiable origin, no signature of its utterance. Barthes writes that "alongside each utterance, one might say that off-stage voices can be heard: they are the codes: in their interweaving, these voices (whose origin is 'lost' in the vast perspective of the *already-written*) de-originate the utterance...."[28] Allusion is mediated, signed, and often entitled. Signature and address are the signs of identifiable utterances. Influential works rarely appear without address, precise location, and explicit or implicit signature, even though all may create a disguise. As the example of parody and forgery indicates, signature, address, and location may be intricate to the point of purposeful evasion, but they are still readable. The continuance of the discourse depends on their readability.

Allusion in the public discourse is a form of address. The compound figure of apostrophe should also be read as a form of public address. As Quintilian and Cicero suggest, the figure indicates, first, a turning away from the immediate audience or subject of an oration, and second, a prosopopeia that completes an address to a person, place, or object.[29] The turn indicates that it is a figure of interruption since it breaks the continuity of any discourse. Wordsworth annotated Richard Payne Knight's *Analytical Inquiry into the Principles of Taste*, where Knight quoted Hugh Blair's criticism of an apostrophe to a hand in Pope's "Eloisa to Abelard," which Blair thought unworthy because "a personified hand is low." Wordsworth agreed that Pope's apostrophes fail but argued that "the meanness of the passage lies in this that the several apostrophes arise not from the impulse of passion; they are not

[28] Roland Barthes, *S/Z*, trans. Richard Miller (New York: Hill and Wang, 1974) 21.

[29] Quintilian, *Institutio Oratoria*, trans. H. E. Butler (Cambridge, Mass.: Harvard University Press, 1921) 3: 397; Cicero, *Ad C. Herennium*, (IV. xv.22) trans. Harry Caplan (Cambridge, Mass.: Harvard University Press, 1954) 283. See also Douglas Kneale's distinction between apostrophe and prosopopeia in "Romantic Aversions: Apostrophe Reconsidered," *English Literary History*, 58 (1991): 141–65.

abrupt, interrupted and revolutionary but formal, and mechanically accumulated."[30] Apostrophe as address may come first in a dedication that forms the boundary of the work, but, as in the cases of the letters of Hazlitt, Southey, and Gifford, it is intended to interrupt or disrupt the other's discourse. The second element in apostrophe, prosopopeia, is also changed in the public discourse. It is not, as Paul de Man defined it, an address "to an absent, deceased, or voiceless entity."[31] Rather apostrophe as prosopopeia speaks to another public signature, by which, if the apostrophe is truly a figure of interruption and revolution as Wordsworth said, the other is caricatured, as the boroughmongering parson, the government critic, or Mr. Higgins. It would even be easy to read a eulogistic apostrophe, such as Southey's to George IV, as the caricature of a public figure, simply on the grounds of its excess. Apostrophe signs the work that it addresses with the mark of a public figure. In 1820 Coleridge annotated a copy of *Conciones ad Populum* to suggest that public persons become personifications: "Except the two or three passages involving the doctrine of Phil. Necessity & Unitarianism I see little or nothing in these outbursts of my youthful Zeal to *retract*, & with exception of some flame-colored Epithets applied to Persons, as Mr. Pitt & others, or rather to Personifications (for such they really were to me) as little to regret" (*Lect.* 25).

The problems of reading allusion as address complicate the reading of traditional literary allusion, often defined as requiring a clear indication of the author's intention and a reasonable certainty that an appropriate audience would recognize the allusion. Even when the allusion may appear to be unconscious on the part of the author and frequently unrecognized by the reader, literary allusion functions as a figure to elaborate the interior of a work.[32] In the public discourse, the allusion may not only be to a literary work of a previous generation; it may be to a nonliterary work of a contemporary. Such allusions import public issues into the private work. A work read in isolation as exclusively private may, through a set of inconspicuous allusions to public matters, be changed by recognition of the public allusions, which cannot be discovered by reading only the work. Thus in discursive, mediated, signed, titled, and sometimes apostrophic allusion, al-

---

[30] *Margin.* 3: 404. I have simplified this transcription. There is some uncertainty whether this is Wordsworth's or Coleridge's comment (*Margin.* 3: 400–401)

[31] Paul de Man, "Autobiography as De-Facement," *The Rhetoric of Romanticism* (New York: Columbia University Press, 1984) 75.

[32] James K. Chandler tests Wasserman's definition of allusion and argues that "as Romantic lyricism reflects an emerging doctrine of unconscious association, so Romantic allusiveness reflects a doctrine of literary influence" ("Romantic Allusiveness," *Critical Inquiry* 8 [1982]: 479). Jonathan Bate has argued that Romantic allusions to Shakespeare are often unconscious (*Shakespeare and the English Romantic Imagination* [Oxford: Clarendon Press, 1986] 35–36). See also Lucy Newlyn's discussion of Romantic allusion as a "crossing over from one frame of reference to another" (*Paradise Lost and the Romantic Reader* [Oxford: Clarendon Press, 1993] 5).

lusion that is both mocking and, in Wordsworth's words, revolutionary, one cannot assume an informed audience in the late twentieth century as part of the definition of allusion, particularly since the historical discourse is largely unread and forgotten.

Discursive allusion is mediated and located, often inconspicuous because of our historical distance from the age, a distance that has conspired with twentieth-century esthetics, which reads a history without footnotes, as Cleanth Brooks read Keats's "Ode on a Grecian Urn." Romantic poetry is deeply allusive in its paratext, its locations, and its internal figures. Those allusions are mediated, both because they are determined by another proximate text, occasionally indicated by direct address, and because they are in the public press. The exterior may be present to the text and present in the text. John Hollander has explicated the figure of transumption, the figure of interpretive allusion, by its mediation, by the ways in which a third figure mediates between an original and the later figure.[33] In the case of a discursive reading, that mediation is done in a public arena, immensely complicated in its relations and intricately filiated among a number of different fields and subjects. When literary allusion is read in the context of literary history, its mediation is exclusively literary, but when allusion is read in the public discourse, its mediation is necessarily public. Mediated discursive allusion turns from the purely literary, interior, and personal to a public space, where it takes its significance. When a poet alludes to Milton or to Shakespeare, one must ask "Whose Milton or Shakespeare?" just as when a poet alludes to Virgil or the Bible, one must ask "Whose Virgil?" and "Whose reading of the Bible?" In reading literary allusion, one commonly answers these questions by saying that if Keats or Wordsworth alludes to Milton, it is surely Keats's or Wordsworth's Milton, and the evidence for such a reading comes from their other poetry, letters, journals, and private writing.

But in reading discursive allusion, the answer must come from the public discourse. To ignore the Milton of the public discourse is to remain unaware of that mediation and the public nature of private poetry. Milton is surely the model of the visionary poet, but he is also publicly cited as the republican and regicide, both in literary and in nonliterary works. His poetry is often read through his republican prose. A large part of Thomas Erskine's defense at Thomas Paine's trial for writing the second part of the *Rights of Man* contained quotations and allusions to "great men, whose works are classics in our language, taught in our schools, and printed under the eye of the Government." He began with Milton "a great authority in

---

[33] John Hollander, *The Figure of Echo: A Mode of Allusion in Milton and After* (Berkeley: University of California, 1981) 133. See also Harold Bloom's use of metalepsis in *A Map of Misreading* (New York: Oxford University Press, 1975) 139.

all learning.—It may be said, indeed, he was a Republican, but that would only prove that Republicanism is not incompatible with virtue. . . ."[34] Coleridge confirmed the identification in 1802: "Milton was a pure Republican, and yet his notions of government were highly aristocratic" (*EOT* 1: 370). When citing Milton in his early political prose, Coleridge read Milton's poetry in the light of his political prose. In 1801, looking back on those who defended liberty in the 1790s in the face of suspension of Habeas Corpus and the attempts of the government to restrict free speech and free assembly, he applied *Paradise Lost* to contemporary dissent:

> We respect the persons, and the rank, we revere the talents, and above all, the services of Opposition. We remember with grateful admiration the patient endurance, and the intrepid courage, with which they defended the Laws and Constitution of their country, and the rights of all mankind, in "evil days" and among "evil tongues." In the trying hour, when liberty was, as it were, fixed on the cross of shame and public abhorrence, amid the earthquake, that rent, and the darkness, that covered, the whole earth; they persisted to acknowledge, and proclaim, the divinity of its mission. (*EOT* 1: 284)

As in the case of Wordsworth's use of Virgil's "paulò majora canamus" to introduce the "Ode" in 1807 or Coleridge's and Byron's use of the Introduction to Book VII of *Paradise Lost*, the allusions are mediated by the public debates.

"This Lime-Tree Bower My Prison": "No Unmeaning Signature"

To read a Romantic lyric in the public discourse is to place it in the complex network of published writing that spreads far beyond what Habermas narrowly defined as the public sphere. Romantic poems have been read in the second half of the twentieth century as pure lyrics, Coleridge's Conversation Poems, Wordsworth's "Tintern Abbey," and Keats's odes for examples, all of which have in common the first-person speaker, a setting at a particular place and a particular time, and address to another person. These subjective meditations on nature and human imagination obscure striking similarities between the conventions of the subjective Romantic lyric and an essential genre of the public discourse, the letter, which is local and located, addressed, signed, allusive, and mediated. However subjective and individual Romantic lyrics appear in modern editions, removed from their initial publication and stripped of their paratexts, their form is fundamentally public. As Habermas has pointed out, the letter was the primary form of a subjectivity as the "innermost core of the private" that "was al-

---

[34] *The Whole Proceedings on the Trial . . . Thomas Paine* (1793), in *The Prosecution of Thomas Paine: Seven Tracts, 1793–98*, ed. Stephen Parks (New York: Garland, 1974) 158.

ways already oriented to an audience."[35] At the level of their allusive structure, Romantic lyrics are public places, and private meditations are mediated public forms.

Coleridge's "This Lime-Tree Bower My Prison" is typical of the lyrics
that have been read as subjective meditations, yet in its first publication
it is a public declaration of social and political principles, obscured in
Coleridge's later republication of the poem. I shall re-site the poem at its
borders in 1800, the point at which the public and the private become in-
tertwined and read the private poem and its public stance in its paratextual
allusions. "This Lime-Tree Bower" was first published in the second volume of Southey's *Annual Anthology* (1800). Two earlier untitled versions
survive in manuscript: one in a letter to Southey of July 17, 1797 (*CL* 1:
334–36) and a second in an undated letter to Charles Lloyd, now in the Berg
Library. These versions were available to a small circle of friends. The first
was part of a long letter describing the rambles of Wordsworth, Dorothy,
and Lamb and included a footnote to remind Southey that "I am a
Berkleian," and another that seems designed for a general audience: "The
ferns, that grow in moist places, grow five or six together & form a complete 'Prince of Wales's Feather'—i.e. plumy." The version sent to Lloyd
was almost devoid of commentary except for a note, now partially de-
stroyed, on the sound of flying rooks.[36]

Both in its private and public forms, the poem was surrounded by the
paratext of a letter. Originally a response to Wordsworth's drafting "The
Ruined Cottage" in the summer of 1797 containing a blessing for Charles
Lamb,[37] it was transmitted in letters to Southey and Lloyd shortly after it
was first drafted and was later published in *The Annual Anthology* surrounded with the full paratext of a public letter. Its full title was "This
Lime-Tree Bower My Prison, / A Poem, / Addressed to Charles Lamb, of
the India House, London." It came with an Advertisement that sites the
poem:

> In the June of 1797 some long-expected Friends paid a visit to the Author's
> Cottage; and on the morning of their arrival he met with an accident, which
> disabled him from walking during the whole time of their stay. One evening,
> when they had left him for a few hours, he composed the following lines in the
> Garden Bower.[38]

---

[35] Jürgen Habermas, *The Structural Transformation of the Public Sphere*, trans. Thomas
Burger and Frederick Lawrence (Cambridge, Mass.: MIT Press, 1991) 49.

[36] Stillinger dates the version in the letter to Lloyd as later than the one in the letter to
Southey (*Coleridge and Textual Instability* [above, n. 7] 45).

[37] See my *Coleridge and Wordsworth: A Lyrical Dialogue* (Princeton: Princeton University
Press, 1988) 114–16.

[38] *The Annual Anthology*, ed. Robert Southey (Bristol, 1800) 2: 140. Quotations from "This
Lime-Bower" are from this version.

After the final line of the poem, Coleridge signed the poem "ESTEESI." Address and signature point both inward toward the poem by quoting it and outward toward other writing by allusion. The extended title of address and the signature were removed in *Sibylline Leaves*, where the poem was placed in the classification of "Meditative Poems in Blank Verse" and where the surviving site of the poem is the private bower.

The poem's paratext changes its genre from a "conversation poem" or "greater Romantic lyric," both twentieth-century definitions, or from a "meditative poem in blank verse," to the genre of a public letter. The addition of an Advertisement changes its utterance from a private blessing to a public statement, since the word *advertisement* itself originates in announcements in the public square by town criers. Advertisement is a trope of public mediation, an adverting toward the subject, but at the same time an averting (from its medieval French origin in *avertissement*), a turning away. The *OED* thus lists one historical meaning of *advertisement* as a warning or admonition. For example, the Advertisement to *Lyrical Ballads* warns a reader against expecting traditional poetry. The word *advertisement* thus alerts a reader, not only to the public location of the themes, but also a certain evasiveness in the poem itself—a turning toward and away at the same time—an evasiveness required by the political pressures of the day. The adverting and averting announce its rhetoric.

Southey's *Annual Anthology*, suggested to him by William Taylor and modeled on the German almanacs, was published in two volumes in 1799 and 1800. On November 10, 1799, Coleridge encouraged Southey to structure the second volume carefully: "The great & master fault of the last anthology was the want of arrangement / it is called a Collection, & meant to be continued annually; yet was distinguished in nothing from any other single volume of poems, equally good" (*CL* 1: 545). Southey thought of the volume as a miscellaneous repository "for my lesser ballads" and responded to Coleridge on December 15 that he saw no "advantage from method— mixed is best."[39] Although Southey thought of the volume as trivial, his preface to the first volume stated that many of the poems were first published in the *Morning Post*, one of the primary targets of the *Anti-Jacobin*, so the political leanings of the authors would have been obvious to a contemporary audience. *The Annual Anthology* may itself have been a response to other anthologies, *The Poetry of the Anti-Jacobin* and *The Beauties of the Anti-Jacobin*, which collected the parodies of Jacobin verse published in the *Anti-Jacobin, or Weekly Examiner*. When Southey was composing the volume, Coleridge offered "Christabel," if he could complete it; the poems in his *Fears in Solitude* volume, if Johnson would give up the copyright; and anything that Southey wanted from the *Morning Post* (*CL* 1: 552). Southey se-

[39] *New Letters of Robert Southey*, ed. Kenneth Curry (New York: Columbia University Press, 1965) 1: 181, 207.

lected fifteen Coleridge poems and a number of epigrams along with his own poems and those of others: Joseph Cottle, William Taylor, Charles Lloyd, Amelia Opie, among others.[40] Ten of Coleridge's poems came from the *Morning Post*, including "Fire, Famine, and Slaughter" and "The Mad Ox." Hazlitt, at least, regarded it among Southey's Jacobin publications. In 1817, attacking Coleridge's defense of Southey in the *Courier* over the *Wat Tyler* episode, Hazlitt responded that Southey's "Joan of Arc, his Sonnets and Inscriptions, his Letters from Spain and Portugal, his Annual Anthology, in which was published Mr. Coleridge's 'Fire, Famine, and Slaughter,' are a series of invectives against Kings, Priests, and Nobles, in favour of the French Revolution, and against war and taxes up to the year 1803" (Howe 7:181). In a cartoon ridiculing Southey printed at the time of the Wat Tyler episode, *The Annual Anthology* is curled up under *Wat Tyler* as one of Southey's radical publications (*EOT* 2: 472).

The original versions of "This Lime-Tree Bower" were in private letters, but the published poem shares a public space with the other poems associated with the *Morning Post*, locations unmistakably connected with dissent, antiwar sentiment, hatred of wealth and luxury, and the hope for equality, causes which both Burke and the editors of the *Anti-Jacobin* classified as Jacobin. Its address to Charles Lamb in 1800 is another of its political gestures. In the *Anti-Jacobin's* poem "New Morality," Lamb is linked with Coleridge, Southey, Charles Lloyd, and Joseph Cottle, as a follower of the French theophilanthropist Lépeaux, and in the Gillray cartoon of the poem published in August 1798, Lamb was portrayed along with Lloyd as "toad and frog," reading from their volume *Blank Verse by Toad and Frog*. In addition he was included in "The Anarchists.—An Ode," published in the *Anti-Jacobin Review* in September 1798. The allegorical figure of Anarchy protects dissidents:

> See! faithful to their mighty dam,
> C——dge, S—th-y, L—d, and L—be,
> In splay-foot madrigals of love,
> Soft moaning like the widow'd dove,
> Pour, side by side, their sympathetic notes;
>   Of equal rights, and civic feats,
>   And tyrant Kings, and knavish priests,
> Swift through the land the tuneful mischief floats.
>   And now to softer strains they struck the lyre,
>   They sung the beetle, or the mole,
>   The dying kid, or ass's foal,
>   By cruel man permitted to expire.

(1: 366)

[40] Kenneth Curry, "The Contributors to *The Annual Anthology*." *Papers of the Bibliographical Society of America* 42 (1948): 50–65. See also *Margin*. 1: 88–90.

Burton Pollin accounted for Lamb's inclusion in the *Anti-Jacobin*'s attacks by reference to *Blank Verse* by Charles Lloyd and Charles Lamb published in 1798.[41] Lamb had contributed to Coleridge's early volumes of poetry, and his contributions to *Blank Verse* were purely personal poems such as the laments over his mother's tragic death. While in 1797 Coleridge's address to Lamb was a personal reference, in 1800 when it was published, Lamb's tragedy had become public by publication of his poems. Coleridge's reference in 1797 is to Lamb's private letters; his reference in 1800 is to Lamb's and Lloyd's public poems, and Lloyd's poems stood squarely in the reformist camp.

Blank Verse began with a dedication to Southey signed by "C. Lloyd": "In offering these Poems to you I am simply consulting my feelings. The greater part of them were written beneath your roof, and owe their existence to its quiet comforts." The first half of the volume contains Lloyd's poems, introduced by a separate title page. The first poem in Lloyd's collection is a letter "To ******. Written in Worcestershire, July 1797." Both the verse and the notes summarize Jacobin themes:

> The world to me
> Seemeth the prison-house of man, where Power
> And loathlier Wealth inflict on trembling slaves
> The rackings of despair!
>
> (7)

Finding solace only in solitude and nature Lloyd ponders a utopian society:

> Often in no uninterested mood
> I've told thee that there were of noble souls
> Who deem'd it wise, e'en in the morn of youth,
> To quit this world!

A footnote explains that "this alludes to a plan projected by S. T. Coleridge and Robert Southey, together with some common friends, of establishing a society in America, in which all individual property was to be abandoned" (9). Lloyd adds a note to the phrase "elect of Heaven," to describe the social visionaries' reward: "Wherever the word elect is used in the following pages, the authors by no means intend the arbitrary dogma of Calvinism. They are both believers in the doctrine of philosophical necessity, and in the final happiness of all mankind. They apply the word elect therefore to those persons whom *secondary causes*, under providence, have fitted for an immediate entrance into the paradisiacal state" (11). Lloyd's philosophy

[41] Burton R. Pollin, "Charles Lamb and Charles Lloyd as Jacobins and Anti-Jacobins," *SIR* 12 (1973): 633–47. See *Blank Verse by Charles Lloyd and Charles Lamb* (1798), intro. Donald H. Reiman (New York: Garland, 1798). Quotations are to this edition by page number.

came from Priestley and Hartley directly through Coleridge. Pollin connects this note with a Godwinism that Lloyd shared with Lamb. The poem concludes with a hope for a utopian future "when *equal man / Shall deem the world his temple*" (12–13). Another Lloyd poem, "London," is clearly derived from "This Lime-Tree Bower," which Lloyd had received in a letter from Coleridge. Amid the "tainted scenes" "of the "proud city," the speaker recognizes that he who retires to "majestic solitude" will gain wisdom, hold "high converse with the present God / (Not mystically meant), and feels him ever / Made manifest to his transfigur'd soul." Lloyd's note to "present" in the phrase "present God" reads "The doctrine of Berkeley, of which the Author is a believer, is here alluded to" (61), which originated in Coleridge's note to the letter version of "This Lime-Tree Bower" sent to Southey.

Coleridge's public apostrophe to "gentle-hearted Charles" in *The Annual Anthology* version of "This Lime-Tree Bower" is to the Charles Lamb of *Blank Verse*, who has suffered a personal loss, and to Lloyd's opening poem:

>   thou had'st pin'd
> And hunger'd after nature many a year
> In the great city pent, winning thy way
> With sad yet patient soul, thro' evil and pain
> And strange calamity!

Coleridge's solace is also sought by Lloyd's solitary man in nature. There is nothing exclusively biographical, interior, or psychological about these associations. When Coleridge addresses "Charles Lamb" in *The Annual Anthology*, he addresses the figure associated with the Godwinians, the pantisocrats, and the West Country radicals. Unfortunately for Lamb, his own writings had little to do with his public signature, for it was a matter of his public associations and the locations of his poems, not his words. "Charles Lamb" was a mediated figure. Both the paratext's address and the text's apostrophe point to a public context in which private meditation has unmistakable public significance beyond Coleridge's blessing on Lamb.

Most of the poems in *The Annual Anthology* were signed by initials or anagrams. Five of Coleridge's were signed "ESTEESI," the vocalization of his transliteration of the Greek letters ΕΣΤΗΣΕ, representing "S. T. C.": "A Christmas Carol," "Ode to Georgiana, Duchess of Devonshire," "To a Friend, who had declared his intention of writing no more poetry," "The British Stripling's War-Song," and "This Lime-Tree Bower." The first two of these were explicitly anti-war poems. In English letters, Coleridge's signature would have been easily read as his initials, especially in *The Annual Anthology*, since other authors were similarly identified, and since a list of the contributors to the first volume was published in Southey's biographical sketch in the second volume of *Public Characters* (1799–1800). The only poem that Coleridge insisted be signed with his name was "The Mad Ox," an allegory of the French Revolution as an ox goaded into a destructive rampage by the townspeople (*CL* 1: 573). "The Mad Ox," along with nine other Coleridge poems, had appeared in the *Morning Post*, where Coleridge had signed his name to "The Visions of the Maid of Orleans," published on December 26, 1797 and "France: An Ode," published on April 16, 1798 as "The Recantation: An Ode." It would have been easy for an astute reader to identify the author of "This Lime-Tree Bower," through its address to Lamb and its signature. It would have been obvious that the author opposed the current war against France and sympathized with the spirit of the French Revolution, if not its acts.

Coleridge's use of "ESTEESI" as his public signature and motto began late in 1799 and continued in his newspaper verse over the next few years, sometimes in English letters, sometimes in Greek. In Greek it was intelligible to a limited circle of readers, the audience that Coleridge intended, but it obscured his personal authorship and could not be widely read. His signature is a code for the educated, and by restricting his audience, Coleridge avoided the government's fear of disseminating seditious thought. Coleridge explained its significance to William Sotheby in 1802:

> Ἕστησε signifies—*He hath stood*—which in these times of apostasy from the principles of Freedom, or of Religion in this country, & from both by the same persons in France, is no unmeaning Signature, if subscribed with humility, & in the remembrance of, Let him that stands take heed lest he fall—. However, it is in truth no more than S. T. C. written in Greek. *Es tee see*—

E. L. Griggs suggests that the transitive "he hath placed" is a more accurate translation of what Coleridge called Punic Greek, which he probably pronounced "punning" Greek in "A Character" (c. 1825), a comic self-portrait:[42]

> Thus, his own whim his only bribe,
> Our Bard pursued his old A. B. C.
> Contented if he could subscribe
> In fullest sense his name Ἕστησε;
> ('Tis Punic Greek for 'he hath stood!')
> Whate'er the men, the cause was good;
> And therefore with a right good will,
> Poor fool, he fights their battles still.

(*CP* 1: 453)

---

[42] *CL* 2: 867. See Tim Fulford's analysis of the signature in *Coleridge's Figurative Language* (New York: St. Martin's Press, 1991) 28–34. E. K. Chambers suggests that to be an accurate translation of "he hath stood" Coleridge's Greek "should have been Ἕστηκε" (*Samuel Taylor Coleridge: A Biographical Study* [Oxford: Clarendon Press, 1938] 161), but then Coleridge's puns would have been lost.

By itself, the word *Punic* indicates "Carthaginians," the ancient people proverbial for treachery and deception. Thus one should be alert to a duplicity in the signature. There may even be an obscure pun on the Etesian winds that blew across the Mediterranean from the North described by the ancient Greeks, especially since the poem was later reprinted in *Sibylline Leaves*—the fragments scattered by the winds. Whether read as "he hath stood" or "he hath placed," the word indicates not a personality, but a position, a location which, as he explained to Sotheby, defines him as a friend of freedom authorized by a religion rejected by other English Jacobins and equally distinct from the French, whom Coleridge saw as having forsaken both liberty and religion. Although in the public discourse he was associated with Thelwall, Godwin, and Paine, he rejected their atheism.[43] Accused of apostasy and unprincipled wavering, and recognizing that Daniel Stuart, the editor of the *Morning Post*, was interrogated by the government in 1798 and that Joseph Johnson, his publisher, went to jail in 1799, Coleridge had to be cautious about his public signature, yet at the same time he was reckless enough to subscribe publicly to seditious causes. He tried to define, for a limited audience, a public standing, which his contentious and factious readers transformed either to vacillation or to French Jacobinism. Either like the Parliamentarians whom he satirized, Coleridge oscillated, or, like the correspondents with whom he exchanged blessings, he persisted publicly in support of a seditious cause. With humor and seriousness, assertion and evasiveness, honesty and deceit, principled publicity and plastic policy, Coleridge signed "This Lime-Tree Bower" to claim his location.

Like the relationship between address and apostrophe in "This Lime-Tree Bower," that between poem and signature is complex because Coleridge's "he hath stood" repeats and translates the lines at the center of the poem. The paratextual signature identifies the poem's central trope of standing, of taking a stand, even though its standing is purposefully evasive:

> So my Friend
> Struck with deep joy may stand, as I have stood,
> Silent with swimming sense; yea, gazing round
> On the wide landscape, gaze till all doth seem
> Less gross than bodily, a living thing
> Which acts upon the mind—and with such hues
> As cloath the Almighty Spirit, when he makes
> Spirits perceive his presence.

Paratextual signature transcribes the poem; it translates and transliterates while it cites. The trope of standing is both inside and outside the poem. Coleridge's signature indicates that it is a poem about standing and taking

---

[43] See Chapter 3, pp. 77–78, 82–83.

a politically transgressive stand. His explanation of his Greek signature includes a paraphrase of St. Paul: "let him that stands take heed lest he fall" (I Cor. 10: 12). The trope of standing also alludes to *Paradise Lost*: God's admonition describing man, "I made him just and right, / Sufficient to have stood, though free to fall" (*PL* III, 98–99); Satan's regret that "other Powers as great / Fell not, but stand unshak'n" (*PL* IV: 63–64); and Raphael's principle, "Because we freely love, as in our will / To love or not; in this we stand or fall" (*PL* V, 540–41).

Coleridge's standing is among the dissidents—he stands by his religion and morality while others such as Godwin and Thelwall forsake theirs for a moral freedom that Coleridge despised. While Coleridge took his stand with "the wise and pure" (62), the phrase "I have stood" recalls Luther's declaration before the Diet of Worms in 1521, "Here I stand," a defiant refusal to renounce his writings. In December 1800, approximately the time "The Lime-Tree Bower" was published, Coleridge wrote in a notebook "Luther—a hero, one fettered indeed with prejudices; but with these very fetters he would knock out the Brains of a modern Fort Esprit" (*CN* 1: 864), and in an entry of November 1803 he listed Luther among those with "Revolutionary Minds" (*CN* 1: 1646). Coleridge stands opposed to established religion and the government; he takes his stand with the Bristol dissidents and Unitarians. In *The Annual Anthology*, the poem with address, locating and warning advertisement, and signature is an allusive network. In both manuscripts of 1797 and printed poem of 1800, landscape is "a living thing / Which *acts* upon the mind." In a letter to Thelwall of Oct 14, 1797 he quoted these lines, to counter Thelwall's materialism:

> I can *at times* feel strongly the beauties, you describe, in themselves & for themselves—but more frequently *all things* appear little—all the knowledge, that can be acquired, child's play—the universe itself—what but an immense heap of *little* things?—I can contemplate nothing but parts, & parts are all *little*—!—My mind feels as it ached to behold & know something *great*—something *one & indivisible*—and it is only in the faith of this that rocks or waterfalls, mountains or caverns give me the sense of sublimity or majesty!—But in this faith *all things* counterfeit infinity!—"Struck with the deepest calm of Joy" I stand. . . . (*CL* 1: 349)

This comment has often been extracted from the letter to illustrate Coleridge's theology and poetic imagination, but replaced in its context in the letter to Thelwall, it gives the trope of standing a significance that it has in its first publication. It distinguishes Coleridge from the reformers whom he sees as atheists and materialists, yet, as Hazlitt recognized, it does not alter his political views.

Coleridge revised *The Annual Anthology* version, perhaps shortly after publication, and deleted the lines "a living thing / Which *acts* upon the mind—

and with such hues / As cloath the Almighty Spirit, when he makes / Spirits perceive his presence." He then drafted substitutes:

> Less gross than bodily, within his soul
> Kindling unutterable Thanksgivings
> And Adorations, such perchance as rise
> Before the Almighty Spirit, when he makes
> Spirits perceive his presence.

> (*Margin*. 1:95)

Although these substitute lines were not incorporated in the *Sibylline Leaves* version and the lines "a living thing / Which *acts* upon the mind" were retained, Coleridge was uneasy about the implications of the 1800 printed version. The idea that nature acts on the mind has a slight taint of pantheism and Priestleyan materialism, in spite of Coleridge's claim of being a Berkeleyan in the 1797 note to the poem, which implies an opposing immaterialism. As a result the lines were removed in versions after *Sibylline Leaves*. These corrections in *The Annual Anthology* were never incorporated in the poem, but they clearly replace a somewhat risky theology with a more orthodox one. Where does Coleridge stand publicly on these issues? And what difference does it make? In the eyes of the government, one vague piety may be as good as another. Surely none of these various versions would be actionable. However, since they are associated with the circle of Bristol Unitarians and have the air of Priestley's thought, they are suspect to those who insist on strict religious orthodoxy. Unitarianism in 1797 was politically dangerous because to deny the Trinity was to run the risk of blasphemous libel. Not until William Smith engineered the Unitarian Toleration Act through parliament in 1813 were some of these restrictions on free speech lifted.[44]

If the poem in 1800 is read with its paratext, its title and signature transform it to a declaration about emerging from a prison and taking a public stand. "This Lime-Tree Bower" cannot be merely a meditative poem on nature's language, whether Berkeleyan or Priestleyan, because its paratext mediates the poem, making it into a poem about the involvement of the private in the public. The poem traces Coleridge's emergence from a private bower and prison, a blindness, a visionary deprivation, and a grave dispossession, through the agency of the Wordsworths and Lamb, whose private

---

[44] Richard W. Davis, *Dissent in Politics, 1780–1830. The Political Life of William Smith, M P.* (London: Epworth Press, 1971) 190–93. See also William Wickwar, *The Struggle for the Freedom of the Press, 1819–32r* (London: George Allen: Unwin, 1928) 22 and Peter Kitson, "The Whore of Babylon and the Woman in White: Coleridge's Radical Unitarian Language," in *Coleridge's Visionary Languages*, ed. Tim Fulford and Morton Paley (Woodbridge: The Boydell Press, 1993). For a concise description of the Bristol Unitarians, see Nigel Leask, *The Politics of Imagination in Coleridge's Critical Thought* (New York: St. Martin's Press, 1988) 19–45.

calamity itself had become a public issue in *Blank Verse*. "This Lime-Tree Bower" repeats the earlier emergence in "Reflections on Having Left a Place of Retirement." The bower is a type of retirement, of absence and privacy where Coleridge is "bereft of promised good."[45] The "promised good" he has lost is not merely individual vision or a validation of private autonomy, but a public good, because privacy in the beginning of the poem is a deprivation, not a possession. The economics of this version of "This Lime-Tree Bower" reads privacy as vacancy, the absence of value. The private is figured as blindness. Coleridge imagines a public realm that one enters, not to pursue one's own self interest, one's own possessions, but a realm that one enters to compensate for one's dispossessions. When Coleridge signed his first volume of poetry, he added "Of Jesus College, Cambridge" to claim a public space, but later in *The Annual Anthology* he claimed a membership in an entirely different kind of public with a distinct pantisocratic air.

Coleridge imagines the Wordsworths and Lamb emerging from the dell, which is the composite *topos* of private bower and prison. Theirs is an emergence similar to that of "Reflections on Having Left a Place of Retirement" and of the call in "Ode on the Departing Year" to private Woes and Joys:

> From every private bower,
> And each domestic hearth,
> Haste for one solemn hour;
> And with a loud and yet a louder voice
> O'er the sore travail of the common earth
> Weep and Rejoice![46]

Lamb and the Wordsworths will view what Coleridge has viewed—a panorama of the "many-steepled tract magnificent," a portion of English landscape certainly, but also the book or *tractatus* of nature with a public significance. The secluded and private dell of their walk and Coleridge's bower have become local landscape, which in turn has become the book of dissenting patriotism. The Wordsworths and Lamb stand where Coleridge has stood, indicating a patriotism that retains suggestions, through its allusive structure, of the pantisocracy mentioned in Lloyd's and Lamb's *Blank Verse*. A group of West Country radicals constitutes this standing: Coleridge, Southey, Wordsworth, Lloyd, Lamb, Cottle, and others. It is, however, a standing not within the established Church but within nature and a standing that distinguishes a political and social position among the reformers but distinct from reformers who accepted atheism and amorality. Coleridge's "I have stood" becomes a collective "we have stood" in the

---

[45] In the version in the letter to Southey, the word *bereft* is *bereav'd* (*CL* 1: 336), suggesting a death and oddly enough a loss of authority as in the loss of an ecclesiastical office, the original meaning of *bereav'd*.

[46] Coleridge, "Ode on the Departing Year" (Bristol, 1796) 6, strophe 2.

"tract magnificent" and a "here I stand" within the second volume of *The Annual Anthology* with the other Bristol poets.

Coleridge invokes light to illuminate the landscape and Lamb:

> Ah slowly sink
> Behind the western ridge, thou glorious Sun!
> Shine in the slant beams of the sinking orb,
> Ye purple heath-flowers! richlier burn, ye clouds!
> Live in the yellow light, ye distant groves!
> And kindle, thou blue ocean!

The foliage is "pale beneath the blaze" of the sun where a

> deep radiance lay
> Full on the ancient Ivy, which *usurps*
> Those fronting elms, and now with blackest mass
> Makes their dark branches gleam a lighter hue
> Thro' the late Twilight . . . .

The invocation recalls Milton's invocation of Light at the beginning of Book III of *Paradise Lost*, "Hail holy light," and the hymn to God further on in Book III:

> Amidst the glorious brightness where thou sit'st
> Thron'd inaccessible, but when thou shad'st
> The full blaze of thy beams, and through a cloud
> Drawn round about thee like a radiant Shrine,
> Dark with excessive bright thy skirts appear.
>
> (*PL* III, 376–80)

The reference to *Paradise Lost* is not obvious as is it in other paradigmatic cases of allusion and is one that Jonathan Bate might call unconscious allusion, but in this instance it is an allusion mediated by the public and non-literary discourse.[47] Coleridge was fond of quoting the line "Dark with excessive bright," and he transmutes it into the poem's imagery where the lime-tree bower changes from a prison into a location that, like the deep dell, is full of light. The point of tracing the allusion, however, is not merely to align Coleridge with Milton's devout prayer for inspiration, with Milton's vision in blindness that models Coleridge's fear of a time "when age / Had dimm'd mine eyes to blindness," but rather to trace Coleridge's use of "Dark with excessive bright" in its public context, to read it as allusion mediated by public issues.

Coleridge quoted the phrase often and used it in the fifth of his *Lectures on Revealed Religion* (1795): "Plato, the wild-minded Disciple of Socrates

---

[47] Bate, *Shakespeare and the English Romantic Imagination* (above, n. 32) 35–36.

who hid Truth in a dazzle of fantastic allegory, and is dark with excess of Brightness had asserted that whatever exists in the visible World, must be in God in an infinite degree. . . . a mysterious way of telling a plain Truth, namely that God is a living Spirit, infinitely powerful, wise and benevolent." Coleridge asserted a visionary and quasi-Trinitarian truth in Plato, while at the same time he suspended belief in Trinitarian Christianity. He explained in the *Biographia* that he had been "a Trinitarian (i.e., ad normam Platonis) in philosophy, yet a zealous Unitarian in Religion" (*BL* 1: 180). He turned in the next paragraph to attack Christian churches in the name of dissent and Unitarianism:

> But though Plato dressed Truth in the garb of Nonsense, still it was Truth, and they who would take the Trouble of unveiling her, might discover and distinguish all the Features, but this would not answer the ends of the Priest. . . . the Gospels are so obvious to the meanest Capacity that he who runs may read. He who knows his letters, may find in them everything necessary for him. Alas! he would learn too much, he would learn the rights of Man and the Imposture of Priests, the sovereignty of God, and the usurpation of unauthorized Vicegerents. . . .[48]

The rest of Coleridge's concluding paragraph contains a vigorous attack on Bishop Horsley, the author of *Tracts in Controversy with Dr. Priestley* (1794):

> But these principles which I hope and trust, begin to spread among true Christians are so obnoxious to our spiritual Noblemen, that Bishop Horsley has declared to his Clergy, that Papists are more their brethren than Protestant Dissenters. . . . He who sees any real difference between the Church of Rome and the Church of England possesses optics which I do not possess— the mark of antichrist is on both of them. (*Lect.* 209–10)

Coleridge's invocation to light invokes Milton's similar prayer, yet that allusion and address is mediated by Coleridge's use of Milton's figure for political purposes. Darkness with excessive light is the possession of Milton, Coleridge, and Lamb, and it boldly shines in opposition to aristocracy and established religion. Plato, too, is a Bristol radical. The blessing that Coleridge utters on Lamb, awakening the heart to "Love and Beauty," and the hope that he will be one "to whom / No sound is dissonant, which tells of life," echoes Coleridge's claim in the fifth lecture that "from Wisdom [Logos] and matter proceeds Nature, or the Spirit of universal Life" (*Lect.* 208). Read through these mediated allusions, Coleridge's blessing is not only a private gesture, but also a public stance, a Unitarian and dissenting stance against an established order that has corrupted Christianity. Do not the Priests, Coleridge asks, "sell the Gospel—Nay, nay, they neither sell,

---

[48] *Lect.* 208–9. The phrase "he who runs may read" is adapted from Habbakuk 2: 2.

nor is it the Gospel—they forcibly exchange Blasphemy for the first fruits, and snatching the scanty Bread from the poor Man's Mouth they cram their lying Legends down his Throat!" (*Lect.* 210–11).

Coleridge takes his stand by turning from established government and religion in an utterance that is marked by apostrophe, the figure that implies a turn, as Wordsworth said, that is "abrupt, interrupted, and revolutionary," an oppositional intrusion in the public discourse. As such, apostrophe enacts an apostasy—not quite a Satanic opposition as in *Paradise Lost*—but an apostasy defined literally as a movement away from a *stasis* and *status*. Coleridge stands in opposition both to the government and other radicals who advocate materialism, atheism, and immorality. His apostrophe to Lamb is a healing blessing for Lamb's personal affliction and at the same time it locates Lamb among the Bristol radicals and defends him from the charges of the *Anti-Jacobin*. It rewrites the public signature of Charles Lamb and relocates it from the community of London radicals like Godwin and Thelwall, in the "great city pent," to the community of the West Country reformers.

"This Lime-Tree Bower" is a different poem in 1800 than later in 1817 when it is a "meditative poem in blank verse." Its earlier paratext and its allusions transform its genre into a public letter and imply that the private Romantic lyric poem is fundamentally a public form of address in which the public and private are intricately entwined. They transform a private and subjective vision of nature's illuminations into a poem of public standing marked by evasive turning. His private blessing becomes a declaration of his political stance. Coleridge images the private individual in the public world, in the "tract magnificent." The trope of emergence is less significant than the trope of standing. The subjective "I" of the poem becomes the public signature, and perhaps even somewhat windy, "ESTEESI." The poem's paratext and figures allude to other literary and nonliterary utterances both historically distant and so intimidatingly present that they require an evasive stance. Paratext is the location of the poem's mediation and repeats and translates the text, mediating its allusions and locating it in the public discourse so that its allusions, its apostrophes and apostasies, become discursive; it changes, in other words, the rhetoric by which we read privacy of poems.

Chapter Three

THE POLITICS OF "FROST AT MIDNIGHT"

"FROST AT MIDNIGHT" is a political poem if it is read in the public context of *Fears in Solitude* and the political debates of the 1790s, but before I ask about the significance of a Romantic lyric, I want to ask about its location: Where is it? And who conspired to put it there? A lyric's location influences its significance, and to change a poem's location is to change its significance, sometimes radically, both for our understanding of its original historical period and for our own construction of Romanticism. Coleridge wrote "Frost at Midnight" in late February 1798. It is commonly read as an intensely subjective, meditative lyric written in isolated retirement and reflecting the individual consciousness of its author; or it is read in the context of Coleridge's other Conversation Poems, such as "The Eolian Harp" and "This Lime-Tree Bower," where it echoes the themes of the other "Meditative Poems in Blank Verse" with which Coleridge classified it in *Sibylline Leaves* (1817); or it is read in the context of Wordsworth's lyrics, particularly "Tintern Abbey." It was first published in the fall of 1798, however, as the final poem in a slim quarto volume that contained two other explicitly political poems: "Fears in Solitude" and "France: An Ode." Coleridge wrote these two poems early in 1798 and published "France: An Ode" in the *Morning Post*, where its title was "The Recantation: An Ode," on April 16. The radical bookseller Joseph Johnson published the quarto in the early fall, after Coleridge met him in late August or early September while he was on his way to Germany with Wordsworth (*CL* 1: 417–18, 420). In *Fears in Solitude*, "Frost at Midnight" concludes a volume composed as Coleridge's public defense of his caricature drawn in the Tory press. It is not only a meditative poem, a poem of healing, but it is also a public speech act, a defense in the court of public opinion. A full understanding of it in 1798 must take into account both the genre of its private meditation and the conventions of its public utterance.

I locate "Frost at Midnight" in the context of the other two poems in the volume and locate the volume in the context of political debates. In a reading of a poem as an integral and individual artifact, the process of interpretation relies only on the poem itself. In the method of reading that I am exploring, the meaning of a poem depends on the themes and figures that exist in the public discourse before the poem is written, on the allusive structure of its public language, and on the paratextual frame formed by the volume's other poems. I compare Coleridge's poems with other written material not often considered in traditional explication, political pamphlets, which implies that a Romantic lyric participates in the political rhetoric of the day. There is a complex play between the poem's figures and those in the public discourse.

I portray the public Coleridge and the public location of the poem. Our reconstructions of Coleridge in this century are based on the publication of his notebooks and letters, by our knowledge of the scholarship that has traced his reading, and by our knowledge of his later career. None of these were available to his contemporaries, whose debates constitute the context of its publication and whose comments trace the history of its reception. The story of its public context and reception is, in 1798, a particularly complex instance of tendentious interpretation and deliberate misrepresentation. To conduct an inquiry into the publication and reception of the poem is not necessarily to determine either the translucence of its figures or the consistency of its political principles. The debate to which it contributes is neither rational nor consensual. "Frost at Midnight" in *Fears in Solitude* partakes, in other words, of the genres and rhetoric of public debate, as well as the rhetoric of symbolism and allegory by which it is usually read.

For a reading of "Frost at Midnight" in the public discourse, the crucial dates are those of the composition of the volume in late August or early September 1798, when Coleridge first met Joseph Johnson. The dates of the writing of the poem are relatively insignificant, because the purposes of publication are more important than Coleridge's original intentions in drafting the individual poems. In late August, when the volume was composed, both author and publisher were under attack from the press and the government. Johnson, whose public signature appeared on the title page, had been placed on trial in the court of the King's Bench and convicted on July 17 for selling Gilbert Wakefield's *A Reply to Some Parts of the Bishop of Llandaff's Address to the People of Great Britain*. His indictment reads in part: "Joseph Johnson late of London Bookseller being a malicious seditious and ill-disposed person and being greatly disaffected to our said sovereign Lord the King . . . wickedly maliciously and seditiously did publish and cause to be published a certain scandalous malicious and seditious libel. . . ." Although he had been found guilty, sentencing was postponed for many months for obvious reasons. At the hearing on his sentence, he would have to produce evidence of his good behavior in any plea for leniency. His sworn statement at the hearing in November claimed that "where he could take the liberty of doing it, he has uniformly recommended the Circulation of such publications as had a tendency to promote good morals instead of such as were calculated to mislead and inflame the Common people."[1] The government was less concerned with the content of the publication and the re-

---

[1] Gerald P. Tyson, *Joseph Johnson: A Liberal Publisher* (Iowa City: University of Iowa Press, 1979) 159–61.

ception among the educated and privileged than it was with the circulation to the common people.

Since the end of 1797, Coleridge himself had been under attack in the *Anti-Jacobin, or Weekly Examiner*, which began publication in November to attack the opposition press. On July 9, 1798, it published a satirical poem called "New Morality,"[2] in which Coleridge was ridiculed along with Southey, Charles Lloyd, and Charles Lamb for being both Jacobins and atheists, followers of the French deist La Révellière Lépeaux.

> The Directorial Lama, Sovereign Priest,—
> Lepaux:—whom atheists worship;—at whose nod
> Bow their meek heads *the men without a God*.
>
>   Ere long, perhaps, to this astonish'd Isle,
> Fresh from the shores of subjugated Nile,
> Shall Buonaparte's victor fleet protect
> The genuine Theo-Philanthropic sect,—
> The Sect of Marat, Mirabeau, Voltaire,
> Led by their Pontiff, good La Reveillere
> —Rejoic'd our CLUBS shall greet him, and install
> The holy Hunch-back in thy dome, St. Paul!
> While Countless votaries thronging in his train
> Wave their Red Caps, and hymn this jocund strain:
>
> (*PAJ* 234–35)

Louis La Révellière-Lépeaux was elected president of the French Assembly in 1795, joined the Committee of Public Safety, and became president of the Directory. Known for his hatred of Christianity, he proposed to replace it with theophilanthropy. On August 1 James Gillray published an elaborate caricature of the worshipers of Lépeaux based on "New Morality." Near the center is a Cornucopia of Ignorance from which flow such works as Wollstonecraft's *Wrongs of Women* and Tooke's *Speeches* along with the *Monthly Magazine*. On either side of the Cornucopia are two human figures with asses' heads, one braying from a paper labeled "Colridge Dactylics" and the other with a copy of *Joan of Arc* sticking out of its pocket, intoning from "Southey's Saphics." Both are behind a dwarf blowing a trumpet and holding a copy of the *Morning Post* with the headline "Forgeries." Behind the hunched figure of Lépeaux stands the goddess of philanthropy with her feet trampling a paper entitled "Ties of Nature." She is embracing the entire globe with such force that she seems to be squeezing

---

[2] "New Morality" was written by Canning, Frere, Gifford, and Ellis ("Authors of the Poetry of the *Anti-Jacobin*," *Notes & Queries*, 3 [May 3, 1851]: 348–49.) Mary Dorothy George gives a full description of the cartoon based on "New Morality" in her *Catalogue of Political and Personal Satires Preserved in the Department of Prints and Drawings in the British Museum, Vol. VII, 1793–1800* (London: British Museum, 1942) 468–72, item 9240.

it to death. Although both "New Morality" and Gillray's caricature were published after "Fears in Solitude" was written, they are ample evidence that Coleridge's name was infamous enough for him to have been a target of the Tory satirists. Thus a volume apparently presenting both author and publisher of *Fears in Solitude* as patriots and Christians would tend to take the heat off both. The volume would be a public defense against attacks on both that were published only weeks before the volume was composed.

Coleridge's reputation as a West Country radical rested on his lectures in Bristol in 1795, *The Watchman* of 1796, and his associations with the *Morning Post*. In December 1797 he began to contribute poems to the *Morning Post*, some of which were signed with his own name, and in January he started to contribute political essays. On December 26, he published *The Visions of the Maid of Orleans. A Fragment, by S. T. Coleridge*, a continuation of his contribution to Southey's *Joan of Arc*. The *Morning Post* extract claims that Joan received divine election to her mission to rid France of the English and includes an episode of her youth in which she comforts a man dying of the cold, who has fled his town set on fire by the English.[3] Coleridge's sympathy was unmistakable, and it must have been so to his readers, because the editor included a notice on February 10: An Englishman makes very silly objections to *Joan of Arc*" (*EOT* 3: 286). The objections may have been to the idea that France, and not England, was the agent of divine justice. On January 9 a set of "Queries" was published in the *Morning Post*. Coleridge's name was not on them, but they were reprinted from *The Watchman*. It would not have been difficult to identify the author. The first reads, "Whether the wealth of the higher classes does not ultimately depend on the labour of the lower classes?" Another asks, "When the root yieldeth insufficient nourishment, whether wise men would not wish to top the tree, in order to make the lower branches thrive?" The final one asks "Whether there might not have been suggested modes of employing two hundred millions of money to more beneficial purposes than to the murder of three millions of our fellow-creatures (*EOT* 1: 11–12). If Johnson was put on trial, would Coleridge be next?

The public discourse that the volume entered was composed of a rhetoric of purposeful duplicity, distortion, and personal attack.[4] Coleridge was constantly in the sights of the *Anti-Jacobin*, which contains many attacks on him

---

[3] *The Visions of the Maid of Orleans* was later incorporated into "The Destiny of Nations." The only copy of the *Morning Post* for this date that I have been able to locate is in Chicago at the Newberry Library. David Erdman describes the text in "Unrecorded Coleridge Variants," *Studies in Bibliography* 11 (1958): 143–62.

[4] Terrance Hoagwood argues that "the poetic and philosophic forms of duplicity are derivative repetitions, even products, of duplicitious forms in the social field of political action" (*Politics, Philosophy and the Production of Romantic Texts* [DeKalb: Northern Illinois University Press, 1996] 31).

although often he is not mentioned by name. Written by Gifford, Canning, Frere, with contributions and oversight from Pitt, then Prime Minister, its major aim stated in its Prospectus was to expose the errors in the opposition press, which it ranged under three categories: lies, misrepresentations, and mistakes. It promised to present "Lies of the Week; the downright, direct, unblushing falsehoods, which have no colour or foundation whatever, and which must at the very moment of their being written, have been known to the writer to be wholly destitute of truth."[5] Yet its own rhetoric was that of parody and distortion. The early numbers contained essays on Jacobin poetry, whose major targets were Southey and Coleridge. On December 18 it included a parody of Southey's "The Soldier's Wife: Dactylics":

> Weary way-wanderer languid and sick at heart,
> Travelling painfully over the rugged road,
> Wild-visag'd Wanderer! ah for thy heavy chance!
>
> Sorely thy little one drags by thee bare-footed,
> Cold is the baby that hangs at thy bending back,
> Meagre and livid and screaming its wretchedness.
>
> *Woe-begone mother, half anger, half agony,
> As over thy shoulder thou lookest to hush the babe,
> Bleakly the blinding snow beats in thy hagged face.
>
> *This stanza was supplied by S. T. COLERIDGE.[6]

The *Anti-Jacobin*'s parody is prefaced by the following comment: "Being the quintessence of all the Dactylics that ever were, or ever will be written."

> Wearisome Sonnetteer, feeble and querulous,
> Painfully dragging out thy demo-cratic lays—
> Moon-stricken Sonnetteer, "ah! for thy heavy chance!"
>
> Sorely thy Dactylics lag on uneven feet:
> Slow is the syllable which thou wouldst urge to speed,
> Lame and o'erburthen'd and "screaming its wretchedness!"

The next stanza, indicated only by a line of asterisks, is omitted with the following note: "My worthy friend, the Bellman, had promised to supply an additional stanza but the business of assisting the Lamplighter, Chimney sweeper, &c. with Complimentary Verses for their worthy Masters and Mistresses, pressing on him at this season, he was obliged to decline it" (*PAJ*

---

[5] The *Anti-Jacobin*, 4th ed., revised, reset, and corrected (London: 1799) 1: 8 (cf. above, Chapter 2, n. 11).

[6] Southey, *Poems*, intro. Jonathan Wordsworth (1797; rept. Oxford: Woodstock Books, 1989) 145.

22–23). The Bellman is, of course, Coleridge, who had published *The Watchman*. In the 1790s "bellman" was a slang term for a newspaperman, and in 1813 Leigh Hunt referred to Coleridge as "The Bellman" in his satire on Southey, "On the New Poet-Laureat."[7] The reference to the lamplighter may be an allusion to the practice of the French revolutionaries of hanging their victims on lampposts.[8]

Not only was Coleridge's poetry parodied in the *Anti-Jacobin*, but his journalism was ridiculed as well. An article in the *Morning Post* for February 24, identified as Coleridge's by David Erdman in his edition of *Essays on His Times*, was quoted in the *Anti-Jacobin* on March 5. Coleridge had written that "the insensibility with which we now hear of the most extraordinary Revolutions is a very remarkable symptom of the public temper, and no unambiguous indication of the state of the times. We now read with listless unconcern of events which, but a very few years ago, would have filled all Europe with astonishment" (*EOT* 1: 20). The *Anti-Jacobin* quoted, with some errors, this passage and commented: "Where he found this 'insensibility,' we know not, unless among the *Patriots* of the *Corresponding Society*.—For our parts, we have a very lively feeling of the transaction [the entry of the French armies into Rome], which for perfidy and inhumanity, surpasses whatever we have yet seen or heard of." Later in his article Coleridge had written "In the midst of these stupendous revolutions, the Nobility, Gentry, and Proprietors of England, make no efforts to avert that ruin from their own heads, which they daily see falling on the same classes of men in neighboring countries" (*EOT* 1:22). The *Anti-Jacobin* sniffed in response to this: "Never, probably, in any period, in any Country, were such Efforts made, by the very descriptions of men this worthy tool of *Jacobinism* has pointed out as making no exertions."[9]

In March and April 1798, government pressure on dissent forced the radical press to become more circumspect and duplicitous in its rhetoric. When Coleridge published "France: An Ode" as "The Recantation" in the *Morning Post*, Daniel Stuart's editorial policy had been shifting against French militarism. As David Erdman has written in his introduction to *Essays on His Times*, Coleridge's shift away from sympathy with France was first evident in the editorial policy of the *Morning Post*. Stuart had published attacks on the ministry and printed detailed accounts of the charges against the conspirators in early March. He was immediately called before the government to explain how he had obtained the information. From early March, as Erdman recounts it, the *Morning Post* became far more mod-

---

[7] See Chapter 5, pp. 136–37.

[8] Burke explains that the National Assembly meets "under the terror of the bayonet, and the lamp-post, and the torch" and was horrified by the revolutionary cry "for *all* the BISHOPS to be hanged on the lamp-posts" (*RRF* 118, 123).

[9] The *Anti-Jacobin* 1 (1799) 579–80.

erate and circumspect in its editorial policy toward both France and the English ministry. Coleridge's ode was prefaced by this note: "The following excellent Ode will be in unison with the feelings of every friend of Liberty and foe to Oppression; of all who, admiring the French Revolution, detest and deplore the conduct of France towards Switzerland." Taking a hint from the title of Coleridge's poem "Parliamentary Oscillators," Erdman remarks, "Both editor and poet, in their different ways, recanted while saying that they did not, and oscillated more than they recanted" (*EOT* 1: lxxxi). On April 23, 1798, one week after Coleridge's "Recantation" was published, the *Anti-Jacobin* gloated that the *Morning Post* "has wisely shrunk from our severity, reformed its Principles in some material points, and in more than one of its last columns, held a language which the *Whig Club* and *Corresponding Society* will not soon forgive" and concluded, "If we could but cure this Paper of its inveterate habits of Lying and *Swearing*, and give it a few accurate notions of *meum* and *tuum*, we should not despair of seeing it one day an *English* Opposition Paper."[10] There is some serious doubt about what precisely Coleridge was recanting and whether the title "The Recantation" reflects an indecisive wavering in Coleridge's political principles, a momentary capitulation to government pressure, a calculated dodge by recasting his public signature, or a repetition of his earlier views.

The *Anti-Jacobin*, however, could claim only some of the credit for the turn of the *Morning Post*. The government had turned up the heat on the paper. The occasion of Coleridge's "Fears in Solitude" was the arrest on March 1, 1798, of John Binns, of the London Corresponding Society, and the Rev. James Coigley and Arthur O'Connor, of the United Irishmen. Coigley had a letter to the French government recommending the French invasion of Ireland (*EOT* 1: lxxvii). Nicholas Roe describes an abortive French invasion at Fishguard on the southwest coast of Wales on February 22, 1797. The French landed twelve hundred soldiers, who immediately surrendered. Papers found with their officers indicated that their orders were to attack and burn Bristol and other English ports.[11] E. P. Thompson writes that "March and April, 1798, saw the greatest *levée* of the Volunteers in the whole decade. Most local volunteer corps were founded with some little oratorical flourish, some resolution of loyalty, but the North Petherton Corps, which drew upon the services of those who lived in Stowey, was founded in April with a quite unusual flourish of patriotic combat." Thompson adds wryly, "The poets, when they went to Germany, were hopping the draft."[12] "France: An Ode" was published in the *Morning Post* a

---

[10] The *Anti-Jacobin* 2 (1799) 193.

[11] Roe, Nicholas, *Wordsworth and Coleridge: The Radical Years* (Oxford: Clarendon Press, 1988) 251–57.

[12] "Disenchantment or Default? A Lay Sermon," in *Power and Consciousness*, ed. Conor Cruise O'Brien and William Dean Vanech (New York: New York University Press, 1969) 167–68.

month after news that the French had invaded Switzerland and seemed to mark Coleridge's change of opinions. If it is read in the limited context of the development of Coleridge's political ideas, it may be read primarily as a considered statement of his political principles. Coleridge's shift, if it was that, was therefore not an isolated event but followed the lead of his editor.

"Fears in Solitude," written at the same time as this exchange between the *Morning Post* and the *Anti-Jacobin*, turns the accusations about the rhetoric of the public discourse against the government. Lying and swearing were not confined to the liberal press. While Coleridge's poem attacks Britain for slavery and the slave trade, wealth and greed, atheism and the thoughtless enthusiasm for war, its major theme is the violation of the ninth commandment against bearing false witness, which Coleridge called "one scheme of perjury." Again and again, Coleridge refers to the public language of the pulpit, the court, and the marketplace: accusing, pleading, preaching, muttering, gabbling, and bribing. There is little rational discourse, only acts of calculated deception. What is more important, there is no disinterested discourse, no discourse dissociated from a financial or political interest, no discourse or exchange independent of the intrusion of the government by its parodies and attempts to silence opposition by restricting freedom of the press. The *Anti-Jacobin's* writers may have been the young Tory wits, but the moving spirit was Pitt himself. In the Sixth Lecture on Revealed Religion of June 1796, Coleridge anticipated his complaints by arguing:

> There is scarcely a Vice which Government does not teach us—criminal prodigality and an unholy Splendor surrounds it—disregard of solemn Promises marks its conduct—and more than half of the business of Ministers is to find inducements to Perjury! Nay of late it has become the fashion to keep wicked and needy men in regular Pay, who without scruple take the most awful oaths in order to gain the confidence which it is their Trade to betray. (*Lect.* 221)

Coleridge's immediate target of criticism here is the abuse of the system of government spies, from which he was to suffer himself, and the bribery of witnesses in criminal cases, but his complaints echo the agitation against the Test Acts, which predates the French Revolution. Thus both Coleridge and the *Anti-Jacobin* agreed that the public discourse was conducted by duplicity. While the public debates concern legitimacy and public policy and are constituted by illocutionary speech acts, they are also about those very perjurious statements and about what one may be doing in uttering them.

Coleridge specifically raises the issues of false speaking in "Fears in Solitude":

> We gabble o'er the oaths we mean to break,
> For all must swear—all, and in every place,
> College and wharf, council and justice-court,

All, all must swear, the briber and the brib'd,
Merchant and lawyer, senator and priest,
The rich, the poor, the old man, and the young,
All, all make up one scheme of perjury,
That faith doth reel; the very name of God
Sounds like a juggler's charm.[13]

(*FS* 4)

Truth in "Fears in Solitude" is a matter of honest speaking, of faithful intention, and of the avoidance of deliberate deception. Falsehood is not a mistake or unconscious error, not a misprision or *méconnaissance*. It is not a psychological misrepresentation prompted by desire, as it may be in a lyric that rests its reality on theories of imagination. No generous error is involved. No providential mistake serves a worthier purpose to support imagination. The public discourse involves perjury, knowing the truth and distorting it; libel, signing another's name by caricature; and swearing contrary to both law and scripture. A rational consensus in the public discourse is nowhere to be found.

Perhaps the cruelest attack upon Coleridge came in 1799 when the satirical poems from the *Anti-Jacobin* were republished with the following note that created a public character for Coleridge in the company of other Jacobins:

> Some of these youths were early corrupted in the *metropolis*, and initiated in the mysteries of Theophilanthropism, . . . at that excellent seminary, Christ's Hospital. C——dge was nominated to an exhibition at Cambridge, and the Vice-master (soon after his admission) sent to him, on account of his non-attendance at chapel. This illuminated gentleman affected astonishment that any criminality could attach to him for his non-performance of religious worship, the trickery of Priestcraft, but if his presence was required, *pro forma*, as at a muster-roll, he had no great objection to attend. To the disgrace of discipline, and a Christian University, this avowed Deist was not expelled for such sin. His equalizing spirit and eccentricities have reduced this poetaster occasionally to such difficulties, that almost in want of bread he once addressed a soldier in the Park—"*Are you one of the cut-throats of the despot.*"—The man was at first astonished, but he soon found that his distress had determined him to enlist. His friends have frequently extricated him from this and other embarrassments. He has since married, had children, and has now quitted the country, become a citizen of the world, left his little ones fatherless, and his wife destitute.[14]

---

[13] Subsequent quotations in this chapter are from the 1798 versions of the poems in *Fears in Solitude.*

[14] *The Beauties of the Anti-Jacobin; or Weekly Examiner; Containing Every Article of Permanent Utility in that Valuable and Highly Esteemed Paper, Literary and Political* . . . (London: 1799) 306–7. The collection was edited for "the middle class of society." For Coleridge's response to this attack, see *BL* 1: 67.

This note echoes the accusations against the mysterious group of Illuminati, a secret society of conspirators against religion and monarchy thought to be responsible for the French Revolution; against Rousseau, who disavowed his natural children; and against Tom Paine, who became a citizen of the world. In a copy of *Fears in Solitude* originally in the possession of Sir George Beaumont, next to the line from "Fears in Solitude" in which Coleridge calls on Englishmen to "Stand forth! be men! repel an impious foe" (*FS* 7), Coleridge wrote in 1807 "and at this very time, or rather immediately after the Publication I was declared in the 'Beauties of the Anti-Jacobin' a [traitor] a[nd] proselytizing at that, a runagate from his Country, who had denounced all patriotic feelings."[15] Late in August 1806 Wordsworth informed Sir George Beaumont that Coleridge had returned from Malta, and Beaumont replied, "Joy to you on the approach of our runagate."[16] Wordsworth's "Epistle to Sir George Beaumont . . . 1811" most likely refers to Coleridge: "No tales of Runagates fresh landed, whence / And wherefore fugitive or on what pretence."[17] As Byron knew, "runagate" was a pun upon "renegade," and the Coleridge who left England in 1798 and again in 1804 was tagged as a runagate and renegade in both instances in public and in private.

Coleridge's public response came in *The Friend* for June 8, 1809:

> Again, will any man, who loves his Children and his Country, be slow to pardon me, if not in the spirit of vanity but of natural self-defense against yearly and monthly attacks on the very vitals of my character as an honest man and a loyal Subject I prove the utter falsity of the charges by the only public means in my power, a citation from the last work published by me in the close of the year 1798, and anterior to all the calumnies published to my dishonour. (*Friend* 2: 23)

Coleridge then includes about sixty-five lines from "Fears in Solitude," which include the accusations against him and his defense that he is a patriot, and conclude: "O divine / And beauteous Island! thou hast been my sole / And most magnificent Temple, in the which / I walk with awe."[18] Since he cited *Fears in Solitude* in his defense in 1809, it is reasonable to think that he thought of it in the same way in 1798. If Coleridge's self-

---

[15] The copy is now in the Pierpont Morgan Library, New York, accession number 47225. B. Ifor Evans printed Coleridge's annotations in "Coleridge's Copy of 'Fears in Solitude,'" *Times Literary Supplement* April 18, 1935: 255. Coleridge's note has been heavily inked over but is still legible. The conjectural readings are Evans's.

[16] Mary Moorman, *William Wordsworth: The Later Years* (Oxford: Clarendon Press, 1965) 84.

[17] Lines 61–62 in *WP* 4: 144.

[18] *Friend* 2: 23–25. Barbara Rooke notes, however, that within a week after this article, Southey wrote to a friend that "if he was not a Jacobine, in the common acceptation of the name, I wonder who the Devil was" (*Friend* 2: 26n).

defense began in 1798, not later when he had changed his political alle-giances, his later defense must be regarded in a different light. His self-defense in 1798 was not, as it later appeared, an effort to change the record to cover up his youthful radicalism, to rewrite his youth, but rather it was a necessary self-defense, done at the moment of pressure from both the press and the government and done in concert with others who were under sim-ilar pressure.

That *Fears in Solitude* was designed to answer criticisms of himself and Johnson is confirmed by the first notices printed in the *Analytical Review* (Dec. 1798), published by Johnson, which prints precisely the passage that Coleridge annotated in protest against "New Morality" and the *Anti-Jacobin* in 1809, Coleridge's portrait of domesticity: "Mr. C., in common with many others of the purest patriotism, has been slandered with the ap-pellation of an enemy to his country. The following passage, we presume, will be sufficient to wipe away the injurious stigma, and show that an ad-herence to the measures of administration is not the necessary consequence of an ardent love for the constitution.

> 'Spare us yet awhile,
> Father and God! O spare us yet awhile!
> O let not english women drag their flight
> Fainting beneath the burden of their babes,
> Of the sweet infants, that but yesterday
> Laugh'd at the breast! Sons, brothers, husbands, all
> Who ever gaz'd with fondness on the forms,
> Which grew up with you round the same fire side,
> And all who ever heard the sabbath bells
> Without the infidel's scorn, make yourselves pure!
> Stand forth! be men! repel an impious foe . . .
>
> . . . .
>
> And O! may we return
> Not with a drunken triumph, but with fear,
> Repenting of the wrongs, with which we stung
> So fierce a foe to frenzy!'"[19]

The reviewer said that "Frost at Midnight" does "great honour to the poet's feelings, as the husband of an affectionate wife, and as the father of a cra-dled infant." The publisher reads the author as a patriot, who can prove that he is a patriot because he is not an atheist.

"Frost at Midnight" concludes with six lines that were later deleted. The "silent icicles" will shine to the moon

---

[19] I have printed the quotation, with variants in Coleridge's text, from the *Analytical*, in *RR*.

> Like those, my babe! which, ere to-morrow's warmth
> Have capp'd their sharp keen points with pendulous drops,
> Will catch thine eye, and with their novelty
> Suspend thy little soul; then make thee shout,
> And stretch and flutter from thy mother's arms
> As thou would'st fly for very eagerness.
>
> *(FS 23)*

The public significance of "Frost at Midnight" in the fall of 1798 is that it presented a patriotic poet, whose patriotism rested on the love of his country and his domestic affections. Coleridge specifically instructed Johnson to send a copy to his brother, the Reverend George Coleridge, even though, as Coleridge noted sometime after 1803, his brother was unhappy with the dedicatory poem in *Poems* (1797): he "was displeased and thought his character endangered by the Dedication."[20] As the reviewer in the *Monthly Review* (May 1799) put it, "Frost at Midnight" displays "a pleasing picture of virtue and content in a cottage," hardly an incisive critical comment for late-twentieth-century readers, until one recognizes that the word *content* implies the negation of its opposite. Coleridge is not discontent, not ill-disposed to the existing state of society; he is not, therefore, seditious. The reviewer echoes the convention that an affirmative voice vote in the House of Lords was registered by the word *content*, which Byron invoked in *Don Juan* as the "servile Peer's 'Content'" (14: 464).

Considering the political intentions of the volume, intentions present in 1798 and not reconstructed later to hide a youthful radicalism, is it possible to draw conclusions about Coleridge's political principles as they appeared in the public discourse? Isn't the public debate that "Frost at Midnight" enters full of duplicity? Does not the volume intend to present Coleridge both as a loyal patriot, who loves his country, and as a devoutly religious man, on the one hand, and on the other, as one who continues to support the Jacobin ideals of liberty that he has always held? The evidence of the volume and the letter that Coleridge sent to his brother George in March that he had "snapped [his] squeaking baby-trumpet of Sedition" (*CL*, 1: 397) suggest that the invasion of Switzerland and government pressure on Stuart had forced him to change his views. In the private letter he announced that "I deprecate the moral & intellectual habits of those men both in England & France, who have modestly assumed to themselves the exclusive title of Philosophers & Friends of Freedom. I think them at least *as* distant from greatness as from goodness. If I know my own opinions, they are utterly untainted with French Metaphysics, French Politics, French Ethics, & French Theology" (*CL* 1: 395).

Considering Coleridge's 1795 lectures, this comment is less of an apology or announcement of new views than it is a confirmation of his original

---

[20] *CP* 1: 173. Coleridge's marginal comment is in *Poems* (1797) now at Yale.

positions. In the same letter he comments upon his public persona, his public signature: "I am prepared to suffer without discontent the consequences of my follies & mistakes—; and unable to conceive how that which I am, of Good could have been without that which I have been of Evil, it is withheld from me to regret any thing: I therefore consent to be deemed a Democrat & a Seditionist. A man's character follows him long after he has ceased to deserve it" (*CL* 1: 397). At the same time that Coleridge claims to have become a loyalist, he is willing to be considered a democrat and seditionist. In part, *Fears in Solitude* wants to have it both ways and is a public utterance crafted for widely different audiences and dominated by the threat of legal action against seditious writing. Its author is a public figure who is both a friend of liberty and a loyal patriot, someone who enters a public dispute that is far more rhetorical than reasonable, far more duplicitous than disinterested. Defensive duplicity stands guard over dissent.

At the same time that he seemed to recant his former praise of the French Revolution, he continued to publish poems in the *Morning Post* expressing sympathy with France. On July 30, 1798 he published "A Tale," the story of the mad ox, which, as a note explains, represents the French Revolution:

> AN Ox, long fed on musty hay,
>   And work'd with yoke and chain,
> Was loosen'd on an April day,
> When fields are in their best array,
> And growing grasses sparkle gay
>   At once with sun and rain.
>
> The grass was sweet, the sun was bright—
>   With truth I may aver it;
> The beast was glad, as well he might,
> Thought a green meadow no bad sight,
> And frisk'd,—to show his huge delight,
>   Much like a beast of spirit.
>
> "Stop, neighbors, stop! why these alarms?
>   "The ox is only glad!"
> —But still, they pour from cots and farms—
> "Halloo!" the parish is up in arms,
> (A *hoaxing* hunt has always charms)
>   "Hallo! the ox is mad."

The ox is chased through the town:

> The Ox drove on right thro' the town;
>   All follow'd, boy and dad,

> Bull-dog, parson, shopman, clown!
> The publicans rush'd from the crown,
> "Halloo hamstring him! cut him down!"—
> —They drove the poor Ox mad.[21]

The poem concludes with the admission that now the beast of the Revolution is indeed mad and must be controlled, as does "France: An Ode" but the attitude toward the Revolution is quite different. "France: An Ode" portrayed the Revolution rising like the allegorical figure of wrath, not the animal gladness of the ox:

> When France in wrath her giant limbs uprear'd,
> And with that oath which smote earth, air, and sea,
> Stamp'd her strong foot and said, she would be free,
> Bear witness for me, how I hop'd and fear'd!

(FS 14)

The picture of the ox liberated in gladness and goaded into madness displays both a greater sympathy with France and a liberal attitude that Whigs and Friends of Freedom had held for some time. One wonders at the degree of recantation that the public Coleridge has actually declared. The political language in Coleridge's response to the government press is tempered to suit the intentions of those who use and abuse it. Coleridge's oscillations should be re-read as the acrobatic feat of remaining in the public debates, when other radical voices had been either silenced or exiled. Coleridge's opinions were individual and did not conform strictly to the party divisions constructed by Burke and the *Anti-Jacobin* in which one side was French, materialist, atheist, libertine, and democratic and the other was English, idealist, Christian, moral, and monarchist.

Utterances in the public debates are complex and even contradictory. For an obvious example, the word *patriotism* is about as ambiguous as dissent could desire. "Fears in Solitude" was reviewed in the *Analytical Review* as displaying the "purest patriotism." The *Monthly Review* (May 1799) echoed the evaluation: "Of his country he speaks with a patriotic enthusiasm, and he exhorts to virtue with a Christian's ardor. . . . No one can be more desirous of promoting all that is important to its security and felicity." But what does *patriot* mean? In the first edition of his *Dictionary*, Dr. Johnson defined a patriot as "one whose ruling passion is the love of his country," but in the fourth edition he added a contrary definition: "a factious disturber of the government." A correspondent in the *Anti-Jacobin*, who signed himself "A Batchelor," had his own definition: "By pretty long habit of ob-

---

[21] "A Tale," later reprinted as "Recantation: Illustrated in the Story of the Mad Ox," is here reprinted from the *Morning Post*, July 30, 1798 with the corrections listed by David Erdman (above, n. 3; "Variants" 154).

servation, I have at length arrived at the skill of concluding from a man's politics the nature of his domestic troubles." The inflamed passions and gloomy dispositions of the discontented are caused by sexual frustration. The Batchelor concludes that "*a* Patriot *is, generally speaking, a man who has been either a* Dupe, a Spendthrift, *or a* Cuckold, *and, not unfrequently*, all together" (1: 260–61). The Batchelor has been reading Swift's *Tale of Tub* and thinks of a patriot as someone whose height of felicity is being a "fool among knaves" and whose acquisitions include the perpetual "possession of being well deceived," and whose great achievements in new systems and conquests can be easily traced to sexual frustration.[22] In a somewhat different and Miltonic key, Coleridge agrees with the Batchelor's analysis. In "Fears in Solitude," he accused both radicals and conservatives: "We have been too long / Dupes of a deep delusion" (*FS* 8). Among those deceived, Coleridge includes the radical iconoclasts as well as the conservative idolaters, who demand total submission to the present government. *Fears in Solitude* thus presents Coleridge as a patriot, but what kind of patriot? Both, of course, depend on which of Coleridge's readers is doing the reading.[23]

Another related, and more complex, set of keywords surrounds the domestic affections in "Frost at Midnight." Does the love of local landscape and family form the basis of a patriotism similar to Burke's or does it lead to a love of all humanity that is characteristic of radical writing? The value of patriotism enters the English public discourse on the French Revolution with Dr. Richard Price's sermon "A Discourse on the Love of our Country, Delivered on November 4, 1789" before the "Society for Commemorating the Revolution in Great Britain." Price argues that the love of one's country is not based on the "soil or the spot of earth on which we happen to be born; . . . but that community of which we are members . . . who are associated with us under the same constitution of government." The love of one's country "does not imply any conviction of the superior value of it to other countries, or any particular preference of its laws and constitution of government." Finally he concludes that "in pursuing particularly the interest of our country, we ought to carry our views beyond it. We should love it ardently, but not exclusively. We ought to seek its good, by all the means that our different circumstances and abilities will allow; but at the same time we ought to consider ourselves as citizens of the world, and take care to maintain a just regard to the rights of other countries."[24]

In response to Dr. Price, Burke's *Reflections on the Revolution in France* countered that inherited monarchy went hand in hand with the inherited

---

[22] Jonathan Swift, *A Tale of a Tub*, ed. Herbert Davis (Oxford: Blackwell, 1939) 108–10.

[23] For eighteenth-century meanings of *patriotism*, see Carl Woodring, *Politics in the Poetry of Coleridge* (Madison: University of Wisconsin Press, 1961) 87–89.

[24] *Burke, Paine, Godwin, and the Revolution Controversy*, ed. Marilyn Butler (Cambridge: Cambridge University Press, 1984) 25–26.

property, and that the love of one's country and government is bound to the
love of one's family:

> By a constitutional policy, working after the pattern of nature, we receive, we
> hold, we transmit our government and our privileges, in the same manner in
> which we enjoy and transmit our property and our lives. . . . In this choice of
> inheritance we have given to our frame of polity the image of a relation in
> blood; binding up the constitution of our country with our dearest domestic
> ties; adopting our fundamental laws into the bosom of our family affections;
> keeping inseparable, and cherishing with the warmth of all their combined and
> mutually reflected charities, our state, our hearths, our sepulchers, and our al-
> tars. (*RRF* 84)

In Coleridge's Introductory Address to *Conciones ad Populum* (1795), he, like
Burke, grounds benevolence and patriotism in domestic affections, but his
definition of benevolence as universal is precisely the opposite of Burke's:

> The searcher after Truth must love and be beloved; for general Benevolence
> is a necessary motive to constancy of pursuit; and this general Benevolence is
> begotten and rendered permanent by social and domestic affections. Let us be-
> ware of that proud Philosophy, which affects to inculcate Philanthropy while
> it denounces every home-born feeling, by which it is produced and nurtured.
> The paternal and filial duties discipline the Heart and prepare it for the love
> of all Mankind. The intensity of private attachments encourages, not prevents,
> universal Benevolence. (*Lect.* 46)

The thought is repeated in the third of his Lectures on Revealed Religion
(1795), where it introduces a criticism of Godwin: "Jesus knew our Nature—and that expands like the circles of a Lake—the Love of our Friends,
parents and neighbours lead[s] us to the love of our Country to the love of
all Mankind. The intensity of private attachment encourages, not prevents,
universal philanthropy—the nearer we approach the Sun, the more intense
his Rays—yet what corner of the System does he not cheer and vivify" (*Lect.*
163). Coleridge's immediate criticism in these passages is not of Burke, but
of Godwin's "proud philosophy" and indifference to personal and domestic affections. In the next paragraph he ridicules the "Stoical Morality which
disclaims all the duties of Gratitude and domestic Affection" and addresses
Godwinians like Thelwall, to whom he used the same words in a private letter: "Severe Moralist! that teaches us that filial Love is a Folly, Gratitude
criminal, Marriage Injustice, and a promiscuous Intercourse of the Sexes
our wisdom and our duty. In this System a man may gain his self-esteem
with little Trouble, he first adopts Principles so lax as to legalize the most
impure gratifications, and then prides himself on acting up to his Principles" (*Lect.* 164–65). In "Modern Patriotism" in *The Watchman*, Coleridge
concludes the same words with a question: "But you act up to your princi-

ples.—So much the worse! Your principles are villainous ones! I would not entrust my wife or sister to you—Think you, I would entrust my country?"[25] Coleridge's consistent rejection of materialism, atheism, and immorality separates him from Godwin, Thelwall, and other radicals, but that does not mean that his invocation of the domestic affections places him in Burke's camp. For Burke the domestic affections formed the basis of the British Constitution, a decidedly national allegiance, while Coleridge viewed them in the 1790s as the basis of a universal benevolence and love of all humanity.

The *Anti-Jacobin*, not surprisingly, takes Burke's and not Coleridge's position. "New Morality" turns Coleridge's image of the sun for the love of humanity against him. The feelings of the "universal man" run "through the extended globe"

> As broad and general as th'unbounded sun!
> No narrow bigot *he*;—*his* reason'd view
> Thy interests, England, ranks with thine, Peru!
> France at our doors, *he* sees no danger nigh,
> But heaves for Turkey's woes th'impartial sigh;
> A steady Patriot of the World alone,
> The Friend of every Country—but his own.

(PAJ 224)

In the eyes of the defenders of tradition and prejudice, Coleridge then should stand in the ranks with Dr. Price and his followers who ask "What has the love of their country hitherto been among mankind? What has it been but a love of domination; a desire of conquest, and a thirst for grandeur and glory, by extending territory, and enslaving surrounding countries? What has it been but a blind and narrow principle, producing in every country a contempt of other countries, and forming men into combinations and factions against their common rights and liberties . . . ?"[26] Finally, in the first of the series on Jacobin poetry (Nov. 20, 1797), the *Anti-Jacobin* ticks off the characteristics of the Jacobin poet:

> The Poet of other times has been an enthusiast in the love of his native soil.
> The *Jacobin* Poet rejects all restriction in his feelings. *His* love is enlarged and expanded so as to comprehend all human kind.
> The old poet was a warrior, at least in imagination; and sung the actions of the heroes of his country, in strains which "made Ambition Virtue," and which overwhelmed the horrors of war in its glory.
> The *Jacobin* Poet would have no objection to sing battles too—but *he* would take a distinction. The prowess of Buonaparte, indeed, he might chant in his

---

[25] *Watchman* 99n. See also Coleridge's letter to Thelwall (*CL* 1: 213).
[26] Butler (above, n. 24) 25–26.

loftiest strain of exultation. *There* we should find nothing but trophies, and triumphs, and branches of laurel and olive, phalanxes of Republicans shouting victory, satellites of despotism biting the ground, and geniuses of Liberty planting standards on mountain-tops. (*PAJ* 3–4)

"Frost at Midnight" as a portrait of the domestic affections enters this debate in 1798, but how was it possible for a reader to know whether what the *Monthly Review* called this "pleasing picture of virtue and content in a cottage" reflects the ideology of Price, or Burke, or Coleridge, or Lépeaux, or Paine, or Priestley, or Bishop Berkeley? Is the public Coleridge the Watchman, the Bellman, the lamplighter, the patriot or the Jacobin, the Christian or the theophilanthropist? What is Coleridge's public signature? Coleridge's and Johnson's friends would have read "content in a cottage" as portraying the domestic affections as the ground for universal benevolence. Coleridge clearly hoped that his brother would have read it in an opposite way, as a rejection of sedition and atheism. The *Critical Review* (Aug. 1799) would not buy it at all: "But those who conceive that Mr. Coleridge has, in these poems, recanted his former principles, should consider the general tenor of them. The following passage surely is not written in conformity with the fashionable opinions of the day," and then the reviewer begins his citation with the lines "From east to west / A groan of accusation pierces heaven!" The citation continues through Coleridge's catalogue of crimes: slavery, greed, atheism, lying, and the glorification of war. The *Anti-Jacobin* may have read the reference in "Frost at Midnight" to the "eternal language, which thy God / Utters" as an allusion to Thomas Paine's *Age of Reason*: "The word of God is the creation we behold; And it is *this word* . . . that God speaketh universally to man" (*Lect.* 95n.), clearly the sentiments of a practicing theophilanthropist. In 1799 when the *Anti-Jacobin* republished "New Morality," its footnote on Coleridge described him as "an avowed Deist," which to their Church-and-King crowd meant that Coleridge was an atheist and a follower of Paine. Combined with their slanderous note about his going to Germany and leaving his family destitute, the note interprets Coleridge as a Jacobin in the camp of Rousseau and Paine.

The issues of patriotism, content, and domestic affections are parts of a crucial social struggle, keywords in a political debate. Their various meanings existed in the public discourse before Coleridge wrote "Frost at Midnight." When he wrote it, he was certainly aware of their meaning, because he himself had contributed to the debate as early as 1795. Coleridge's public references to the domestic affections have as much to do with public issues as they do with his own domestic affections. The language of "Frost at Midnight" in 1798 is the creation of that public discourse, not exclusively the creation of private circumstances or private meditation. "Frost at Midnight" is a private poem with public meanings because it has a public location. Its public reception responds to the poem's mediated rhetoric. Its figures take their significance from the allusiveness of the dialogue, not from referentiality or from the rhetoric of symbol and allegory, which at this date Coleridge had not defined. Since it was placed, in 1798, in the public discourse, it cannot represent rural retirement as an evasion of political issues, although the poem is certainly evasive. "Frost at Midnight" is not only the meditation of an private consciousness, but the testimony of a public figure; it is a poem that is changed from our received readings through an acknowledgment of its historical location.

Jack Stillinger has pointed out to me that when the printer set up copy for *Sibylline Leaves* (1817), "Frost at Midnight" was included among "Poems Connected with Political Events," following "France: An Ode" and "Fears in Solitude," the reverse of the order of these first two poems in 1798, and preceding "The Mad Ox." Coleridge wrote at the top of the proof "How comes this Poem here? What has it to do with Poems connected with Political Events?—I seem quite confident, that it will not be found in my arranged Catalogue of those sent to you—. It *must*, however, be deferred till it[s] proper place among my domestic & meditative Poems—& go on with the Mad Ox." Although it may simply have been a printer's error, it is doubtful that he would have made such a mistake without some cause, most probably the connection of the poems in the 1798 volume, which was reprinted in 1812. The printer may have made a mistake according to the list that Coleridge sent him, but he had good reason to make such a mistake in thinking "Frost at Midnight" a political poem. Coleridge ended his note with the comment "Besides, the Copy, I shall send, is very much altered and improved,"[27] so that when the poem was shifted from the category of political poems to its final category among "Meditative Poems in Blank Verse," it was also revised. In 1798 "Frost at Midnight" had political resonances lost when Coleridge changed its location.

If *Fears in Solitude* was crafted as a public defense against the charges in the *Anti-Jacobin* and elsewhere, then how would one read "Frost at Midnight" and the entire volume? It is not enough to read each individual poem in isolation, particularly in their later versions where some of the more radical political statements have been removed; it is equally inadequate to read just the volume itself, because reading just the volume relies implicitly on the generic expectations of literary convention. The volume responds to other writing and incorporates speech acts that are not exclusively literary. As a statement in the public discourse, the volume is not merely a collection of literary works, an anthology of odes and meditative poems, but rather something shaped as a public genre, a defense in the court of public

---

[27] The proofs are in the Beinecke Library at Yale. See Jack Stillinger, *Coleridge and Textual Instability* (New York: Oxford University Press, 1994) 55.

opinion against accusations made about Coleridge's public standing and character. In publishing "Frost at Midnight" in *Fears in Solitude*, Coleridge is as much concerned with legitimating his public character as he is in musing on nature's beauty, as much concerned with rewriting his public signature as with recognizing his subjectivity. The public themes of volume include prophecy and recantation, perjury, oath-taking, and social sympathy, all subjects of heated discussion in the political debates. His defense is to rewrite his caricature sketched in the public discourse by distancing himself from those who "expect / All change from change of constituted power" (*FS* 8), those who hope for a kind of "wild justice," as he put it in *Conciones ad Populum* (*Lect*. 38), and from the idolaters who support the government.

"Fears in Solitude" includes the accusations against Coleridge from the government supporters:

> Others, meanwhile,
> Dote with a mad Idolatry; and all,
> Who will not fall before their images,
> And yield them worship, they are enemies
> Ev'n of their country!—Such I have been deem'd.
>
> (*FS* 9)

Coleridge's first defense is to accuse his accusers of idolatry. Implicitly following Erskine's defense of Paine in which he spent most of his address to the court reading from noted literary authorities, Coleridge delivers a literary response, carefully crafted as a recantation in which he recasts and repeats his earlier political utterances. The idolatry that Coleridge refuses and that he associates with the supporters of the government is not merely the theatrical show of military and monarchic power, but the idolatry he identifies in the second of his Lectures on Revealed Religion, where he implicitly identifies idolatry with that of the ancient Hebrews and Mexicans:

> They who affect to consider Idolatry as one of the harmless Absurdities shew a strange ignorance of History and Antiquities—Between the Rites of the Inhabitants of Canaan, and the Mexican rites as existing at the time of the Spanish Conquests—a very considerable similarity is observable. In the Empire of Mexico, the very lowest accounts rate the annual number of human sacrifices at 20,000—and the majority of Historians at a number incredibly great. (*Lect*. 142)

Coleridge continues: "We become that which we believe our Gods to be. Atheism is a blessing compared with that state of mind in which men expect the blessings of Life not from the God of Purity and Love by being pure and benevolent; but from Jupiter the lustful Leader of the mythologic Banditti, from Mercury a Thief; Bacchus a Drunkard, and Venus a Harlot" (*Lect*. 142–43). From the perspective of the lectures and the political debates of the 1790s, idolatry and its literary embodiment in allegory is not simply a shadowy and harmless rhetoric that has lost all its substance in literary convention, as Coleridge would later argue.[28] If allegory is regarded solely in a literary tradition, it is simply a stale convention, but idolatry is a public rhetoric. Coleridge's and Southey's *Joan of Arc* (1796) uses allegory to expose such idolatry. Allegory is pernicious to Coleridge in the 1790s not because it is an arbitrary picture language, as he described it later, but because it is associated with blood sacrifice, violence, and war. These are the idols that Coleridge refuses to worship, and his refusal constitutes sedition in the eyes of the government. Coleridge's recitation of the accusation adds iconoclast to the list of his public signatures.

The inclusion of these accusations against his dissenting iconoclasm in "Fears in Solitude" is preceded by the observation that the whole of the public discourse is one "scheme of perjury," of lying and swearing, of uttering "oaths we mean to break." The accusations of iconoclasm are partially disarmed as part of the rhetoric of the legal system that is commonly perjurious. Lies are deliberate but sanctioned by the practice of swearing and oath taking. Coleridge agrees with dissenters who reject oaths and swearing altogether. At the end of the third Lecture on Revealed Religion, he cites the Sermon on the Mount in Matthew, where the commandment against bearing false witness is revised: "Ye have heard that it hath been said by them of old time, Thou shalt not forswear thyself, but shall perform unto the Lord thine oaths: But I say unto you, Swear not at all: neither by heaven; for it is God's throne: Nor by the earth; for it is his footstool" (Matt. 5: 33–35). Coleridge comments that this is a "text which I conceive interdicts all Oaths of every description. It is not required that a Good Man should swear, and to a bad man you are only offering a motive to additional Wickedness" (*Lect.* 165). Like other dissenters, Coleridge was appalled that "Power can pay Perjury": "Hired swearers were not perhaps so numerous in former days, as (we may judge by the sate trials) they are now. But our ancestors however had read, that when the rulers and high-priests were interested in making a man appear guilty, even the spotless innocence of the Son of God could not preserve him from false witnesses" (*Lect.* 291). Godwin shared Coleridge's dislike for "federal oaths." In a chapter "Of Tests" in *Political Justice*, he parodied the government's message:

> It is vehemently suspected that you are inimical to the cause in which we are engaged: this suspicion is either true or false; if false, we ought not to suspect you, and much less ought we to put you to this invidious and nugatory purgation; if true, you will either candidly confess your difference, or dishonestly prevaricate; be candid, and we will indignantly banish you; be dishonest, and we will receive you as bosom friends. (*PJ* 2: 623)

[28] "The Statesman's Manual," in *Lay Sermons*, ed. R. J. White (Princeton: Princeton University Press, 1972) 30.

The legal system that accuses Coleridge and others who oppose war, slavery, and economic oppression is, therefore, founded upon a system of oaths, lies, idolatry, and corrupt Christianity.

Coleridge's first defense against the accusations is that the legal system is corrupted not only by wealth but also by perjury and idolatry, the practice of validating false witness by oaths. His second is to issue a recantation supported by a self-portrait as a devout patriot who loves his native landscape and family. His recantation in *Fears in Solitude* is focused and specific. "France: An Ode" was first titled "The Recantation: an Ode," and Coleridge chose the word *recantation* carefully with an eye not only to its common English meaning, but to its Latin root in *cantare*, "to sing." Coleridge's poetry does not recant a whole set of political principles or even a political position, but a specific utterance. He is denying and singing again his earlier "Ode on the Departing Year" (1796), but as some reviewers of the 1798 *Fears in Solitude* noted, it may not be a recantation of his other political sympathies; it is partially a recantation in the root sense of a re-singing, a repetition, or reaffirmation. "France: an Ode" specifically refers to "Ode on the Departing Year":

> Yet still my voice unalter'd sang defeat
> To all that brav'd the tyrant-quelling lance,
> And shame too long delay'd, and vain retreat!
> For ne'er, O Liberty! with partial aim
> I dimm'd thy light, or damp'd thy holy flame;
> But blest the paeans of deliver'd France,
> And hung my head, and wept at Britain's name!
>
> (*FS* 15).

He recants by invoking freedom's forgiveness.

In a copy of *Sibylline Leaves*, where "Ode on the Departing Year" immediately precedes "France: an Ode," Coleridge wrote the following note at the end of "Ode on the Departing Year": "Let it not be forgotten during the perusal of this Ode that it was written many years before the abolition of the Slave Trade by the British Legislature, likewise before the invasion of Switzerland by the French Republic, which occasioned the Ode that follows, a kind of Palinodia."[29] A "palinode" is literally a re-singing, or singing again, a word of Greek origin. Calling "France: An Ode" a "Palinodia" in the note and referring to the poem in the *Biographia* as "FRANCE, *a Palinodia* (*BL* 1: 200) indicates that what he is recanting and repeating in "France: An Ode" is specifically "Ode on the Departing Year," which must be read in its 1796 and 1797 versions to make any sense of the recantation. Coleridge is

---

[29] *CP* 1: 168. See also *The Complete Poetical & Dramatic Works*, ed. James Dykes Campbell (London: 1893) 588.

not recanting an entire set of political principles, which may be difficult to define because of his evasiveness, but a specific section of "Ode on the Departing Year" that prophesied England's destruction. In the 1796 version of "Ode on the Departing Year," Coleridge predicted the destruction of England:

> O doom'd to fall, enslav'd and vile,
> O ALBION! O my mother Isle!
> Thy valleys, fair as Eden's bowers,
> Glitter green with sunny showers;
> Thy grassy Upland's gentle Swells
> Echo to the Bleat of Flocks;
> (Those grassy Hills, those glitt'ring Dells
> Proudly ramparted with rocks)
> And Ocean 'mid his uproar wild
> Speaks safety to his Island-child,
> Hence for many a fearless age
> Has social Quiet lov'd thy shore;
> Nor ever sworded Foeman's rage
> Or sack'd thy towers, or stain'd thy fields with gore.
> Disclaim'd of Heaven! mad Av'rice at thy side,
> At coward distance, yet with kindling pride—
> Safe 'mid thy herds and corn-fields thou hast stood,
> And join'd the yell of Famine and of Blood.
> All nations curse thee: and with eager wond'ring
> Shall hear DESTRUCTION, like a vulture, scream!

In versions after 1803 Coleridge revised the first line to read, "Not yet enslaved, not wholly vile" to change the entire meaning of the 1796 passage, which predicts conquest and destruction from a vengeful foreign nation. The negative "Not yet" recants the earlier version of the poem. The fears of "Fears in Solitude" are that the prophecy of "Ode on the Departing Year" will come true, a prophecy Coleridge intends to recant. "Fears in Solitude" simply holds out the possibility of destruction:

> And what if all-avenging Providence,
> Strong and retributive, should make us know
> The meaning of our words, force us to feel
> The desolation and the agony
> Of our fierce doings?—
>
> (*FS* 7)

In later versions of "Ode on the Departing Year," he omitted a long note included in the 1797 and 1803 versions, which reads in part:

We have been preserved by our insular situation, from suffering the actual horrors of War ourselves, and we have shewn our gratitude to Providence for this immunity by our eagerness to spread those horrors over nations less happily situated. In the midst of plenty and safety we have raised or joined the yell for famine and blood. Of the one hundred and seven last years, fifty have been years of War. Such wickedness cannot pass unpunished. We have been proud and confident in our alliances and our fleets—but God has prepared the canker-worm, and will smite the *gourds* of our pride.[30]

In "Fears in Solitude" his introduction of the accusations against him is preceded by his accusations against his country in the terms of "Ode on the Departing Year": "Thankless too for peace, / (Peace long preserv'd by fleets and perilous seas) / Secure from actual warfare, we have lov'd / To swell the war-whoop, passionate for war!" (*FS* 5)

Fears in Solitude, written after a real threat of invasion, is a public recantation, a palinode, only of the prediction of invasion and ruin for Britain contained in "Ode on the Departing Year." As some reviewers of the 1798 *Fears in Solitude* noted, it may not be a recantation of Coleridge's other political positions. Although France's victories were accompanied by slaughter, he still held hopes for true liberty, but France's invasion of Switzerland, also in February 1798, dispelled those hopes and proved the French as much idolaters as the English who raise the cry for war. On other public issues in *Fears in Solitude*, Coleridge repeats his earlier positions. He does not change his opposition to imperialist war, which Burke defined as the position of English Jacobins. Nor does he change his opinions on the excesses of wealth and privilege, slavery, and the corruption of the legal system and religion. Any one of these issues would have labeled him a Jacobin in 1798.

France has succumbed to an idolatry that has diverted its quest for freedom. In the final stanza of "France: An Ode," Coleridge addresses liberty: "But thou nor swell'st the victor's strain, nor ever / Didst breathe thy soul in forms of human pow'r" (*FS* 18), a line he interpreted in the *Morning Post* reprinting of the poem on October 14, 1802, as indicating that "that grand *ideal* of Freedom which the mind attains by its contemplation of its individual nature, and of the sublime surrounding objects (see Stanza the First) do not belong to men, as a society, nor can possibly be either gratified or realized, under any form of human government; but belong to the individual man, so far as he is pure, and inflamed with the love and adoration of God in Nature" (*CP* 1: 244). But the final stanza in *Fears in Solitude* is not this specific. The phrase "forms of human power" can mean the idols of human power, the false gods of military destruction. Burke surely would

---

[30] *CP* 1: 167. E. H. Coleridge lists this as in the versions of 1796, 1797, and 1803, but I do not find it in the 1796 quarto.

have been troubled to read on the preceding page that Liberty does not swell "the victor's strain" and

> Alike from all, howe'er they praise thee,
> (Nor pray'r, nor boastful name delays thee)
> Alike from priesthood's harpy minions,
> And factious blasphemy's obscener slaves,
> Thou speedest on thy subtle pinions,
> To live amid the winds, and move upon the waves!
>
> (FS 18)

In "Fears in Solitude" and "France: an Ode," Coleridge changes his vision of England's destruction, but he repeats his love of liberty.

Coleridge's second defense against being called a Jacobin, deist, theophilanthropist, and runagate is to portray himself as a lover of domesticity who retains his religious faith, whatever his sectarian allegiances may be. Coleridge words his defense with enough ambiguity to avoid the stigma of both Jacobin materialism and loyalist idolatry. To the authors of the *Anti-Jacobin* he remained a "worthy tool of Jacobinism," and to his publisher he remained a patriot. In his crafted defense Coleridge opposes the public discourse composed of idolatry, lies, perjury, and false swearing to a language of nature, domesticity, and patriotism, but it is not a simple opposition of the public and the private, because the latter is always involved in the public discourse. "Frost at Midnight" concludes the volume and the defense, and although it begins as a solitary meditation, it is, in 1798, a meditation on public issues, in the root meaning of meditation as a healing or curing; in "Fears in Solitude" the "spot amid the hills" is a "spirit healing nook." If "Frost at Midnight" is read as an isolated artifact, Coleridge is removed from the intrusive noise of active life and permitted to think philosophically about nature's language, the ministry of frost. But if the entire volume is read as one poem, the meditations of "Frost at Midnight" echo those at the beginning of "Fears in Solitude":

> many thoughts,
> Made up a meditative joy, and found
> Religious meanings in the forms of nature!
> And so, his senses gradually wrapp'd
> In a half-sleep, he dreams of better worlds.
>
> (FS 2)

The "better worlds" may be heaven, the *locus* of his "future being" as he expressed it in "Fears in Solitude," or an earthly paradise. At the end of "Fears in Solitude" he is grateful that

                              by nature's quietness
               And solitary musings all my heart
               Is soften'd, and made worthy to indulge
               Love, and the thoughts that yearn for human kind.

                                                          (*FS* 11–12)

An older meaning of "yearn" is "to sympathize with" or "to pity." The "solitary musings" of "Fears in Solitude" are the "abstruser musings" of "Frost
at Midnight" where he meditates on the silence of the "numberless goings
on of life"—specifically in this volume, the current political events.
Coleridge's "abstruse musings" take on a public tone, especially since, on
the facing page, exactly in the same position as Coleridge's line on his vexed
meditation, is the final line of "France: An Ode" on the significance of nature: "O Liberty, my spirit felt thee there!" Yet in the public discourse "abstruse" thinking sounds suspiciously like the abstract metaphysics that
Burke saw as Jacobin: "I cannot stand forward, and give praise or blame to
any thing which relates to human actions, and human concerns, on a simple view of the object, as it stands stripped of every relation, in all the naked-
ness and solitude of metaphysical abstraction" (*RRF* 58).

    The relation between the calm and the vexation in "Frost at Midnight"
is the same as it is at the beginning of "Fears in Solitude" when calm solitude turns abruptly to thoughts of war: "it is a melancholy thing / For such
a man, who would full fain preserve / His soul in calmness, yet perforce
must feel / For all his brethren" (*FS* 2). If one reads the entire volume of
Fears in Solitude as a single composition, are the "abstruser musings" of
"Frost at Midnight" and the "solitary musings" of "Fears in Solitude" a
meditation on the love of all humanity and universal benevolence, or are
they on the "eternal language" of nature? If the love of humankind and the
love of nature are the same, and if the thoughts of humanity and universal
benevolence in "Fears in Solitude" remain with Coleridge throughout the
volume, then the "abstruser musings" of "Frost at Midnight" may be precisely the kind of thinking that Burke feared.

    Coleridge is vexed and disturbed with the extreme calm, a calm that dis-
rupts the healing of meditation. In the volume his calm is disturbed, not
only because he is isolated from a language of nature that is the signature
of liberty and divinity, but also because that language, in the two earlier
poems, justified his persistent re-singing of dissenting views. He wishes to
be able to read nature's language symbolically, but his phrase "the numberless goings on of life" signifies that human liberty is threatened. Since
"Frost at Midnight" is preceded by two political poems that worry specifically about war and invasion, the "goings on of life" must refer to the present political anxieties. The space between the poems in this volume,
widened by Coleridge himself in *Sibylline Leaves* and extended to an un-

bridgeable chasm in twentieth-century criticism, does not, in 1798, act as a bounding line separating one poem from another. Within the poem itself the "numberless goings on of life" are present in "Sea, hill and wood"—the elements of nature, but in the context of the first two poems, the potential French invasion changes the reference of the phrase.

The first forty-seven lines of "Frost at Midnight" in the 1798 quarto version constitute one verse paragraph with no break similar to the later break between the present moment and his recollections of school. While the later version of "Frost at Midnight" is an exercise of individual memory troubled by a lapse of continuity indicated by the paragraph break and the sharp turn indicated by "But O!" the earlier version moves more smoothly without the abrupt turn from the solitude of his fireside, where his fears take root, to a society where church bells are "the poor man's only music." The love of domesticity leads to a love of society, represented as a country fair, a local attachment to warm Burke's heart. Yet the associations curiously are made through the image of the film on the grate, which a note explains "in all parts of the kingdom these films are called *strangers*, and supposed to portend the arrival of some absent friend." If friends are strangers, strangers must be friends, and the circle of sympathy widens beyond the narrow domestic, and perhaps even national, circle. In *Fears in Solitude* his thoughts "yearn for human kind."

Toward the end of "Frost at Midnight," Coleridge hopes that Hartley will "see and hear / The lovely shapes and sounds intelligible / Of that eternal language, which thy God / Utters." God is the "Great universal Teacher" (*FS* 22) But whose universality are we talking about? Coleridge may allude to the divine visible language of nature that Bishop Berkeley defines in *Alciphron* and to which Coleridge himself alludes in a note to "This Lime-Tree Bower" when he explains to Southey in 1797 that "I am a Berkleyan":

> The great Mover and Author of nature constantly explaineth Himself to the eyes of men by the sensible intervention of arbitrary signs, which have no similitude or connexion with the things signified; so as, by compounding and disposing them, to suggest and exhibit an endless variety of objects differing in nature, time, and place; thereby informing and directing men how to act with respect to things distant and future, as well as near and present. In consequence . . . you have as much reason to think the Universal Agent or God speaks to your eyes, as you can have for thinking any particular person speaks to your ears.[31]

Other readers might quote Spinoza or Priestley as the source of Coleridge's quasi-pantheistic lines. But if the poem is located within a political context

---

[31] *Alciphron* in *The Works of George Berkeley, Bishop of Cloyne*, ed. A. A. Luce and T. E. Jessop (London: Nelson, 1950) 3: 157.

in which nature is the home of liberty, universality becomes a problem. What is the universal teacher teaching? The works of Tom Paine, or the works of Edmund Burke?

In his review of the *Biographia*, Hazlitt said of Coleridge's political writings: "His style, in general, admits of a convenient latitude of interpretation" (Howe 16: 129). Coleridge's latitude wasn't merely convenient; it was necessary. Coleridge was dodging because the heat was on him and his associates Stuart and Johnson, from the government and the hostile press. It is common for those who try to maintain opposition in times of repression to speak a type of double talk; it is the nature of public debate. The latitude Hazlitt observes does more than measure the poles of his political oscillations. It also describes a field of possible contexts in which his poetic and political utterances were received and read, the contexts that determined the public significance of "Frost at Midnight" in 1798.

Chapter Four

THE MARINER'S EXTRAVAGANCE AND
THE TEMPESTS OF *LYRICAL BALLADS*

DOMINANT twentieth-century opinion of "The Ancient Mariner" separates esthetics and its allies, psychology and philosophy, from politics and credits Coleridge's emergence as a great poet to his liberation from polemical poetry and newspaper writing. Humphrey House's *Clark Lectures* (1953) represents common opinion: "It has been observed by Dr. Tillyard how very unpolitical 'The Ancient Mariner' is. 'Frost at Midnight' (dated February 1798—that is while the 'Mariner' was still being written) is, if possible, less political still." Carl Woodring's *Politics in the Poetry of Coleridge* (1961) echoes House, expressing severe reservations about David Erdman's claims for the political significance of "The Ancient Mariner": "When Dr. Erdman reasons that Coleridge was 'objectifying the dereliction and dismay of the times in an imaginatively controlled nightmare *The Ancient Mariner*,' he goes beyond what we can demonstrate to the skeptical."[1] With a few notable exceptions, particularly William Empson and Jerome McGann,[2] critics have read "The Ancient Mariner" as either a story of crime and punishment, a narrative of spiritual death and rebirth, as in Robert Penn Warren's essay, or as a psychological tale of personal disintegration, as in Edward Bostetter's *Romantic Ventriloquists*.[3] In both the symbolic and the psychological readings, "The Ancient Mariner" is removed from its historical contexts of 1798 and 1817 and read as a separate and integral poem, explicated with writings of Colerdige that appeared a full twenty years after

[1] Humphry House, *Coleridge: The Clark Lectures, 1951–52* (London: Rupert Hart-Davis, 1953) 85–86. Carl Woodring, *Politics in the Poetry of Coleridge* (Madison: University of Wisconsin Press, 1961) 33 quotes *Blake: Prophet against Empire* (Princeton: Princeton University Press, 1954) 293.

[2] William Empson, "The Ancient Mariner," *The Critical Quarterly* 6 (1964): 298–319; Jerome McGann, "The Ancient Mariner: the Meaning of the Meanings," *Critical Inquiry* 8 (1981), reprinted in his *The Beauty of Inflections: Literary Investigations in Historical Method and Theory* (Oxford: Clarendon Press, 1985) 135–72. See also Patrick J. Keane, *Coleridge's Submerged Politics*: The Ancient Mariner *and* Robinson Crusoe (Columbia, Mo.: University of Missouri Press, 1994).

[3] Robert Penn Warren, "A Poem of Pure Imagination: An Experiment in Reading," in his *Selected Essays* (New York: Random House, 1958) 198–305; Edward Bostetter, "The Nightmare World of *The Ancient Mariner*," *SIR* 1 (1962): 241–54, reprinted in *The Romantic Ventriloquists* (Seattle: University of Washington Press, 1963).

its original publication. The discourses of esthetics and politics are completely separate.

"The Ancient Mariner" is a poem with political significance, but that significance cannot be recognized unless the poem is located within the public debates raging over the events and principles of the French Revolution
and within the context of Coleridge's and Wordsworth's protest poetry. Its
location in *Lyrical Ballads* (1798), the insistently literary paratext that the
other poems provide, and the allusions within the poem align it with the
public discourse in the 1790s. A reading that limits evidence to the poem
itself or attempts to connect its figures literally with public events or political theory is undermined by the appearance of the poem itself in 1798.
With the archaic spellings and the absence of the later gloss, the poem is,
visually, a fake, a counterfeit similar to the poems of Chatterton and
Macpherson. Any attempt to identify its ideology, periods of history represented, or cultural significance must account for the poem's appearance. As
Charles Burney realized in his review, the poem is not an innocent imitation of an earlier style but a counterfeit history. He deplored the tendency
"to go back to the barbarous and uncouth numbers of Chaucer" and remarked that "*Rust* is necessary quality to a counterfeit old medal; but, to
give artificial rust to modern poetry, in order to render it similar to that of
three or four hundred years ago, can have no better title to merit and admiration than may be claimed by any ingenious forgery."[4] If it is a counterfeit, it can have no history, nor can it represent history because a
counterfeit or forgery has no time, no tense, except the present. An acknowledged forgery has its own moment distinct from that which it imitates. That moment cannot represent an earlier historical period because a
counterfeit or forgery announces its inauthenticity. If "The Ancient
Mariner" of 1798 is read as an imitation of a native English tradition, it is
located in the public discourse, not as representative of an earlier historical
period, but as a part of a debate over the value of literary history and tradition deeply involved in the public discourse in 1798.

"The Ancient Mariner" reveals its contemporary significance from its location in 1798: the circumstances of its composition, the varying emphases
of its reception, and the allusiveness of its style. I read the discourse that it
enters in 1798 in *Lyrical Ballads*. My intention is not to substitute a political reading for an esthetic one, but to read politically to argue that an
esthetic reading is limited by its own boundaries and, by excluding a consciousness of social issues, cannot read literature's public mediation. To dis-
place the one with the other would be to substitute one enabling blindness
for another. The complex situation of literature in the 1790s is that the discourse of esthetics is often figurative of the discourse of politics, and that
the tropes of the literary are often the public rhetoric of law courts and pub-

---

[4] Charles Burney, Review of *Lyrical Ballads, Monthly Review* (June 1799: 203) in *RR*.

lic addresses. Nor is my purpose to insist, here and elsewhere in these chapters, on a materialism that reduces itself to a literalism and thus can detect a willful ignorance and a consciousness eager to evade the responsibilities of social engagement. I prefer to read displacement as figuration, since figuration implies a troubled presentness to awareness that displacement tends to discount and find culpable.

Lyrics take their significance from their location. In the case of "The Ancient Mariner," I read Coleridge's decisions about publication. My claim is not that "The Ancient Mariner" is in itself a poem of explicit political commentary—Woodring's skepticism is appropriate for such claims—but that if one reads the poem carefully as one fragment of the public discourse, its significance changes. It is not a poem that avoids or evades political issues for the secure comforts of retirement or a dreamworld to which Coleridge escapes; it is a poem that enters the public debates. In reading the public poem, one must read the nuances of words reviewers used to describe it and the literary history that was constructed to authorize it. I then use the rhetoric of the poem's reception and the history that is forged to support it as a way of reading the public figures of "The Ancient Mariner" in *Lyrical Ballads*. The language that reviewers use to describe the poem is crucial; "The Ancient Mariner" is "German," "extravagant," "obscure," "unintelligible," "absurd," a "rhapsody" and a "farrago," a set of terms opposed to the more conventional ones of "elegant," "proper," "classical," and "tasteful." The vocabulary of its reception derives from the discourse that precedes and is contemporary with the writing of the poem. Insofar as it is extravagant, it is an appropriate introductory poem for *Lyrical Ballads*, whose major theme is that of wandering, placelessness, and homelessness and whose major tropes are those of vagrancy and tempest.

I begin a survey of the context of "The Ancient Mariner" with Hazlitt's "On the Living Poets" from his *Lectures on the English Poets* (1818), which characterizes the Lake School of poets: "This school of poetry had its origin in the French revolution, or rather in those sentiments and opinions which produced that revolution; and which sentiments and opinions were indirectly imported into this country in translations from the German about that period." Later in the same lecture, Hazlitt said that Coleridge's "Ancient Mariner is his most remarkable performance, and the only one that I could point out to any one as giving an adequate idea of his great natural powers. It is high German, however, and in it he seems to 'conceive of poetry but as a drunken dream, reckless, careless, and heedless, of past, present, and to come,' "[5] unmindful, in other words, of time and history. The political keyword in these comments is *German*, one that is repeated again and again in contemporary reviews of "The Ancient Mariner." Hazlitt, who began writing for the *Edinburgh Review* in 1815, may have been drawing on

---

[5] Howe 5: 161, 166. Howe identifies the quotation from *Measure for Measure* IV, ii, 148–52.

Francis Jeffrey's famous review of Southey's *Thalaba* in the *Edinburgh* (Oct. 1802), where he characterized the poetry of Southey, Coleridge, and Wordsworth:

> The peculiar doctrines of this sect, it would not, perhaps, be very easy to explain; but, that they are *dissenters* from the established systems in poetry and criticism, is admitted, and proved indeed, by the whole tenor of their compositions. Though they lay claim, we believe, to a creed and a revelation of their own, there can be little doubt, that their doctrines are of *German* origin, and have been derived from some of the great modern reformers in that country.

It may seem odd that Hazlitt's and Jeffrey's emphasis falls upon Germany and not France as the origin of the politics of the Lake School, but Jeffrey is quite specific by enumerating "the sources from which their materials have been derived"; one that he cites is the "simplicity and energy . . . of Kotzebue and Schiller." Jeffrey adds "A splenetic and idle discontent with the existing institutions of society, seems to be at the bottom of all their serious and peculiar sentiments."

In his *Lectures on the Age of Elizabeth* (1820), Hazlitt explains his association of "the Goethes, the Lessings, the Schillers, the Kotzebues" as "the only incorrigible Jacobins, and their school of poetry is the only real school of Radical Reform." The German drama goes

> all the lengths not only of instinctive feeling, but of speculative opinion, and startling the hearer by overturning all the established maxims of society, and setting at nought all the received rules of composition. It cannot be said of this style that in it "decorum is the principle thing." It is the violation of decorum, that is its first and last principle, the beginning, middle and end. It is an insult and defiance to Aristotle's definition of tragedy. The action is not grave, but extravagant. . . . We are no longer as formerly heroes in warlike enterprise; martyrs to religious faith; but we are all the partisans of a political system, and devotees to some theory of moral sentiments.

Having noted that in the German drama seamstresses express noble sentiments and aspire to wed nobles, that noble women commit adultery with similarly ideal sentiments, and that young nobles turn robbers, Hazlitt summarizes the discourse of the German drama:

> All qualities are reversed: virtue is always at odds with vice, "which shall be which:" the internal character and external situation, the actions and the sentiments, are never in accord: you are to judge everything by contraries. . . . The world and every thing in it is not just what it ought to be, or what it pretends to be; or such extravagant and prodigious paradoxes would be driven from the stage. . . . Opinion is not truth: appearance is not reality: power is not beneficence: rank is not wisdom: nobility is not the only virtue: riches are not happiness: desert and success are different things: actions do not always speak of

the character more than words. We feel this, and do justice to the romantic extravagance of the German Muse.[6]

Hazlitt was not alone in his evaluation. Before "The Ancient Mariner" was
published, T. J. Mathias wrote in "The Shade of Alexander Pope":

> Lo, from the abyss, unmeaning Spectres drawn,
> The Gothick glass, blue flame, and flick'ring lawn!
> Choak'd with vile weeds, our once proud Avon strays,
> When novels die, and rise again in plays:
> No Congress props our Drama's falling state,
> The modern ultimatum is, 'Translate,'
> Thence sprout the morals of the German School:
> The Christian sinks, the Jacobin bears rule.

A note to these lines explains that "the modern productions of the German
stage, which silly men and women are daily translating, have one general
tendency to Jacobinism. . . . They are too often the licensed vehicles of immorality and licentiousness, particularly in respect to marriage."[7]

Jeffrey's extended comparison of the Lake poets to a sect of dissenters
connects them with the German Illuminati. Crabb Robinson explains the
organization:

> During the heat of the first Revolution in France, two works appeared, one in
> England, by Professor Robison of Edinburgh, and the other, the more volu-
> minous, in France, by the Abbé Barruel, with the common object of showing
> that the Revolution and all the horrors consequent on it were the effect of a
> conspiracy deliberately planned and carried out on the Continent of Europe
> by an Order of Infidels, who, by means of secret societies, planned to destroy
> all thrones, overturn all altars, and completely upset the established order of
> things. The society to which this scheme was ascribed had the name of *The Il-
> luminati.* . . . The Kantian philosophy was one of their instruments. Indeed
> more or less, every union of men, and every variety of thought, opposed to
> monarchy and popery had about it the suspicion of "Illumination." And of this
> tremendous evil the founder and archdeacon was Adam Weishaupt.[8]

---

[6] Howe 6: 360–62. Hazlitt's quotations echo Milton, "On Education" and *Macbeth* III, iv,
127, where Lady Macbeth says that night is "almost at odds with morning, which is which."

[7] John Livingston Lowes quotes Mathias's poem in *The Road to Xanadu* (Boston: Houghton
Mifflin, 1927) 539. The *Anti-Jacobin Review*'s review of "The Shade of Alexander Pope" (Mar.
1799) prints part of the quotation and the note.

[8] *Diary, Reminiscences, and Correspondence of Henry Crabb Robinson*, ed. Thomas Sadler (London, 1869) 1: 192. See Abbé Barruel, *Memoirs, Illustrating the History of Jacobinism*, trans.
Robert Clifford (London, 1798); John Robison, *Proofs of a Conspiracy against all the Religions
and Governments of Europe Carried on in the Secret Meetings of Free Masons, Illuminati and Reading Societies*, 4th ed. (New York, 1798); and a rebuttal, Jean-Joseph Mounier, *On the Influence
Attributed to Philosophers, Free-Masons, and to the Illuminati on the Revolution in France* (London,
1801). For Coleridge's reading of Weishaupt's commentary on Kant, see *CN* 1: 1724n.

Writing of secret Irish revolutionary societies, Coleridge, in the *Courier* of
Sept. 29, 1814, explained that

> the Bavarian Weishaupt attempted to combine the secret oaths and filiated so-
> cieties of Free Masonry, with the discipline, education, and mechanized obe-
> dience of the disciples of Loyola; and succeeded so far as to furnish some few
> hints and materials for that monstrous romance of the Illumino [sic] with
> which the fanatics, Barruel and Robison, astonished and terrified the good
> people of England, Ireland, and Vienna. (*EOT* 2: 382)

Discussion of the Illuminati was common in the press in the 1790s. On January 17, 1798 the *Morning Post* described the Illuminati as "enlightened"
men who "wished to impress mankind with a sense of their dignity, and thus
to produce a revolution, the result of reason," while the *Anti-Jacobin Review*
in August 1798 stigmatized them as "vile instruments of the most desper-
ate race of miscreants that ever disgraced humanity" (217).

Jeffrey's allusion to the "great modern reformers" in Germany is tinged
with a bit of sarcasm. Whether or not Jeffrey intended to allude to the Illuminati in his identification of the Lake School's German origin, his accusations are quite precise. The source of their opinions may be found, to a
large extent, in the German drama of Kotzebue and Schiller. In this association Jeffrey may be following the contemporary reviews of *Lyrical Ballads*, several of which used the word *German* to describe "The Ancient
Mariner." Southey's comment is perhaps the most famous. In the *Critical
Review* for October 1798, he called it "a Dutch attempt at German sublimity," which may have been the occasion for Hazlitt's more sympathetic re-
joinder that it is "high German." Earlier in his review, Southey had complained of "The Idiot Boy" as a "Flemish picture in the worthlessness of its
design and the excellence of its execution. From Flemish artists we are sat-
isfied with such pieces; who would not have lamented, if Corregio or Rafaelle
had wasted their talents in painting Dutch boors or the humors of a Flemish wake?" To Southey the subject matter was unworthy, but he was well
aware of what "German sublimity" implied to his readers, particularly that
of German drama. In a letter written a few months after the review was published, he commented that "the German plays have always something ridiculous, yet Kotzebue seems to me possessed of unsurpassed and unsurpassable
genius. I wonder his plays are acted here; they are so thoroughly Jacobinical in tendency. They create Jacobinical feelings, almost irresistibly. In every
one that I have yet seen . . . some old prejudice or old principle is attacked."[9]

In some cases the reviewers' comments on the poem's German style were
prompted by a sentence in the Advertisement to *Lyrical Ballads*, which said
that "the Rime of the Ancyent Marinere was professedly written in imita-

---

[9] *Selections from the Letters of Robert Southey*, ed. John Wood Warter (London, 1856) 1: 68.

tion of the *style*, as well as of the spirit of the elder poets."[10] Earlier in the Advertisement Wordsworth had warned that readers will find less to complain of "the more conversant the reader is with our elder writers." Wordsworth found his traditions in early poetry, but Southey denied that "The Ancient Mariner" was written in the style of an English ballad: "We are tolerably conversant with the early English poets; and can discover no resemblance whatever, except in antiquated spelling and a few obsolete words." To Southey the style was not English, but German. An anonymous reviewer in the *Analytical Review* for December 1798 echoed Southey's criticism: "We are not pleased with it: in our opinion it has more of the extravagance of a mad german poet, than of the simplicity of our ancient ballad writers." This harsh judgment comes as something of a surprise because the *Analytical* was published by Joseph Johnson, the radical bookseller, who in the same months was publishing Coleridge's *Fears in Solitude*. To the *Analytical*, "The Ancient Mariner" was not only German, which meant Jacobin, but its German extravagance was contrasted with English simplicity.

The word *extravagant* occurs repeatedly in describing the poem in particular and German literature in general. Reviewing *Sibylline Leaves* in November of 1817, the *British Critic* remarked on Coleridge's "wildness of imagination" that is "apt to degenerate into extravagance." In 1828 Thomas Colley Grattan recorded a conversation with Coleridge, who related an anecdote at Mrs. Barbauld's "a few days after" *Lyrical Ballads* was published in which "Pinkerton the geographer" ridiculed "The Ancient Mariner." Since the volume was published anonymously, Coleridge could join in the ridicule without revealing himself as the author. After Pinkerton described the poem as "an extravagant farrago of absurdity," "detestable," and "odious," Coleridge responded that it was "intolerable," "abominable," and "loathsome."[11] Coleridge's anecdote may or may not be accurate, but his repeating the word "extravagance" echoes its use in reviews and, with Coleridge's acknowledgment, types the poem as extravagant. In its root meaning, *extravagance* suggests excessive wandering and vagrancy, unbounded voyaging beyond the proper bounds of political, religious, and moral order. To be extravagant is to violate boundaries, to transgress, and to search for (or be forced into) the political sublime, a world of disorder and fragmentation.[12] Its appeal for Coleridge is obvious. The German po-

[10] All quotations from *Lyrical Ballads* are from Jonathan Wordsworth's reprint of the first volume of 1798 (Oxford: Woodstock, 1990). References are to pages.

[11] *TT* 2: 495. Since Coleridge was in Germany a few days after the publication of *Lyrical Ballads*, the story is at least partly fabricated.

[12] Kurt Heinzelman quotes the final chapter of Thoreau's *Walden*: "I fear chiefly lest my expression may not be *extra-vagant* enough, may not wander far enough beyond the narrow limit of my daily experience, so as to be adequate to the truth of which I have been convinced" (*The Economics of the Imagination* [Amherst: University of Massachusetts Press, 1980] 30).

litical sublime partook of none of the French militant atheism and materialism.

A similar unfavorable judgment was contained in a brief notice in the *Monthly Magazine*, to the effect that "the author of '*Lyrical Ballads*' has attempted to imitate the style of our old English versifiers, with unusual success: '*The Auncient Marinere*,' however, on which he particularly prides himself, is in our opinion, a particular exception." The harsh judgment is surprising considering Wordsworth's and Coleridge's original intention to submit the poem to the *Monthly* to pay the expenses of a walking tour, and considering the *Monthly's* political principles, which began in 1796 when its first number announced its purpose to give "aid to the propagation of those liberal principles respecting some of the most important concerns of mankind, which have been either deserted or virulently opposed by other Periodical Miscellanies." It also had a particular interest in German literature. Its second number contained William Taylor's translation of Bürger's "Lenore." Considering the popularity of Burger's poem, which also appeared in at least four other translations within the year, including one by Walter Scott, Coleridge's expectation that the *Monthly* would admire "The Ancient Mariner" was reasonable. The *Monthly's* opinion can be briefly summarized: "Not British."

Perhaps the most common comment in the reviews was that the poem was obscure. Southey wrote that "many of the stanzas are laboriously beautiful; but in connection they are absurd or unintelligible." The reviewer for the *British Critic* (Oct. 1799) complained of a "kind of confusion of images, which loses all effect, from not being quite intelligible." In the *Monthly Review* (June 1799) Charles Burney described it as "the strangest story of cock and bull that we ever saw on paper," in which there was a "rhapsody of unintelligible wildness and incoherence,"—in other words a poem of no determined form. As Burney, a musicologist, surely knew, the rhapsody as a literary and musical form is a miscellaneous collection of fragments without order or bounds, something stitched together. Anne Ferry quotes the definition of *rhapsody* from Elisha Coles's *An English Dictionary* (1717): "a confused Collection."[13] These reviews are probably the origin of Wordsworth's note to the poem in the second edition which identified its defects: "the imagery is somewhat too laboriously accumulated" and "the events having no necessary connection do not produce each other."[14] There is, in other words, no narrative.

To many readers the poem was disordered and therefore unintelligible, but it was a significant unintelligibility, because obscurity had significance. When Sheridan rejected Coleridge's play "Osorio" in the months that Co-

---

[13] Anne Ferry, *The Title to the Poem* (Stanford: Stanford University Press, 1996) 167.
[14] *Lyrical Ballads*, ed. R. L. Brett and A. R. Jones (London: Metheun, 1963) 277.

leridge was beginning "The Ancient Mariner," Coleridge transmitted Sheridan's objections to Thomas Poole: "his *sole* objection is—the obscurity of the three last acts" (*CL* 1: 358). "Osorio" ended with the rebellious Moors in possession of the Spanish citadel, and with a speech by Alhadra, their leader, who boasted that if she had one hundred men she could "shake the kingdoms of this world" (*CP* 2: 596). Not an ounce of obscurity in that speech. Sheridan's use of the word *obscure* (if that was his word and not Coleridge's) suggests, not that Coleridge's play was absurd or nonsensical, but that it was disordered and politically dangerous, which it certainly was. That which is a rhapsody, or obscure, or unintelligible, or extravagant in the 1790s is highly suspicious and dangerous to the civil peace. The fragmented rhapsody was not narration but the oratorical figure of legendary *narratio* as Cicero defined it: "The legendary tale comprises events neither true nor probable."[15] Read as a part of the public discourse, "The Ancient Mariner" is not narration, but legendary *narratio*, a rhetorical figure located in a work addressed to the public.

In an age when one expects most reviews to be determined by political allegiances, it is curious to find liberal journals finding fault with "The Ancient Mariner." Their grounds for not admiring it appear to be esthetic. The reviews mark a day in which it was becoming increasingly possible to weigh judgments of esthetics as evenly as questions of politics. It is even more odd to find The Reverend William Heath in the *Anti-Jacobin Review* (April 1800) praising *Lyrical Ballads* in a language that indicates an opposite esthetic and political evaluation. The volume "has genius, taste, elegance, wit, and imagery of the most beautiful kind. 'The ancyent Marinere' is an admirable 'imitation of the style as well as of the spirit of the elder poets.' . . . indeed the whole volume convinces us that the author possesses a mind at once classic and accomplished and we, with pleasure, recommend it to the notice of our readers as a production of no ordinary merit." The *Anti-Jacobin Review* read the imitation of the elder writers as "classic," as an English, not German, volume, and as an elegant, not extravagant, collection. The word *elegant* points, not only to the esthetic qualities of refinement and beauty, but also the political categories of that which is proper, since the word means *propriety* as well as beauty and grace. Thus, in the public discourse, to describe a poem as "German," "extravagant," or "absurd" or to call it a "farrago" or "rhapsody" is to imply that it is politically dangerous and the opposite of "elegant," "classical," "proper," and "tasteful."

The surprise in finding the *Anti-Jacobin Review* praise the poem as English and elegant rather than extravagant is greater when one realizes that the predecessor of the *Anti-Jacobin Review*, the *Anti-Jacobin; or Weekly Ex-*

---

[15] *Ad Herennium* (I. viii. 13), trans. Harry Caplan (Cambridge, Mass.: Harvard University Press, 1931) 23.

aminer, had included in its numbers for June 4, and June 11, 1798, a parody of a German play, which it called *The Rovers*, to ridicule the fashion for German drama that coincided with Coleridge's enthusiasm for Schiller and the writing of "The Ancient Mariner." It is in part a parody of Schiller's *Robbers*, and the prologue announces its subjects:

> To-night our Bard, who scorns pedantic rules,
> His Plot has borrow'd from the German schools;
> —The German schools—where no dull maxims bind
> The bold expansion of the electric mind.
> Fix'd to no period, circled by no space,
> He leaps the flaming bounds of time and place:
> Round the dark confines of the forest raves,
> With *gentle* Robbers stocks his gloomy caves;
> Tells how Prime Ministers are shocking things,
> And *reigning Dukes* as bad as tyrant Kings;
> How to *two* swains *one* nymph her vows may give,
> And how *two* Damsels with *one* Lover live!
> Delicious Scenes!—Such scenes *our* Bard displays
> Which, crown'd with German, sue for British, praise.
>
> (*PAJ* 168)

A footnote to the Prologue's reference to *The Robbers* explains that it is a "German Tragedy, in which Robbery is put in so fascinating a light, that the whole of a German University went upon the highway in consequence of it." Overleaping boundaries is, of course, a Satanic occupation. The *Anti-Jacobin*'s line "He leaps the flaming bounds of time and place" is borrowed from Gray's "The Progress of Poetry": "He passed the flaming bounds of place and time,"[16] which refers to *Paradise Lost* and Satan's entry into Eden: "Due entrance he disdain'd, and in contempt, / At one slight bound high overleap'd all bound / Of Hill or highest Wall . . . " (*PL* IV, 180–82). "Milton" in the public discourse is frequently a republican and regicide, to Tory and radical alike.

Schiller's *Robbers* was first translated by A. F. Tytler and published in 1792. Tytler's translation, or perhaps it would be better to call it an adaptation, tones down many of the attacks on the ruling classes and particularly the Church, yet still includes many revolutionary speeches. Charles Moor, the older son of a Count, is disowned and disinherited through the evil plots of younger brother Francis. When he becomes an outlaw, his purposes are not only to live by plunder but to revenge himself upon the corrupt society that cast him out. He becomes literally an incendiary. Even before he is finally

---

[16] *The Poems of Thomas Gray, William Collins, and Oliver Goldsmith*, ed. Roger Lonsdale (New York: Norton, 1969) 174.

cast off by his father, Charles exclaims: "What a damn'd inequality is the lot of mankind!—While the gold lies useless in the mouldy coffer of the miser, the leaden hand of poverty checks the daring flight of youth, and chills the fire of enterprise."[17] When he receives a letter from his younger brother telling him that he has been disowned, he cries: "Oh! that I could blow the trumpet of rebellion through all nature, and summon heaven, earth and seas against this savage race" (46). When he is surrounded in the forest by government authorities, he is accused of many crimes. His response boldly acknowledges his crimes:

> It is true I have assassinated a Count of the empire.—It is true I have burnt and plundered the church of the Dominicans.—It is true I have set fire to your bigotted town, and blown up your powder magazine.—But I have done more than all that.—Look here (*holding out his right hand*) look at these four rings of value.—This ruby I drew from the finger of a minister whom I cut down at the chace, at his prince's feet. He had built his fortune on the miseries of his fellow creatures, and his elevation was mark'd by the tears of the fatherless and the widow.— This diamond I took from a treasurer-general, who made a traffic of offices of trust, and sold honors, the rewards of merit, to the highest bidder.— This Cornelian I wear in honour of a priest whom I strangled with my own hand, for his most pious and passionate lamentation over the fall of the Inquisition.— I could expatiate at large, Sir, on the history of these rings if I did not repent already that I have wasted words on a man unworthy to hear me. (96–97)

Finally, when a new recruit arrives to join the band, he says:

> I seek for men who can look death in the face—who can play with danger as with a tamed snake—who prize liberty above life and fame—whose names speak comfort to the oppress'd, who can appall the bold and make the tyrant shudder! (115)

Tytler's adaptation was denied a license for the stage. In Coleridge's public lecture "The Plot Discovered," which protested against the Two Bills, Suspension of the Habeas Corpus Act and the Seditious Meetings Act, he complained that the enactment of the bills would silence John Thelwall's lecturing: "The public amusements at the Theatre are already under ministerial controul. And if the tremendous sublimity of Schiller, if 'the Robbers' can be legally suppressed by that thing yclept a Lord Chamberlain, in point of literary exhibition it would be unreasonable for Mr. Thelwall to complain" (*Lect.* 296–97). The first production of *The Robbers* in England was given as a private performance at Brandenburgh House a few months before the *Anti-Jacobin*'s parody appeared. The performance was noticed in the *Morning Chronicle* somewhat sourly on May 31: "The Democratic

---

[17] *The Robbers*, trans. A. F. Tytler (London, 1792) 26.

points of this heavy play were mostly cut out, but the tendency remains." A text of the performance was published, as its Preface explains, "in order that any persons who may have read the exact Translations of it from the German, may be enabled to judge of the ungenerous and false aspersions of Newspaper Writers . . . that it was played there with all the Jacobinical Speeches that abound in the original." Hannah More got wind of this performance and expressed disapproval in her *Strictures on the Modern System of Female Education* (1799). She was shocked that "persons of quality" appeared in such "distorted and unprincipled compositions which unite the taste of the Goths with the morals of Bagshot."[18]

1798 and 1799 marked the high point of the vogue for German drama, precisely at the moment when the *Anti-Jacobin* struck. In the 1798–99 theater season in London, there were no fewer than eight Kotzebue plays in translation on the stage, including Sheridan's adaptation of *Pizarro*.[19] Although *Pizarro* was a great success, critics looked with increasing fear upon plays that seemed to encourage the worst excesses of Jacobinism: adultery, ridicule of the church, and a heavy dose of political freethinking. There was a rapid decline in the popularity of such plays for both their melodramatic quality and their political implications at the time of the fear of French invasion. When in the Preface to *Lyrical Ballads* Wordsworth referred to "sickly and stupid German Tragedies, and deluges of idle and extravagant stories in verse," his reference is clearly to this vogue and the sensationalism and extravagance that the nation finally came to see in it.[20]

Such criticism as *The Rovers* in the *Anti-Jacobin* was partly responsible for the decline in taste for German drama. *The Rovers* was prefaced by a letter from a Mr. Higgins, the supposed author, who is, in part, Coleridge, who had published in the *Monthly Magazine* some sonnets under the pseudonym of Nehemiah Higginbottom and an early sonnet in praise of Schiller. As is clear from his letter, Mr. Higgins had friends in Germany who were members of the Illuminati:

> I have turned my thoughts more particularly to the German Stage; and have composed, in imitation of the most popular pieces of that country, which have already met with so general reception and admiration in this,—a Play: which,

[18] For the reception of Schiller in England, see L. A. Willoughby, "English Translations and Adaptations of Schiller's 'Robbers,'" *Modern Language Review*, 16 (1921): 304 and Margaret Cooke, "Schiller's 'Robbers in England," *Modern Language Review* 11 (1916): 156–75. Information on its first performance and reviews is contained in Sybil Rosenfeld, *Temples of Thespis: Some Private Theatres and Theatricals in England and Wales* (London: Society of Theatre Research, 1978) 67–68.

[19] *The London Stage: 1660–1800. Part 5, 1776–1800*, ed. Charles Beecher Hogan (Carbondale: Southern Illinois University Press, 1968) 2097–98.

[20] *The Prose Works of William Wordsworth*, ed. W.J.B. Owen and Jane Worthington Smyser (Oxford: Clarendon Press, 1974) 1:128.

if It has a proper run, will, I think, do much to unhinge the present notions of men with regard to the obligations of Civil Society; and to substitute in lieu of a sober contentment, and regular discharge of the duties incident to each man's particular situation, a wild desire of undefinable latitude and extravagance,— an aspiration after shapeless somethings, that can neither be described nor understood,— a contemptuous disgust at all that *is*, and a persuasion that nothing is as it ought to be—to operate, in short, a general discharge of every man (in his own estimation) from every tie which laws divine or human, which local customs, immemorial habits, and multiplied examples impose upon him; and to set them about doing what they like, where they like, when they like, and how they like,— without reference to any law but their own will, or to any consideration of how others may be affected by their conduct. (*PAJ* 162–63)

The optimistic Mr. Higgins then outlines the assumptions on which his play is written:

Destroy the frame of society,—decompose its parts,—and set the elements fighting one against another,—insulated and individual,—every man for himself (stripped of prejudice, of bigotry and of feeling for others) against the remainder of his species;—and there is then some hope of a totally new *order of things*—of a *Radical Reform* in the present corrupt System of the World. (*PAJ* 164)

Implicit in this parody is the notion that following Godwin's recommendations for a rational society will result in what Hobbes described as a life lived in the state of nature in which each individual lives in a state of perpetual war with every other individual. Charles Moor in *The Robbers* calls for violent warfare as a means for liberation and national honor; he cries "Liberty or Death." A review in the *British Critic* (January 1799) of the fourth edition of the *Anti-Jacobin, or Weekly Examiner* praised the paper for

attacking, with unparalleled dexterity and humor, that hateful medley of ignorance, vanity, spleen, and irreligion, which under the impudently assumed mask of philosophy and candour, labours to destroy all the endearing charities of life, to weaken or tear asunder all the bands of society, and to render man a selfish, brutified, and unprincipled savage! As part of this general plan, some of these German plays were undoubtedly designed, and as the fashion of translating them was gaining ground very fast, the check given to their credit by the very just ridicule thrown upon them in the 30 and 31st numbers of the paper, may be considered of great public utility. When these originals pass through such hands as those of Mrs. Inchbald, neither their absurdities nor their poison will be permitted to remain.

Coleridge's knowledge of Schiller's *Robbers* dates from November 1794 when he wrote to Southey that he had been reading "this Convulser of the

Heart": "Did he write his Tragedy amid the yelling of Fiends?—I should not like to [be] able to describe such Characters—I tremble like an Aspen Leaf—Upon my Soul, I write to you because I am frightened—I had better go to Bed. Why have we ever called Milton sublime?" (*CL* 1: 122). Shortly after, Coleridge wrote his sonnet "To the Author of 'The Robbers,'" describing Schiller as a "Bard tremendous in sublimity." In the final lines he describes Schiller as a sublime (and maybe mad) poet "Wandering at eve with finely-frenzied eye / Beneath some vast old tempest-swinging wood." When the poem was published as "Effusion XX" in *Poems* (1796), Coleridge added a note: "Schiller introduces no supernatural beings; yet his human beings agitate and astonish more than all the *goblin* rout—even of Shakespeare." The sonnet alludes specifically to a scene in *The Robbers* in which the elder Count, who had been imprisoned by his younger son so that he would starve to death, is liberated:

> SCHILLER! that hour I would have wish'd to die,
> If thro' the shuddering midnight I had sent
> From the dark dungeon of the Tower time-rent
> That fearful voice, a famish'd Father's cry—
> Lest in some after moment aught more mean
> Might stamp me mortal!
>
> (*CP* 1: 72–3)

The *Anti-Jacobin*, which had its sights on Coleridge for many months, parodied in *The Rovers* the same dungeon scene that Coleridge's sonnet praised. Rogero laments: "Eleven years! it is now eleven years since I was first immured in this living sepulchre—the cruelty of a Minister—the perfidy of a Monk—yes, Matilda! for thy sake—alive amidst the dead—chained—coffined—confined—cut off from the converse of my fellow-men."[21] It may be that the *Anti-Jacobin's* Mr. Higgins parodied it because Coleridge had praised it, but there is no doubt that the private domestic relations, which Coleridge and the *Anti-Jacobin* single out, had political overtones in Burke's *Reflections on the Revolution in France*.[22]

When Coleridge conceived of his mariner, who is, like Coleridge's image of Schiller, a man wandering in a tempest, the context for the poem's reception was established in the public press. He intended a supernatural ballad with touches of sublime terror and thought that it would be acceptable for a liberal journal, the *Monthly Magazine*. When he began work on it, he was also busy recomposing and publishing some early poems and prose for the *Morning Post*. When Humphrey House observed that "The Ancient

---

[21] *PAJ* 175. The authors of *The Rovers* borrow from Macbeth, who is "cabined, cribbed, confined" (III, iv, 24).

[22] Coleridge wrote that "the whole system" of German drama "is a moral and intellectual *Jacobinism* of the most dangerous kind" (*BL* 2: 190).

Mariner" and "Frost at Midnight" were not at all political poems, he insisted that work on "The Ancient Mariner" "released Coleridge from some of the burden of his Miltonic responsibilities and helped to split his ambitious synthesizing aim of bringing all human knowledge together in the frame of one or more huge poems" (85). To House, escaping from the historical context benefited Coleridge's esthetic achievement, but, as Hazlitt, Jeffrey, Southey, and the reviewer for the *Analytical* perceived, "The Ancient Mariner" had precise political overtones. Its German sublimity resided in its gothic terror and in its extravagant, disjointed narrative. It was not merely removed from time as a "drunken dream," as Hazlitt called it in 1818 when he was attacking Coleridge for his metaphysical obscurities, "heedless of past present and to come." To many of its readers it was a Jacobin poem of violated boundaries and errant wandering. It is obviously not a poem of literal political protest in the sense that "The Vision of the Maid of Orleans" is a political poem, but its public significance was unambiguous to many readers. "The Ancient Mariner" is, in the words of the prolific Mr. Higgins, a poem of "a wild desire of undefinable latitude and extravagance."

The Extravagance of "Lyrical Ballads"

Lyrical Ballads of 1798 is a public volume with the extravagant themes traveling, wandering in tempests, homelessness, and vagrancy. The people it depicts are commonly without proper locations or loyalties and thus without law, either outcasts who have transgressed boundaries or convicts who are confined by them. Like the mariner, they have no recognized claim on society. The volume begins with a fantastic tale of a mythical wanderer, the mariner, and continues to tell tales of those who are isolated travelers and solitaries or who are bound in a prison: "The Foster-Mother's Tale," "Lines left upon a Seat in a Yew-tree which stands near the Lake of Esthwaite," "The Female Vagrant," "The Last of the Flock," "The Dungeon," "The Mad Mother," "Old Man Traveling," "The Complaint of a Forsaken Indian Woman," and "The Convict." The volume concludes with "Tintern Abbey," in which tempestuousness is tempered while wandering continues. Vagrancy and wandering are variations of the trope of the quest, and the volume can be read as a record of the disruptions, dislocations, displacements, regressions, and errors in a search for an individual imagination. At the same time, the trope of wandering in a tempest traces disenfranchisement, impropriety, impoverishment, and an extravagance that breaks social bonds. The exclusive attention to one or another reading of the trope, to a single discourse of esthetics or politics, or to a literal focus on explicit themes must suppress the knowledge that one discourse is figurative of another, that one individual poem echoes and recites other poems in the volume. The tropes of wandering and tempestuousness, mediated by the public discourse, allude to both imaginative quest and political disruption. If one reads exclusively for the individual imagination, the opposite of the quest is the error of wandering, of being lost on one's way. If one reads location and the public imagination, the opposite of the vagrant quest is being located, having a home, a place within society. In *Lyrical Ballads* the poor have no location but the road or the prison.

If one discourse figures another, if the literary figures the public, the anonymous innocence of *Lyrical Ballads* presents problems for a historical reading. The temptation to read *Lyrical Ballads* as an escape from the historical and topical, or as a purposeful evasion of social issues, is strong because of the volume's entrancingly simple paratext, which appears to avoid public location by purely literary allusion. In contrast to other volumes of poetry published by the Bristol reformers, Coleridge's *Poems on Various Subjects* (1796) and *Poems* (1797), Lloyd and Lamb's *Blank Verse* (1798), Joseph Cottle's *Poems* (1795), Southey's *Poems* (1797) and *Annual Anthology* (1799, 1800) for examples, *Lyrical Ballads* seems removed from the discursive intentions of the other volumes. *Lyrical Ballads* was published anonymously, unsigned either on the title page or in a preface that would construct an author's public character. Although some poems, "The Nightingale" and "Tintern Abbey" among them, are spoken in the first person, and although some poems seem occasional and local, the speaking voice does not respond directly to the public discourse and is not specifically engaged in speaking to someone or some specific work beyond the volume's threshold. Many poems are narrowly dialogic with two voices or characters speaking within the boundaries of individual poems, but none are addressed to other public characters and none overtly use public genres, like the letter, to forge connections with the public discourse. The volume's characters are most often read as esthetic creations and not public figures. Despite the Advertisement's claim that some of the stories are founded on fact, the significance of the poem's figures appears to reside within the imaginations of both author and sympathetic reader as much as they do in the social consciousness.

Lyrical Ballads avoids the appearance of being public in the way that the other volumes of Bristol poets are literally public by their signatures, addresses, and allusions. The brief, warning Advertisement of 1798 offers it as an esthetic transgression and a stylistic experiment to determine "how far the language of conversation in the middle and lower classes of society is adapted to the purposes of poetic pleasure" (i) and while the revolution in style that this implies, inevitably read through the expanded Prefaces of 1800 and 1802, suggests the selection of diction, the phrase emphasizes the "language of *conversation*." One might inquire what kind of conversation *Lyrical Ballads* contains. Don Bialostoski has argued vigorously for a

Bakhtinian interior dialogic reading poems, but can the word *conversation* be extended outside the volume?[23] The phrase hints that the poems are in conversation with others. Further, while the Advertisement and later Preface sympathize with classes whose speech has been excluded from serious and elegant poetry, the issue of language has generally been deflected to questions of poetic style.

The literary, however, here as elsewhere in the public discourse, cannot be separated from other discourses; its very literariness and paratextual simplicity locate *Lyrical Ballads* in a significant present. While the poems in the volume contain footnotes admitting their debts to Young, Milton, and Collins, the Advertisement situates the volume's origins in early English poetry:

> It will perhaps appear to them, that wishing to avoid the prevalent fault of the day, the author has sometimes descended too low, and that many of his expressions are too familiar, and not of sufficient dignity. It is apprehended, that the more conversant the reader is with our elder writers, and with those in modern times who have been the most successful in painting manners and passions, the fewer complaints of this kind will he have to make. (iii)

The prefatory note on "The Ancient Mariner" as an imitation of the style and spirit of "the elder writers" emphasizes the association that Charles Burney thought at best misguided. To be "conversant" with the elder writers is not only to locate oneself in literary history, but also, as Burney suggests, to re-site oneself within the public discourse that valued Pope, Dryden, and Johnson, the Tory satirists who influenced the wits of the *Anti-Jacobin*, as the models of poetic excellence and as the defenders of established order. To select the style of Chaucer's age, as Burney insisted, was to regress to a barbarous age, but it was also to select a native poetic tradition in opposition to the neoclassical style of Tory apologists. For example, in his preface to his four-volume *Life of Chaucer, The Early English Poet* (1803), William Godwin concluded his list of reasons for studying and valuing Chaucer with a similar opposition:

> It seemed probable also that, if the author were successful in making a popular work, many might by its means be induced to study the language of our ancestors, and the elements and history of our vernacular speech; a study at least as improving as that of the language of Greece and Rome.[24]

Godwin's *Chaucer* is not a political tract, although it does share Horne Tooke's interest as stated, in *The Diversions of Purley* (1798), in deriving an

---

[23] Don Bialostosky, *Wordsworth, Dialogics, and the Practice of Criticism* (Cambridge: Cambridge University Press, 1992).

[24] William Godwin, *Life of Geoffrey Chaucer*, 2d ed. (London 1804) 1: v–vi.

English grammar from a native tradition. In most places it is difficult to assign a political ideology to his discussions of the genres of romance or of the state of society, although he locates Chaucer and his age within an idea of history as a progressive liberation from ignorance, superstition, and tyranny:

> It has been well observed that the English language rose with the rise of Commons; an event which first discovers itself in the reign of John, and which was ascertained and fixed under Edward I. Chaucer perhaps perceived, and was the first to perceive, that from this era the English tongue must necessarily advance in purity, in popularity and dignity, and finally triumph over every competitor within the circuit of its native soil. (1: 334)

Godwin's argument that the English language "rose with the rise of Commons" acknowledges that language and liberty prefigure one another. Poetry and politics advance together, as they did in Dante's Italy, and Godwin defends Chaucer as a court poet favored by patronage, because he avoided praise of military glory associated with the classical poets, in the public discourse of the day a thinly veiled allusion to the Tory Satirists:

> When he compliments his patrons in what may be called his laureat compositions, it is a courtship or a marriage, a personal misfortune or a death, which he selects for his topic; and not achievements in arms, or the robbery and desolation of unoffending thousands. We shall be guilty of great injustice to Chaucer, if we do not recollect, among his most honourable commendations, the feature by which he is thus singularly distinguished from the whole band of the Greek and Roman bards his masters, the trouveurs and troubadours his contemporaries, and the Italian poets who came after him and who constitute the principle glory of the sixteenth century. (2: 221)

The *Anti-Jacobin*, as I have mentioned in Chapter 3, contrasts "the old poet" who is a "warrior, at least in imagination" with the Jacobin poet who would sing the praises only of Buonaparte. Chaucer in this context is not quite a Jacobin poet, but he possesses a Godwinian and Coleridgean distaste for war. Described in this manner, Chaucer would be a Jacobin poet in Burke's eyes, even though Godwin praised at great length the virtues of chivalry as a progressive social force. Leigh Hunt had no doubt. He wrote in the *Examiner* for March 9, 1817 that Chaucer was a "Reformer in his day," and "set his face both against priestly and kingly usurpation." The allusions to "the elder poets," which Burney read as allusions to Chaucer, have their contemporary political significance in their obvious opposition to the rhetoric of neoclassical literature and Tory satire. As late as October 1821, *Blackwood's* remained a bit testy about Godwin's *Chaucer*. In an article titled "Chaucer and Don Juan," it complained:

The restless gloom of the philosophical idealist overcasts the page, which might have been the light and elegant memorial of the poet. And instead of dissertation and inquiry concerning these most frightful of all chapter-heads—the *feudal system* and *the middle ages*—we might have been presented with a narrative suitable to the gay and mercurial temper of its subject.

Godwin, it seems, was a cultural critic.

The allusive and mediated tropes of wandering and tempest echo the private within the public at the same time that they describe the figurative links between the discourses of esthetics and politics. The composition of the volume in the spring of 1798 indicates that the tropes of wandering and vagrancy were an organizing principle. The poem that Wordsworth referred to as "Salisbury Plain" was transformed into "The Female Vagrant." "Salisbury Plain" was completed in the spring of 1794,[25] but the version printed as "The Female Vagrant" contains nine stanzas at the end, not in the first version of "Salisbury Plain," that describe the woman's vagrancy in England after her ship returns. They detail her hunger, madness, rest in the hospital, and a brief stay with gypsies. In "Salisbury Plain," although the woman suffers great losses, she is not literally a vagrant as she is when she returns "homeless near a thousand homes" (79). It is difficult to determine when these stanzas were added. The manuscript evidence is inconclusive, but there is some probability that revisions were made shortly before *Lyrical Ballads* was completed, with the idea of re-siting the poem in the volume. They are stylistically more mature. Wordsworth handles the verse form with less of the tortured syntax and awkward inversions of the earlier drafts. In the spring of 1798, Coleridge and Wordsworth proposed several different volumes to Cottle. When they referred to the poem, it was as "Salisbury plain," not "The Female Vagrant," as though it were the poem of 1794. In March 1798 Coleridge asked Cottle whether he would publish "Wordsworth's Salisbury Plain & Tale of a Woman," probably some form of "The Ruined Cottage" (*CL* 1: 400). Later, on May 9, Wordsworth wrote to Cottle, "I say nothing of the Salisbury Plain, 'till I see you, I am determined to finish it, and equally so that You shall publish,"[26] which may indicate that he was contemplating revisions not completed at that date. Still later, on May 28, Coleridge wrote to Cottle that "W. would not object to the publishing of Peter Bell *or* the Salisbury Plain, singly" (*CL* 1: 411). The continued reference to the poem as "Salisbury Plain" and Wordsworth's promise to finish it may indicate that it had not yet been transformed into

[25] Gill, Stephen, *The Salisbury Plain Poems of William Wordsworth, The Cornell Wordsworth* (Ithaca, Cornell University Press, 1975) 6–7.

[26] *The Letters of William and Dorothy Wordsworth. The Early Years, 1787–1085*, ed. Ernest de Selincourt and Chester Shaver, 2d ed. (Oxford: Clarendon Press, 1967) 218.

"The Female Vagrant." If in March Wordsworth was thinking of "The Female Vagrant" in its early stages as "Tale of a Woman," it had not yet become "The Female Vagrant." The evidence is not conclusive that Wordsworth added the stanzas on vagrancy and changed the title to "The Female Vagrant" late in the spring of 1798 with the purposes of *Lyrical Ballads* in mind, but if he did revise it then, they may have shaped the volume to explore the very social issues of vagrancy and homelessness that he is accused of ignoring.

Elsewhere I have argued that the primary source of "The Ancient Mariner" may be found in Wordsworth's tentative revisions of "Salisbury Plain," specifically in three stanzas drafted in 1795 at Racedown describing the sailor's exasperated commission of a crime, the fear and guilt that plagues him, and the brief restoration of a "second spring," which is followed by a return of terror:[27]

> And little grieved he for the sleety shower
> Cold wind and hunger he had long withstood
> Long hunted down by mans confederate power
> Since phrenzy-driven he dipped his hand in blood
> Yet till that hour he had been mild and good
> And when the miserable deed was done
> Such pangs were his as to relenting mood
> Might melt the hardest since   he has run
> For years from place to place nor known one chearful sun
>
> Yet oft as Fear her withering grasp forbears
> Such tendency to pleasures loved before
> Does Nature   common cares
> Might to his breast a second spring restore
> The least complaints of wretchedness explore
> His heartstrings trembled with responsive tone
> Trembling the best of human hearts not more
> From each excess of pain his days have known
> Well has he learned to make all others ills his own
>
> Yet though to softest sympathy inclined
> Most trivial cause will rouse the keenest pang
> Of terror and oerwhelm   his mind
> For then with scarce distinguishable clang
> In the cold wind a sound of irons rang
> He looked and saw on a bare gibbet nigh
> In moving chains a human body hang

---

[27] Paul Magnuson, *Coleridge and Wordsworth: A Lyrical Dialogue* (Princeton: Princeton University Press, 1988) 37–40, 73–83.

A hovering raven oft did round it fly
A grave there was beneath which he could not descry[28]

The parallels between the two poems are numerous, but one of the most interesting parallels for the purposes of reading literature in the public discourse is the presence of a tempest in both. In "The Female Vagrant" the woman leaves with her family for the American Wars and a storm drives them to war:

> But from delay the summer calms were past.
> On as we drove, the equinoctial deep
> Ran mountains-high before the howling blast.
> We gazed with terror on the gloomy sleep
> Of them that perished in the whirlwind's sweep,
> Untaught that soon such anguish must ensue,
> Our hopes such harvest of affliction reap,
> That we the mercy of the waves should rue.
> We reached the western world, a poor, devoted crew.

(75)

The word *devoted*, according to the *OED*, means both "dedicated" and in an archaic sense "doomed."

In both "The Ancient Mariner" and "Salisbury Plain" a tempest drives the crew to death and desolation and serves as the transition between the security of an ordered society and the extravagance of wandering. The Latin root of *tempest*, a word used in the eighteenth century specifically for social unrest, is *tempus*, a marked and limited time or space, the origin of *temple*, *tense*, *temporality*, *temper*, and *temperate*. and most importantly, *tempest*. The Bastille, after all, was stormed, yet in *Lyrical Ballads*, the tempests are not the irrational actions of an intemperate mob, as common representations would have it. Ronald Paulson writes that "the imagery of the phenomenon of the Revolution itself merged the powerful natural force (Robespierre's *tempête révolutionnaire*, Desmoulins's *torrent révolutionnaire*) with the indistinguishable, vague indeterminate shape of the sovereign people."[29] In *Lyrical Ballads*, however, tempests are the inevitable result of tyrannical acts. Those caught in the tempests are persecuted and pursued by them. The mariner leaves his own country, when his shifting perspective on the church leads him to see the church, the temple, fall into the sea, but his leaving becomes a fall from the temple into a tempest, which drives him to cross the line, the boundary, and transforms him into a wanderer both in and out of

---

[28] Gill, *The Salisbury Plain* (above, n. 25) 115–16. I have simplified Gill's transcription. Note that the gaps are authentic to the original text.
[29] *Representations of Revolution (1789–90)* (New Haven: Yale University Press, 1983) 21.

temporality and historical time. He is in history because he is driven by the tyrannical storm; he is extravagant; and he crosses the boundaries of legitimate order. The female vagrant suffers a similar fate. She loses her home, her legitimate place in society, and falls into an endless vagrancy. The last that her father sees of her home as he leaves with his daughter is "the steeple tower, / That on his marriage-day sweet music made" (72). The narrator of "The Thorn," an old sea captain, first sees Martha Ray when he is driven to seek shelter from a storm.

With the innumerable filiations between "The Ancient Mariner" and "The Female Vagrant," one can read *Lyrical Ballads* as a volume whose themes of wandering and vagrancy intricately involve the discourses of both history and individual imagination, such that distinctions between the public and the private become obscured. The trope of the Romantic imaginative quest finds its opposite in errant wandering, which sometimes halts the quest but also disperses it. The quest continues in immeasurable repetition, both in the sense that it is unpredictable and that it cannot be bound. The failure of the quest is not marked by regression, because the boundaries once crossed cannot be redrawn to mark the *tempus* of an origin; the failure is traced in aimlessness. The thirteen-book *Prelude* is the *narratio* of the mental traveler who transits the boundaries of a childhood *tempus*, who is lost both in innumerable tempests of "redundant energy" that vex "its own creation" and in tempests of the French Revolution, who recalls spots of time as reflections of an original *tempus*, and who is tempered. "The Ancient Mariner," "The Female Vagrant," and other poems in the volume can and have been read by themselves as quest narratives, but they are also legendary *narratio*, the rhetoric of the public discourse as read by contemporaries. A full reading of the volume should elaborate the poems' public geography, both as they are located in an existing discourse and as they are received by reviewers, a discourse that maps its location between poles of the boundaries of social order, with dungeons that parody an original *tempus*, on the one hand, and extravagance on the other. Most early reviews of *Lyrical Ballads* contrast order and disorder, the bound and the unbound, the temperate and the tempest.

In their locations as *narratio*, the tempests in "The Ancient Mariner" and "The Female Vagrant" are both the elements of the biography of a failed quest narrative and of a historical present that forges its own past. Wandering in a "tempest-swinging wood," as Coleridge described Schiller, is not only an allusion to Dante and Spencer's Wood of Errour, but a transformation of wandering from a moral and spiritual state to a state of both revolutionary energy and disenfranchisement and desolation. The trope of tempest is further complicated because in its historical present, in marked time, and in the public discourse, the tempest is construed as boundless extravagance. The storms throughout *Lyrical Ballads* efface its literary boundaries. To fall is to fall into temporality, into history, and quest narrative as *narratio* is public romance in its historical location. Just as the Romantic lyric poem has its origins in the public genre of the letter, so romance in its locations and dislocations of *tempus* and tempest has its public and historical place, whatever its improbable plot and figuration may suggest to literalist readers. By its nature, public romance is deeply rooted in its time and its geography.

The narrative form within *Lyrical Ballads* is public romance. The mariner and the female vagrant begin their narratives, not with childhood and not to find an origin for their individuality, but within a defined physical space of social order. The issue in both is not the influences of childhood on intellectual and imaginative growth, but the change from a defined social geography, dominated in both poems by a church steeple, an emblem of marriage, the Burkean foundation of local and national unity. The home of the female vagrant is the cottage with its garden, and its security rests on her father's "little range of water" (72). The legitimate private security of landed possessions, however, rests in the power of established property to expel others. To be in society is to be located within a geographical *tempus*. To be cast out so that the wealthy can expand their own location is to be banished into a tempest, to fall into temporality. Established order describes its place through banishing others. Order defines itself by disorderly acts of exclusion, and the illusion of privacy, of a stable *tempus*, is dispelled by expulsion. By being cast out, the private becomes the public, since it was always public in the first place, in the first *tempus*.

In "The Female Vagrant" the ocean storm is only a prelude to the tempest of war:

> Oh! dreadful price of being to resign
> All that is dear *in* being! better far
> In Want's most lonely cave till death to pine,
> Unseen, unheard, unwatched by any star;
> Or in the streets and walks where proud men are,
> Better our dying bodies to obtrude,
> Than dog-like, wading at the heels of war,
> Protract a curst existence, with the brood
> That lap (their very nourishment!) their brother's blood.
>
> The pains and plagues that on our heads came down,
> Disease and famine, agony and fear,
> In wood or wilderness, in camp or town,
> It would thy brain unsettle even to hear.
> All perished—all, in one remorseless year,
> Husband and children! one by one, by sword
> And ravenous plague, all perished: every tear

Dried up, despairing, desolate, on board
A British ship I waked, as from a trance restored.

.   .   .   .

Yet does that burst of woe congeal my frame,
When the dark streets appeared to heave and gape,
While like a sea the storming army came,
And Fire from Hell reared his gigantic shape,
And Murder, by the gastly gleam, and Rape
Seized their joint prey, the mother and the child!
But from these crazing thoughts my brain, escape!
—For weeks the balmy air breathed soft and mild,
And on the gliding vessel Heaven and Ocean smiled.

(76–78)

Being cast out, the vagrant's husband can only serve the violent purposes of those who cast him out. He becomes a victim to the wars of the American Revolution. Being a private soldier in the British army serving those in the public sphere is here a poignant contradiction.

The private catastrophe was read by the public voice of reviewers as a public issue. Charles Burney in the *Monthly Review* (June 1799) acknowledged that "The Female Vagrant" was

an agonizing tale of individual wretchedness; highly coloured, though, alas! but too probable. Yet, as it seems to stamp a general stigma on all military transactions, which were never more important in free countries than at the present period, it will perhaps be asked whether the hardships described never happen during revolution, or in a nation subdued? The sufferings of individuals during war are dreadful: but is it not better to try to prevent them from becoming general, or to render them transient by heroic and patriotic efforts, then to fly them forever?

Burney hopes that suffering in tempests is merely transient, merely temporary. The anonymous reviewer in the *British Critic* (Oct. 1799) legitimates the disordered tempest :

"The Female Vagrant" is a composition of exquisite beauty, nor is the combination of events, related in it, out of the compass of possibility; yet we perceive, with regret, the drift of the author in composing it; which is to show the worst side of civilized society, and thus to form a satire against it. But let fanciful men rail as they will at the evils which no care can always prevent, they can have no dream more wild than the supposition, that any human wisdom can possibly exclude all evils from a state which divine Providence has decreed, for reasons the most wise, to be a state of suffering and of trial. The sufferers may be changed, by infinite revolutions, but sufferers there will be, till Heaven shall interfere to change the nature of our tenure on earth.

The *British Critic*'s voice of legitimacy reads the unruly tempest as orderly "suffering and trial," a view that locates justice in an age of chivalry and bases its justice upon "divine Providence." Legitimacy's "tenure on earth," its geographical grip, its binding compass, thus claims a divine sanction for evil at the same time that it claims permanence for both evil and its own tenure; the view of victims caught in the tempests is that order is merely temporary and that human existence is marked by a homeless transience.

Burney's transience of evil and the *British Critic*'s permanent tenure contrast sharply with the conclusions of the narratives in *Lyrical Ballads*. Traditional quest romance ends with either a vision of a heavenly city or the assurance of a self-recognition or personal salvation, but "The Ancient Mariner" and "The Female Vagrant" conclude with stronger statements of the permanence of wandering and transience. The mariner continues, a wanderer telling his tale that silences the hermit's hymns, usurps the hermit's spiritual role, and prevents the wedding guest from attending the wedding, a Burkean sacrament of national and constitutional importance. The mariner's public message that one must love *all* creatures resonates with stormy German ideology and Jacobinism in 1798. The mariner has transgressed boundaries, traveled on an extravagant journey, returned briefly to interrupt a wedding with his tale, only to continue his wandering repeating it. While his tale is one of private experience, it delivers a message so public that it stuns listeners. The wedding guest listens and becomes wiser, but does not respond. To the conservative readers of *Lyrical Ballads*, the mariner is not as much enlightened as illuminated, and they, like the wedding guest, know that the message is public and are stunned by it.

The Female Vagrant ends her story with the prospect of endless wandering:

> Three years a wanderer, often have I view'd,
> In tears, the sun towards that country tend
> Where my poor heart lost all its fortitude:
> And now across this moor my steps I bend—
> Oh! tell me whither——for no earthly friend
> Have I.——She ceased, and weeping turned away,
> As if because her tale was at an end
> She wept;—because she had no more to say
> Of that perpetual weight which on her spirit lay.

(84)

This conclusion of "The Female Vagrant" revises grimmer lines that end the woman's tale in "Salisbury Plain": "no earthly friend / Have I, no house in prospect but the tomb" (34). "The Female Vagrant," less explicitly depressing, conveys a similar burden. The woman has no home and will have no home and consequently has no place in society. What is worse, she has no audience. She has fallen into tempests and the result is a fall into unbounded wandering and into a temporality that will end only in death. At the same time, she falls into her own story, her own *narratio*, her own tense. She ends with the end of her story because there is no responsive sympathy, no public discursive presence for her. The final irony of this public romance is that it begins in her youth with her private possessions, which are a mere illusion in light of the public tenure of land that supports such privacy, and that it ends with her being an outcast of that public tenure, living on the public road, but in a such a privacy that she has only her temporal location and voice for definition.

"The Female Vagrant" concludes with silence "because she had no more to say / Of that perpetual weight which on her spirit lay." The transient evil of war that Burney had noted as the prudent conduct of national policy is to the woman a permanent wound. "Tintern Abbey" concludes *Lyrical Ballads* (1798) with a claim that "the heavy and the weary weight / Of all this unintelligible world / Is lighten'd" (203). There is a tempering by nature and by the "still, sad music of humanity," which chastens and subdues. Tempering restrains excess. Within "Tintern Abbey" the tempering matures a youthful exuberance into sober imagination, but within the entire volume "the music of humanity" alludes to the burdens borne by those condemned to wander. If "the music of humanity" is read exclusively within the boundaries of "Tintern Abbey," its reference is the harmonious joy within the speaker's human heart. Its sadness is for a personal loss for which the poet finds "abundant recompense." Wordsworth himself, perhaps, is responsible for encouraging such a reading by removing "Tintern Abbey," from its context in *Lyrical Ballads* and placing it, in 1815, in the category "Poems of the Imagination." If, however, one restores it to its earlier context, it alludes to the rest of *Lyrical Ballads*. The "still, sad music of humanity" echoes the final lines of "The Female Vagrant" with a poignancy in the word *still* that remembers her final silence.[30] If one pauses over the poem that immediately precedes "Tintern Abbey" in 1798, "The Convict," a poem in Jacobin dactylics that contrasts the torment of the jailed convict with the monarch who is conducted to his chamber "from the dark synod, or the blood-recking field," one finds even a note of bitterness in the allusion to humanity. The speaker of "Tintern Abbey" not only sees, feels, and remembers, he also hears—an oddly intrusive note in a poem commonly read as the utterance of an isolated consciousness. He hears the rest of *Lyrical Ballads*. Since his words allude to the female vagrant's story, he becomes her auditor. His "dizzy raptures" have matured to a more temperate joy by listening, by responding to her as well as to his sister, and he, like the wedding guest, is a "wiser" man. His eye is "made quiet" by listening, by being at-

---

[30] Kenneth R. Johnston provides a similar and fuller reading of "Tintern Abbey" in "The Politics of 'Tintern Abbey,' " *The Wordsworth Circle* 14 (1983): 6–14.

tentive to a public discourse of dissent represented in *Lyrical Ballads* by "The Ancient Mariner" and "The Female Vagrant." As a contribution to the public discourse, the volume anticipates its reviewers and offers its own response to the tales that contrast with those of Burney and the *British Critic*.

Lyrical Ballads publicizes the private anguish of the people it depicts. In some few instances, "The Female Vagrant" and "The Convict," the protest of social conditions, institutions, and classes is direct and unambiguous. Other poems repeat their major tropes, those of extravagance, wandering, tempestuousness, the crossing of boundaries, of violence and violation, yet the public significance of these figures, which crosses the boundaries between the esthetic and the political, cannot be fully read even in the volume itself. They are repeated from poem to poem, and for any single poem the rest of the volume stands as a complex paratext, and the volume echoes the public discourse. Without that allusive ground, the volume remains primarily a document in a purely literary history. With that ground, one can read it more closely within its literary period and thus with a more complex awareness of the resonances of its awareness. It is neither the pure expression of an individual imagination nor a proud assertion of autonomy, but rather an anonymous and collaborative legendary *narratio* in a public address, mediated by the public discourse that it implicitly addresses.

Chapter Five

THE DEDICATION OF *DON JUAN*

PIERRE BOURDIEU has astutely commented that "the fundamental stake in literary struggles is the monopoly of literary legitimacy, i.e., *inter alia*, the monopoly of the power to say with authority who are authorized to call themselves writers; or, to put it another way, it is the monopoly of the power to consecrate producers or products." He adds that "cultural production distinguishes itself from the production of the most common objects in that it must produce not only the object in its materiality, but also the value of this object, that is, the recognition of artistic legitimacy."[1] In this and the following chapter, I map some of the discourse of literary legitimacy explicit and implicit in its discursive practices. Byron's Dedication to *Don Juan* and canto I are more than the witty response to Southey's personal insults. The Dedication and canto I are, in the heavily mediated discourse of the day, a parody of Southey's laureate verse, similar to the *Anti-Jacobin*'s parodies in the 1790s, but they also constitute Byron's claim for poetic legitimacy. What has often been described as Byron's desire for poetic fame can be re-defined as his desire for a place, a location in the public realm. The Dedication implies a map and a geography of spatial and national dimensions. Byron defines his location by being the geographer of the literary world. In the age, however, the literary world is not a separate realm, not a hierarchy separate from the political world, and thus the struggle for literary legitimacy is also a struggle for political and social priority.

The Dedication and canto I can be read historically by reading the Dedication as paratext. The Dedication was not published with the first two cantos in 1819 but was known to a significant audience. The Dedication is a curious instance of an unpublished, and thus in one sense private work, which nevertheless was known to a significant circle of Byron's intimates— the public to whom Byron appealed with his "claim to praise."[2] While the Dedication and canto I as sent to Murray constitute a parody of Southey's laureate poetry, the absence of the Dedication blunts that attack and leaves canto I as a general criticism of moral self-righteousness. The focus on Southey was known to Byron's intimate audience at Murray's, who saw the Dedication in manuscript or who heard of it through word of mouth. That

---

[1] Pierre Bourdieu, *The Field of Cultural Production*, ed. Randal Johnson (New York: Columbia University Press, 1993) 42, 164.

[2] *Don Juan* 1: 1774 in *BP* vol. 5. Subsequent notes in this chapter are to canto and line.

group, which constituted the poem's first public, was the immediate audience for whom Byron wrote and whose language Byron used. The paratextual Dedication defines canto I as a poem that can be located through its audience and its style, a style that originated in the circle of its first reception.

In 1819 the Dedication was public not only because it was known, although unpublished, but also because it drew heavily from the satires on Southey that began in 1813, when Southey was appointed poet laureate. Byron satirized Southey because Southey circulated rumors about a "League of Incest" in 1816 in Switzerland, but there is nothing personal in the Dedication.[3] It offers little opportunity for the most assiduous biographical reader for "reaping allusions private and inglorious" (13: 196). His satire on the Lake poets and Castlereagh was public because it echoed the satires on them in many newspapers and reviews. The style of the Dedication originates in the public media, and the public standing of both Byron and Southey is at stake. The name Byron, or Lord Byron, which did not appear on the title page of the first quarto edition, was attached to the poem by most reviewers and readers, who knew, by one means or another, that he was the author. If one reads *Don Juan* in the context of the public press, "Byron" is a heavily mediated figure. *Don Juan* is perhaps the most public poem of its age, yet without a close historical reading of its absent Dedication, its public nature remains obscure.

As many readers of *Don Juan* have noted, Byron's style is the familiar conversational banter of Regency England, the quizzing social chatter that parodies the epic vanity of the Lake poets and the empty-headed oratory of Castlereagh. Byron remarked, "I rattle on exactly as I'd talk / With any body in a ride or walk" (15: 151–52). Byron's pedestrian muse is not only the muse of instruction but also the muse of parody,[4] and his conscious use of many different languages invites a Bakhtinian analysis of its historical, contextual, and dialogic sources.[5] The Dedication to *Don Juan* draws from the political satires of the periodical press, nursery rhymes, foreign languages, the

[3] *BLJ* 6: 76. Coleridge was included in the Dedication because Byron thought he had circulated Southey's gossip (*BLJ* 6: 83).

[4] For comments on Byron's conversational style, see Elizabeth French Boyd, *Byron's* Don Juan: *A Critical Study* (New York: Humanities Press, 1945, 1958) 46–47; M. K. Joseph, *Byron the Poet* (London: Victor Gollancz, 1964) 188–91; Jerome J. McGann, Don Juan *in Context* (Chicago: University of Chicago Press, 1976) 79; and Peter J. Manning, "*Don Juan* and Byron's Imperceptiveness to the English Word," *SIR* 18 (1979): 207–33. For Byron's invocation of the pedestrian muse, see McGann (69–70) and George M. Ridenour, *The Style of* Don Juan (New Haven: Yale University Press, 1960) 9–10.

[5] For a discussion of the dialogic characteristics in the language of literature, see chapter 5 in Mikhail Bakhtin, *Problems of Dostoevsky's Poetics*, trans. Caryl Emerson (Minneapolis: University of Minnesota Press, 1984) and "Discourse in the Novel" in *The Dialogic Imagination*, trans. Caryl Emerson and Michael Holquist (Austin: University of Texas Press, 1981).

sexual double entendres of current slang, parliamentary debates in England
and Ireland, the jargon of economics and the law, and literary sources:
Shakespeare, Milton, Pope, and even Wordsworth. The mixture of languages with their conflicting ideologies suggests that Byron's intention is to
parody the authority of Southey's position as poet laureate, to ridicule the
unprecedented pride that he took in the office, and to introduce Don Juan
as the natural man, the comic rebel against a canting authority.

A close investigation of the actual sources of Byron's Dedication, however, tells a more complex story. He does not draw his parody directly from
this great variety of sources, and the ideological implications are different
than a Bakhtinian analysis would suggest. The style of *Don Juan* originates
in the social and political banter of Regency society. The words of the Dedication can be traced to a small class of articulate voices writing in the public press and chatting at the tables in the West End, the voices that in the
opinions of Burke and Godwin constitute a public sphere, not to a variety
of subcultures excluded from Regency society. The languages of these subcultures are mediated by the public press and those at the pinnacle of political power. *Don Juan* points to a serious flaw in the common application
of Bakhtin's theories. The language of poetry is rarely a direct and un-
mediated reflection of the class or group where it originates, and its cultural
nuances come as much from its mediation as from its class origin. Bakhtinian parody is destructive of all established authority, and Byron's purpose is
to ridicule Southey, but paradoxically enough, Byron's parody is the language of political and social authority, the satire of the Tory *Anti-Jacobin, or
Weekly Examiner* (1797–8), edited in part by Pitt, of the Whig *Edinburgh Review*, and Leigh Hunt's more radical *Examiner*. Although parody was also
the rhetoric of such radicals as Thelwall, Spence, Eaton, Hone and others,
Byron's sources reflect the limited circle of his immediate audience at
Murray's.

The style of the Dedication, which worries about who is "in and out of
place," argues that Byron, by speaking the language of Regency wit, possesses its authority and thus occupies his natural place simply because he
speaks it, although exiled to Italy. Southey, who occupies an eminent place,
is out of place, or misplaced, because he cannot observe its decorum. He
utters only fulsome praise or ranting condemnations and thus thinks of
himself as "representative of all the race," the race of Britons, the race of
poets, and the race of poets-laureate. In what sense could Southey be representative either in poetry or politics? Whom does he represent politically
or poetically? Whom does he speak for? Where is he and who is he? Byron's
location is defined by a combination of aristocratic birth, university education, Whig politics, and cosmopolitan wit, but it is constituted by no one
of these alone. A better word than *class* to describe Byron's position is his
own word *place*, by which he means "social rank," "government office," "pa-

tronage," and "rank among poets." To have a place, a location, is to have a public, which is not the same thing as having a political party. The subject of the Dedication and canto I of *Don Juan* is place and literary legitimacy, and Byron intends to be its geographer as well as its ironic Geo-grapher. Public poets, like public poems, are defined by their legitimate locations. By choosing the style of *Don Juan*, Byron locates himself in English society, proves that his place is proper, and enters his "claim to praise," a claim to be the first poet of the age:

> This narrative is not meant for narration,
> But a mere airy and fantastic basis,
> To build up common things with common places.
>
> (14: 54–56)

There is, in fact, very little in the Dedication that is original with Byron. Well before he wrote it, his satire existed in the public discourse, in the parodies and caustic reviews of the periodical press, parliamentary debates, and the witty gossip of his day. Byron borrows phrase after phrase directly from these sources. These are not the sources in canonical literature often cited to gloss his satire, although political satire of the period is heavily influenced by Dryden, Swift, and Pope as least as early as the *Anti-Jacobin* in 1797. Their influence is mediated by contemporary political debates. *Don Juan* may draw on Augustan satire, but the Dedication is also topical Regency parody. While the language of the press, Parliament, and the pamphlet wars is not literary in the late-twentieth-century sense, it is highly rhetorical. Paratext functions in *Don Juan*, as it does elsewhere in the poetry of the period, to focus a reading of the text and to provide an allusive frame that connects it with the public discourse. The paratextual Dedication marks the crossroads between the poem's literary qualities and the public.

Many words and phrases in the Dedication are taken from these public sources. The identification of the sources is not intended to debunk Byron by questioning his originality. Rather, it illustrates the particular velocity of his mind. His sources describe a location in English society and the public debates which was established before he wrote. Byron was accused many times of plagiarism, principally by the Tory *Literary Gazette*, which complained in its review of cantos IX–XI that "these cantos set out with a miserable tirade against the Duke of Wellington and Waterloo; and if the author is guilty of his usual crime of plagiarism in them, it is in borrowing the scurrilous trash of the lowest factious newspapers" (Sept. 6, 1823), which refers to Cobbett's *Political Register* and Hunt's *Examiner*, both of which Southey attacked in the *Quarterly Review* in 1816 and 1817. *Blackwood's* was more specific when it complained in a review of cantos VI–VIII in July 1823 that Byron descended "to the composition of heartless, heavy, dull, anti-British garbage, to be printed by the Cockneys, and puffed in the Examiner." The *Examiner* provided Byron with much of his satire, which Byron admitted at the end of canto I, when he claimed that his story was true: "If any person doubt it, I appeal / To history, tradition, and to facts, / To newspapers, whose truth all know and feel" (1: 1617–19). The charge of plagiarism is both splenetic and tendentious, but it catches one truth of the style of the Dedication; it is highly allusive. *Don Juan* may be outrageously individual when placed in literary history or the history of satire, but in the context of the public discourse, it is representative. Byron speaks the language of others because he wishes to locate himself among them and prove that he, and not Southey, Wordsworth, or Coleridge, is the representative English poet who has the authority to define poetry for the age. The strange paradox is that to be the first poet of his age, he must be both representative and original.

The proof of Byron's strategy is in the reading of his public sources. A located historical reading provides the best way to provide a close reading of his poetry. The resonances of his tone can best be understood in their origin. His words are unique at the time of their utterance, and such a reading reveals not only Byron's sources, but their significance to his first readers. Such a reading listens to the language of the public debates as evidence of the historical moment but slights actual historical events. The Dedication is more directly grounded in the words of Leigh Hunt than it is in the performances of Orator Hunt. Reading the Dedication in the public discourse traces Byron's lines to published sources, whether they be original composition in the press or reports of public oratory, such as the parliamentary debates. The public significance of *Don Juan* rests in the public debates that precede it, not in the reviews that it provokes. While reviews of other authors constitute a major portion of the public context, in the case of *Don Juan*, they offer little more than a dreary condemnation of its immorality and skepticism and obscure, rather than reveal, its significance. The reviews of Southey's laureate verse and his *Wat Tyler* contribute more to the Dedication, particularly since in some instances Byron may have known Southey's writing only through those reviews. Wherever possible such a reading traces the private circulation of works.

Whatever is public is published or uttered in a public place, but there is always the complication of the private circulation of a work either by manuscript or by word of mouth. Knowledge of the Dedication and canto I was relatively widespread before the publication of the first two cantos. In June 1819 *Blackwood's* Mr. Odoherty expressed impatience at the delay in publication of *Don Juan*: "If Lord Byron does not publish Don Juan speedily, I will."[6] Byron's primary audience can be defined by tracing private circulation and by identifying the numerous sources of the Dedication. Those

---

[6] The comment is in a letter prefacing a parody of "Christabel." See Frederick L. Beaty, *Byron the Satirist* (Dekalb: Northern Illinois University Press, 1985) 110.

traces circumscribe a society that Byron knew well, a society that extends from Leigh Hunt's journalism on one edge of the political and social spectrum to the Tory writers for the *Quarterly* who gathered at Murray's at the other, a spectrum that defines literary and political London. As a writer for the *Quarterly*, Southey is included in that audience and society but only as the person to whom Byron speaks in the Dedication. Southey is in place because his presence is implicitly acknowledged in the argument that he is out of place. Although the Dedication was suppressed and not published with the first two cantos, Southey knew of its existence. Murray published the first two cantos on July 15, 1819. Having seen a review in a provincial newspaper, Southey wrote to C. H. Townshend on July 20: "I do not yet know whether the printed poem is introduced by a dedication to me, in a most hostile strain, which came over with it, or whether the person who has done Lord Byron the irreparable injury of sending into the world what his own publisher and his friends endeavoured, for his sake, to keep out of it, has suppressed it."[7] Writing to Grosvenor C. Bedford on July 31, Southey noted that "Wynn has told me of Lord Byron's dedication to me." Charles Watkin Williams Wynn was a school friend of Southey, an M.P., and a relative of Lord Grenville. Southey added a postscript: "I hear that 'Don Juan' is published without the dedication. I should like to know who has suppressed it, and why it has been suppressed."[8]

It is not certain when Southey heard of the Dedication. Byron sent off the manuscript of the Dedication and canto I on November 11, 1818. His friends at Murray's, Hobhouse, Davies, Kinnaird, and Frere deliberated over it, until Hobhouse wrote a long letter to Byron on January 5 recommending that it not be published. In the following months it was read by Canning, Rogers, and Moore, among others. On January 19 Byron wrote to Hobhouse agreeing to omit the stanzas on Robert Stewart, Viscount Castlereagh, and the "dry Bob" double entendre in the third stanza. In early May Byron agreed to omit the entire Dedication. There is no evidence that Southey had actually seen a copy of the Dedication, but he did know some details about its history. He wrote to the Reverend Herbert Hill on August 13 that "'Don Juan' came over with a dedication to me, in which Lord Castlereagh and I (being hand and glove intimates!) were coupled together for abuse as 'the two Roberts.' A fear of persecution from the *one* Robert is supposed to be the reason why it has been suppressed."[9] Byron finally suppressed the entire Dedication because the poem was to be published anony-

---

[7] *The Life and Correspondence of Robert Southey*, ed. Rev. Charles Cuthbert Southey (New York, 1850) 4: 352–53. The essential documents of the conflict between Byron and Southey are printed in *The Works of Lord Byron: Letters and Journals*, ed. R. E. Prothero (London, 1904) 6: 377–99.

[8] *Selections from the Letters of Robert Southey*, ed. John Wood Warter (London, 1856) 3: 137–38.

[9] Ibid., 3: 142.

mously. He agreed to suppress the stanzas on Castlereagh because, as Hobhouse had warned him, he was not in England "to fight him":[10] "I would not take advantage of the Alps and the Ocean to assail him when he could not revenge himself" (*BLJ* 6: 104). After all, Castlereagh had fought a duel with Canning in 1809. Byron twice explained his reasons for suppressing the Castlereagh stanzas, both times in private correspondence to Murray. Southey knew both the reason for suppression of the Castlereagh stanzas and the possible suppression of the entire Dedication but did not know at the time of publication in July whether it had been suppressed or not.[11]

Southey mentions that his information came through Wynn, who may have heard of it from his friends or directly from Hobhouse, whom he had known since 1810.[12] Knowledge of the Dedication may have passed through others before it reached Wynn. Southey's knowledge of the reasons for the suppression is more difficult to trace. Since Southey wrote for Murray's Tory *Quarterly Review*, he may have heard it directly from him. There is a probability that Byron's letters to Murray were read by Byron's friends, so that any one of them could have informed Southey about the Castlereagh stanzas. The evidence as to when Southey heard of the Dedication is more uncertain. His belief that *Don Juan* was dedicated to "the two Roberts" suggests that he may have heard of it before the cancellation of the Castlereagh stanzas in late January. If Southey did hear of it before then, the news did indeed travel fast. On the other hand, his uncertainty about the cancellation of the entire Dedication indicates that he had not heard of the final decision, which was made early in May. He may have had more than one informant and may have heard of the fate of the Dedication on several occasions.

In these circumstances, there is very little in Byron's correspondence with Murray and the deliberations over the publication of *Don Juan* that is completely private or confidential. Byron's transmitting manuscripts or letters was a form of private publication to Murray's literary circle, which included people in various political camps. In 1820 Croker wrote to Murray about the rumor that Byron would return to England to lead the radicals if they gained strength: "We were twelve at dinner, all (except myself) people of note, and yet (except Walter Scott and myself again) every human being will repeat the story to twelve others—and so on." The audience for private circulation of this sort would quickly become quite large. In the same year Byron sent a short song to Murray about Hobhouse's political ambitions

---

[10] Peter Graham, ed., *Byron's Bulldog: The Letters of John Cam Hobhouse to Lord Byron* (Columbus, Ohio: Ohio State University Press, 1984) 259.

[11] Details of the negotiations over *Don Juan* are given in Truman Guy Steffan, *Byron's* Don Juan, *The Making of a Masterpiece*, 2d ed. (Austin, University of Texas Press, 1971) 1: 3–29, and *BP* 5: 663–67.

[12] *Byron's Bulldog* (above, n. 10) 50.

and connected them with those of Orator Hunt and Cobbett, whom Byron ridiculed:

> Who are now the People's men?
>   My boy Hobby O!
> Yourself and Burdett, Gentlemen,
>   And Blackguard Hunt and Cobby O![13]

Hobhouse complained about its private circulation that led to its publication: "Had Lord Byron transmitted to me a lampoon on you, I should, if I know myself at all, either have put it into the fire without delivery, or should have sent it at once to you. I should not have given it a circulation for the gratification of all the small wits at the great and little houses, where no treat is so agreeable as to find a man laughing at his friend."[14]

Late in January, when it appeared to Byron that Murray might not publish *Don Juan*, Byron, still insisting on publication, requested that it be printed in fifty copies and circulated to a list that he would provide, a form of private publication to the circle at the great and little houses who would acknowledge that Byron, and not Southey, represented the public and who would admit that Southey, being in place, was decidedly out of place. Privately printing the Dedication would not have been merely private revenge against Southey; it would have been a public act. After the fate of "Fare Thee Well," which was pirated and printed in the newspapers,[15] Byron knew very well what would happen to his privately circulated works. In fact, after Byron's death, when Hobhouse publicly revealed the existence of the Dedication in the *Westminster Review* (January 1825), pirated copies of the Dedication may have appeared.[16] Considering the speed and efficiency of private circulation, Byron must have known that his primary audience and Southey would hear of the Dedication whether or not it was published.

I detail the reception at Murray's of the Dedication and canto I in the final section of this chapter. Byron's audience at Murray's and at the small and great tables of the West End judged him the first poet of the age. His

---

[13] *A Publisher and His Friends: Memoir and Correspondence of the Late John Murray*, ed. Samuel Smiles, (London, 1891) 1: 415–17. Byron's ballad refers, not to Leigh Hunt, but to Henry Hunt, whom *Blackwood's* called Bristol Hunt. Byron wrote to Hobhouse in May 1820: "If you *will* dine with Bristol Hunt—& such like—what can you expect? . . . it is not against the *pure* principle of reform—that I protest, but against low designing dirty levellers who would pioneer their way to a democratical tyranny" (*BLJ* 7: 99). See also *BLJ* 7: 59n., 62–63, 81.

[14] *Murray Memoirs* (above, n. 13) 1: 418.

[15] David V. Erdman, " 'Fare Thee Well'—Byron's Last Days in England," *Shelley and His Circle*, ed. Kenneth Neill Cameron (Cambridge, Mass.: Harvard University Press, 1970) 4: 638–53, rept. in *Romantic Rebels*, ed. Kenneth Neill Cameron (Cambridge, Mass.: Harvard University Press, 1973) 203–27.

[16] McGann doubts their existence before 1832 (*BP* 5: 667).

audience was composed of readers at both ends of the political spectrum.[17]
To enter his claim, Byron places, or locates, both himself and Southey
through apostrophe and address that play on the names and titles Southey
had been given and on the geography of place and patronage. In asking,
"Who is he?" Byron asks, "Where is he?" as did many of Southey's reviewers. I detail, below, reactions to his appointment as poet laureate in 1813 to
early 1814, to reviews of his *The Lay of the Laureate* (1816), and public discussion of the *Wat Tyler* episode of 1817. I also describe the Dedication's
complex mediated allusions to Milton and Castlereagh. In each instance I
focus on the nuances and innuendoes in the words themselves both in the
commentary on Southey and in the Dedication.

"Bob Southey" (1813–14)

Bob Southey! You're a poet—poet Laureate,
    And representative of all the race;
Although 'tis true that you turn'd out a Tory at
    Last,—yours has lately been a common case:—
And now, my epic renegade! what are ye at,
    With all the Lakers in and out of place?
A nest of tuneful persons, to my eye
Like 'four and twenty blackbirds in a pie;

'Which pie being open'd they began to sing'—
    (This old song and new simile holds good)
'A dainty dish to set before the King';
    Or Regent, who admires such kind of food.
And Coleridge, too, has lately taken wing,
    But, like a hawk encumber'd with his hood,
Explaining metaphysics to the nation—
I wish he would explain his Explanation.

                                   (1–16)

    Byron's first draft of the Dedication, completed in September 1818,
began "Southey! you are a poet," but he revised it to "Bob Southey! You're
a poet." The altered apostrophe introduces the name Bob and prepares for
the "dry-bob" joke to follow, but its hint of sexual incapacity is more appropriate to Castlereagh than Southey, as Hobhouse hinted when he wrote
to Byron on January 5, 1819: "Both Scrope [Davies] and myself agreed that
the attack on Castlereagh was much better than that on Southey (which by

---

[17] William St Clair offers an account of Byron's wider audience. *Don Juan* was printed in
pirated and inexpensive editions, which reached very large numbers of readers—far beyond
the limited circle from which its language was taken ("The Impact of Byron's Writings: An
Evaluative Approach," in *Byron: Augustan and Romantic*, ed. Andrew Rutherford [New York:
St. Martin's Press, 1990] 1–25).

the way has the phrase '*dry-Bob*' !!)."[18] Following the lead of Hunt and Hazlitt, Byron refers to Southey by his common and natural name Bob primarily for its political and economic significance and only secondarily for the sexual double entendre. Southey was ridiculed by his name, his public signatures. The satires on Southey as laureate in 1813–14 played upon his signatures by transforming them into apostrophic caricature.

After the death of Henry Pye in 1813 and before the appointment of Southey as the new poet laureate that October, the *Examiner* began a campaign to abolish the office of poet laureate: "If a good poet accepts it, the office disgraces him; if a bad one, he disgraces the office." Whoever accepts it "must be one of the dullest, or meanest, or vainest, or most mercenary of his species."[19] Thus the office itself was a subject of ridicule before Southey accepted it. When Southey was appointed, the *Eclectic Review* politely admitted Southey's stature as a poet but thought that "some objections lie against the place itself, considered in its present degraded state." Remembering the regicide in *Hamlet*, it judged that "a hundred pounds and a butt of sack, were, we confess, monstrous overpayment for such annual strains of stupefying praise as Cibber, Whitehead, and Pye, were wont to pour into the ear of royalty."[20] Similarly, Francis Jeffrey, in the *Edinburgh Review*, described a poet-laureate as "naturally a ridiculous person" and "an object which it is difficult to contemplate with gravity."[21] When Southey's appointment was announced, the *Examiner* hooted its ridicule on September 26:

> The court-laurel,—that sapless and shapeless nonentity, polluted by every species of meanness, ridiculous in its imaginary honour, and despicable in its demand of service,—seemed at last to be gaining its just reputation; and there appeared a chance that if not absolutely abolished, it would at least be despised by every living writer who had not forfeited every body's respect but his own,— when lo!—amidst a flourish of horns from the *Courier* and *Morning Post*,— amidst the shouts of men of the world, and the blushes of the honest and the consistent, it is planted on the primitive head of Mr. Robert Southey.

The *Examiner*'s announcement of Southey's appointment begins with a quotation from his early poem "To My Own Miniature Picture Taken at

---

[18] *Byron's Bulldog* (above, n. 10) 259. Details of revisions are in *Byron's* Don Juan: *A Variorum Edition*, ed. Truman Guy Steffan and Willis W. Pratt, 2d ed. (Austin: University of Texas Press, 1971) 2: 9–20. Byron revised the first line about the same time that he added the stanzas on Castlereagh to the Dedication.

[19] August 29, 1813. Subsequent references to the *Examiner* included in the text are by date.

[20] Rev. of Southey's first laureate poetry in the *Eclectic Review*, 2d series, 1 (April 1814): 431–36, reprinted in *Robert Southey: The Critical Heritage*, ed. Lionel Madden (London: Routledge & Kegan Paul, 1972) 198.

[21] Rev. of Southey's *The Lay of the Laureate*, in the *Edinburgh Review* 26 (June 1816): 441–49, reprinted in *Critical Heritage* (above, n. 20) 215.

Two Years of Age," published in *Poems* (Bristol, 1797): "There were / Who form'd high hopes and flattering ones of thee, / Young Robert." The quotation concludes with Southey's smug identification of the mistakes of his elders: "they deemed, forsooth, / That thou shouldst tread Preferment's pleasant path. / Ill-judging ones" (*SP* 392).[22] Southey himself created, in 1797, a signature as "Young Robert," who would follow his own path and reject patronage. Byron's response is the nursery rhyme "A Song of Sixpence." The contrast between Southey's epic pretensions and the nursery rhyme parodies Southey's pride and is particularly apt in the context of the *Examiner*'s reprinting Southey's poem on his own miniature painted when he was two years old. In the Dedication Byron is speaking to "Young Robert," reflected in the miniature. From the high seriousness of Blake's *Songs* to the high hilarity of Haydon's immortal dinner, nursery rhymes and children's literature were commonly used for mockery. At Haydon's dinner an anonymous comptroller of stamps solemnly asked Wordsworth, whom Haydon had neglected to introduce to Wordsworth, whether "Milton was a great genius" and then whether Newton was "a great genius."

> Wordsworth seemed asking himself: "Who is this?" Lamb got up, and taking a candle, said: "Sir, will you allow me to look at your phrenological development?" He then turned his back on the poor man, and at every question of the comptroller he chaunted:
>
> > "Diddle diddle dumpling, my son John
> > Went to bed with his breeches on."

The comptroller, realizing that Wordsworth did not know who he was, solemnly announced, "I am a comptroller of stamps":

> There was a dead silence, the comptroller evidently thinking that was enough. While we were waiting for Wordsworth's reply, Lamb sung out:
>
> > "Hey diddle diddle,
> > The cat and the fiddle."
>
> (Haydon 318)

Byron used "Hey Diddle Diddle" in a review of Wordsworth's *Poems in Two Volumes* (1807), where he described "Written in March, While resting on the Bridge at the Foot of Brother's Water" as "an imitation of such minstrelsy as soothed our cries in the cradle."[23] "Hey diddle diddle" was first published about 1765 in *Mother Goose's Melody; or, Sonnets for the Cradle*, which contained a note explaining that the poems were "calculated to amuse Children and excite them to Sleep." *The Oxford Companion to Chil-*

---

[22] From 1813 the *Examiner* frequently reprinted Southey's poem.
[23] *Lord Byron: The Complete Miscellaneous Prose*, ed. Andrew Nicholson (Oxford: Clarendon Press, 1991) 9.

dren's Literature explains that it "was equipped with a preface 'By a very Great Writer of very Little Books' and with editorial remarks in a mock scholarly style ('Illustrated with Notes and Maxims, Historical, Philosophical and Critical'), which have sometimes been interpreted as a satire on the editing of ballads in Percy's *Reliques*."[24] Thus even before Lamb's quips and Byron's satire, there was a substantial body of opinion that children's songs were satires on more serious literature. Children's literature, as Geoffrey Summerfield explains, although considered to be "vulgar, immoral, or mentally regressive," persisted through the eighteenth century as a folk culture, "sometimes with the antinomian energies of a counter-culture."[25]

Given the place of children's literature in the late eighteenth century, it is tempting to associate Byron's use of "A Song of Sixpence" as an ideological gesture implied in the mockery of serious literature and to think that *Don Juan* is a thoroughly dialogic work that refuses its own authority at the same time that it attacks Southey's pretensions. But the case is quite otherwise. The joke about Henry Pye is not originally Byron's; he does not take the "A Song of Sixpence" directly from the chatter and prattle of children. The joke originates with George Steevens, who quipped when Henry Pye wrote his first birthday ode: "And when the PYE was opened the birds began to sing; / Was not that a dainty dish to set before the King?"[26] Steevens, a member of Dr. Johnson's club, assisted Johnson with the *Lives of the Poets* and produced his own edition of Shakespeare. His acid wit was so well known that Gifford called him the "Puck of Commentators." *The Oxford Dictionary of Nursery Rhymes* points out that the nursery rhyme was attributed to Steevens in the *Dictionary of National Biography*,[27] but of course it was printed as a children's poem long before Steevens applied it to Henry Pye. Byron's "old song" is the nursery rhyme, and the "new simile," the resemblance between Henry Pye and the king's pie, is Steevens'. Thus, despite the ideological associations with children's literature and the potential dialogic play of conflicting authorities in the Dedication, Byron's language here, as throughout the Dedication, is the language of Regency wit, a form of parody that was the language of authority. Byron's particular pun on Henry Pye comes, not from those who were excluded from the literary world of London, but from within that literary world, although Marcus Wood proves that the use of

[24] Humphrey Carpenter and Mari Prichard, *Oxford Companion to Children's Literature* (Oxford: Oxford University Press, 1984) 363.

[25] Geoffrey Summerfield, *Fantasy and Reason: Children's Literature in the Eighteenth Century* (Athens, Georgia: University of Georgia Press, 1984) xiv–xv. For a detailed examination of the use of children's literature as satire and parody, see Marcus Wood's *Radical Satire and Print Culture, 1790–1822* (Oxford: Clarendon Press, 1994).

[26] T. G. Steffan, E. Steffan, and W. W. Pratt note that the quip was Steevens's (*Lord Byron: Don Juan* [New Haven: Yale University Press, 1982] 565).

[27] *The Oxford Dictionary of Nursery Rhymes*, ed. Iona and Peter Opie (Oxford: Oxford University Press, 1952) 394.

nursery rhymes for satire and parody was common among many classes. He prints Isaac and George Cruikshank's etching "Rhyms for Grown Babies in the Ministerial Nursery" (1809), which uses "A Song of Sixpence" for parody.[28] The implication is that Byron is a part of the literary world, that he is in that place because he can use that language, not that he is aligning himself with those who are outside the public sphere. Byron, not Southey, who is "young Robert," is representative of the literary race.

Byron responded to Southey's appointment in the fall of 1813 with lines that ridicule him for the same reasons that the *Anti-Jacobin* attacked him in 1797:

> Who gains the bays and annual Malmsey barrel—
>   Busby the bright—or Southey the sublime?
> Southey with monarchs has made up his quarrel,
>   Nor pities prisoned Martin's venial crime,
> My Liege, (that same lopped off the head of [Charles]
>   And Southey sang him once upon a [time.)]
> Bob now no more the sapphic patriot [warbles,]
>   And up to Pye's Parnassus he may climb——
> George gives him what—God knows he wanted—laurels,
>   And spares him what—he never spared us—rhyme.[29]

By singling out Marten, Byron not only alludes to Southey's sonnet "Inscription For the Apartment in Chepstow-Castle, where Henry Marten, the Regicide, was imprisoned thirty years," he also alludes to its parody in the first number of the *Anti-Jacobin*, November 20, 1797, "Inscription For the Door of the Cell in Newgate, where Mrs. Brownrigg, the Prentice-cide, was confined previous to her Execution" and to the *Anti-Jacobin's* parody of Southey's "The Widow: Sapphics" in the second number, "The Friend of Humanity and the Knife Grinder" (*PAJ* 5–11). Both of Southey's poems appeared in *Poems* (1797). Byron's first response to Southey's laureateship, perhaps inspired by the *Anti-Jacobin*, is contained in his journal for November 22, 1813: "His appearance is *Epic*; and he is the only existing entire man of letters. . . . His prose is perfect. Of his poetry there are various opinions: there is, perhaps, too much of it for the present generation; posterity will probably select. He has *passages* equal to any thing. At present, he has a *party*, but no *public*—except for his prose writings" (*BLJ* 3: 214). Byron's comments that Southey has a party but no public is repeated throughout his criticism and the criticism of the London literary world as well. After Southey's first laureate poetry in 1814, Byron's opinion of him began to

---

[28] Wood (above, n. 25) 227–28.

[29] *BP* 3: 90–91. McGann notes Byron's use of the *Anti-Jacobin's* parody and calls attention to Byron's dislike of Southey's Sapphics (*BLJ* 3: 122). Byron had a copy of *Poetry of the Anti-Jacobin* in his library and quoted from "The Rovers" (*BLJ* 3: 144). Nicholson (above, n. 23) prints the sales record of Byron's library in 1816, item 251 (240).

change. On March 24, he wrote to James Hogg: "You love Southey, forsooth—I am sure Southey loves nobody but himself, however. I hate these talkers one and all, body and soul. They are a set of the most despicable impostors—that is my opinion of them. They know nothing of the world; and what is poetry but a reflection of the world?" (*BLJ* 4: 85).

When Southey's first laureate poem, *Carmen Triumphale*, was published in 1814, the *Examiner* noted that it was written by "Robert Southey, Esquire, Poet Laureat" and added in parentheses "alas for plain Robert." It contrasted the name on the title page with his earlier, more common name, Robert or Bob Southey. Southey's first lines rejoiced, not about the nation's victories, but about his own preferment: "In happy hour doth he receive / The Laurel, meed of famous Bards of yore, / Which Dryden and diviner *Spenser* wore." Hunt parodied the second stanza, which began: "Wake, lute and harp! My soul take up the strain! / Glory to God! Deliverance for mankind!" (*SP* 447) with the following lines:

> Come pen and ink! My hand take up the *notes*!
>   Glory to Kings! A hundred pounds for Southey!
> Joy,—for all poets, joy!—who turn their coats:
>   But most for thee, the mouthiest of the mouthy:[30]

The "notes" in Hunt's first line are not only the notes of music but the bank notes of his payment, in the second decade of the nineteenth century a debased and dubious form of currency.[31] Byron repeats the charge when he asks in the Dedication "You have your salary—was't for that you wrought?" (45). Toward the end of the first canto, when Byron parodies the Ten Commandments, he repeats the Southey-mouthey rhyme:

> Thou shalt believe in Milton, Dryden, Pope;
>   Thou shalt not set up Wordsworth, Coleridge, Southey;
> Because the first is crazed beyond all hope,
>   The second drunk, the third so quaint and mouthey:
>
> (1: 1633–36)

Byron may have been reminded of Hunt's rhyme by reading the following lines in Southey's *Wat Tyler*, spoken about Tyler himself: "Aye, aye hear him—/ He is no mealy-mouth'd court orator, / To flatter vice, and pamper lordly pride."[32] The joke in Byron's and in Hunt's rhyme is that "mealy-mouthed" originally meant someone who was soft-spoken, timid, and afraid

---

[30] The *Examiner*, Jan. 16, 1814. The italics are in the original. The *Examiner* consistently used the spelling "laureat."

[31] The Bank of England suspended cash payments on banknotes from 1797 to 1819: "Paper money was legal tender that was not convertible to gold" (Kurt Heinzelman, *The Economics of the Imagination* [Amherst: University of Mass. Press, 1980] 117).

[32] R. Southey, *Wat Tyler*, intro. Jonathan Wordsworth (Oxford: Woodstock Books, 1989) 27.

to speak one's own mind, while "mouthey" originally referred to its opposite: someone who is constantly ranting and railling. To Byron, Southey is
someone who is both "quaint" and "mouthey," direct opposites. Hazlitt typ-
ically portrays Southey as a simple antithesis, a contradiction, and Byron
borrows the figure.

Hunt also parodies Southey's line "O England! O my glorious native
Land!":

> O Robert! O my glorious, natural Bob!
> For thou, before thou knew'st a job,
>   Much of man's own freedom didst parade,
>   Making thy friends afraid,
> Thy hope in truth and in an honest fob,
>   Now are thy worst of verses overpaid
>   Thy bending back hath now official raiment,—
> Glory to Kings, thy song! A hundred pounds, thy payment.

To Hunt and the *Examiner*, Southey's place led him to think that "glorious
Bob" stood for England; appointed by the Regent, he thought of himself as
the literary regent, the poet to instruct the age.

In January 1814 the *Examiner* printed a short poem called "The Bellman
v. The Laureat" with the following headnote: "The following lines are
taken from 'a Copy of Verses' by the Beadle of the East Division of the
parish of St. Paul, Covent Garden—'Humbly presented to all his worthy
Masters and Mistresses.'" The *Anti-Jacobin* parodied Southey's "The Soldier's Wife," which had included a stanza by Coleridge, whom the *Anti-
Jacobin* parodied as the Bellman. Then the *Examiner* printed "On the New
Poet-Laureat," spoken by the Bellman.

> "My honest Masters, take care of extremes,
> BOB SOUTHEY, once upon a time, it seems,
> (Too young to know the value of decorum)
> Held in disdain, all crowns, and those who wore 'em;
> For *suffering* them, he saw no reason why;
> And as to *flattering* them, he'd rather die.
> Such was his tone for years, and such his scorning;
> When lo! one fine autumnal blushing morning,
> Changing his *mind* and *coat*, as CRABBE would say,
> He comes to Court—the oddest of the gay,
> And there not only lay his notions by,
> Kissing the REGENT'S hand with down dropt eye,
> But puts the Crown on, that was worn by PYE!
>
> My noble Masters, how could this change be?
>
> .   .   .   .

I'll tell you what it was, My Masters dear—
Pure weakness, and a hundred pounds a year!

. . . .

In what, my candid Masters, I have said,
Do not suppose I've been by malice led;
I would not of his fame the Laureat rob;
Think not your Bellman would speak ill of BOB.
'Tis of his odd extremes I speak alone;
In all things else—his verse, his taste, his tone,
I'm sure I look on BOB's fame as my own."[33]

The Bellman, who writes these verses, is the radical Coleridge caricatured by the *Anti-Jacobin* in 1797, who apologizes for Southey, or "Bob," his common, radical, and youthful name and rhymes it with "rob." Southey coined his own laurels and exchanges his words for money, overcharging the crown. From their early associations as objects of parody and ridicule in the *Anti-Jacobin* to Coleridge's defense of Southey in the *Biographia*, they are intimately linked as the pair of radical poets who turn their coats. The Bellman foretells his own apostasy. In the turns of the public debates, apostrophe answers apostasy. Thus when Byron begins his Dedication to *Don Juan* with the apostrophe to "Bob Southey," he is doing much more than simply preparing for the "dry Bob" joke to follow. He is quoting the Bellman's use of "Bob" and Leigh Hunt's use of "plain Robert" and "natural Bob," pointedly rhymed also with "job" and "fob," while the values of a crown and a bob as money are always present. The Dedication and canto I of *Don Juan* are Byron's expansive version of Hunt's parody of "natural Bob," who has become a "dry-Bob." The opening line of the Dedication is a sharp antithesis, which addresses Southey as both the earlier radical poet and the two-year-old Southey of the miniature, "Young Robert," who scorned "preferment's path," in the first half of the line, and the later Southey, who is poet laureate, in the second half of the line. The allusions amount to simple quotation, because there is no need for Byron to vary the apostrophe or to make it original with himself. Byron's language is the satirical wit of the *Anti-Jacobin* and the *Examiner*, a language that is the currency of Regency London, the medium of social exchange that defines social value and the place and possessions of those who are capable of using it.

"THE LAY OF THE LAUREATE" (1816) AND THE MINSTREL'S RATTLE

As the *Examiner* predicted, Southey responded to such attacks with a vain pride in his office and a defense of the legitimacy of his place. On the oc-

---

[33] The *Examiner*, January 2, 1814. The ellipses are in the original.

casion of the marriage of Princess Charlotte in 1816, he published *The Lay of the Laureate: Carmen Nuptiale*, which he was finishing at the end of April, a few weeks after Byron left England.[34] Southey appeared on the title page as "Robert Southey, Esq., Poet Laureate, Member of the Royal Spanish Academy, and of the Royal Spanish Academy of History," titles that Byron knew, because he parodied Southey's associations with Spanish royalty. Doucet Fischer has pointed out to me that in the Berg Collection in the New York Public Library there is a clipping from the *Morning Chronicle* of March 15, 1816, with Byron's "Ode from the French," a supposed translation, but actually an expression of Byron's radical sentiments. The clipping contains Byron's manuscript corrections indicating that the supposed translator of the poem was "R[obert] S[outhey], P[oet] L[aureate], Q[uarterly] R[eviewer], Member of the Royal Spanish Inq[uistitio]n."[35] Title pages are the locations of public signatures. In the case of the signature of "Ode from the French," Byron parodies Southey's titles pages and titles. Southey's change of his public name from "young Robert" to "Poet Laureate" and "Member of the Royal Spanish Academy" provided Hunt and Byron with material to attack Southey and may have suggested Don Juan as Byron's hero.

The Lay of the Laureate consisted of three parts: a twenty-stanza Proem, in which Southey paraded his laurels in defiance of Hazlitt and Hunt; a dream vision in which Southey assumes the allegorical voices of Britannia, Praxis (or Experience), and the Angel of the Church of England to lecture the Princess on her public and domestic duties; and an Epilogue. The Proem begins, as do Southey's earlier laureate poems, with self-praise, in terms that defy solemnity:

> There was a time when all my youthful thought
>   Was of the Muse; and of the Poet's fame,
> How fair it flourisheth and fadeth not,
>   Alone enduring, when the Monarch's name
> Is but an empty sound, the Conqueror's bust
> Moulders and is forgotten in the dust.

One would think that Southey's assurance that the "Monarch's name" will be "an empty sound" is at the very least unconventional in laureate verse. Stanzas nine and ten of the Proem reflect Southey's indifference to the *Examiner's* criticism:

[34] *Life and Correspondence* (above, n. 7) 4: 169–75. There is no mention of *The Lay of the Laureate* in *BLJ*.

[35] Fischer, Doucet D., and Donald H. Reiman, *Byron on the Continent: A Memorial Exhibition, 1824–1974* (New York: Carl H. Pforzheimer Library and The New York Public Library, 1974) 17.

Yea in this now, while Malice frets her hour,
    Is foretaste given me of that meed divine;
Here undisturbed in this sequestered bower,
    The friendship of the good and wise is mine;
And that green wreath, which decks the Bard when dead,
That laureate garland crowns my living head.

That wreath which in Eliza's golden days,
    My Master dear, divinest Spenser wore,
That which rewarded Drayton's learned lays,
    Which thoughtful Ben and gentle Daniel bore,
Grin Envy through thy ragged mask of scorn!
In honour it was given, with honour it is worn!

Southey's Proem invited parody. James Hogg burlesqued it in the *Poetic Mirror* (1816) as "The Curse of the Laureate: *Carmen Judiciale*," which plays on the older sense of the word *lay* as law and religious faith.[36] Hunt was also quick to respond. On August 4, 1816, he printed Southey's Proem in a left-hand column in the *Examiner*, with a parody in the right-hand column entitled "The Laureate Laid Double," along with an epigraph from *A Midsummer Night's Dream*, "Bottom, thou art translated," and a long footnote that reprinted again Southey's "To My Own Miniature Picture Taken at Two Years of Age." Hunt never claimed authorship of the parody. It was not signed with his usual mark of the pointing hand, and he never reprinted it in any of his collected editions of poetry, so his authorship is not absolutely certain. Southey's Proem is "laid double" on the page to illustrate Southey's duplicity. The *Examiner*'s parody of Southey's first stanza ridicules Southey's youthful pride:

There was a time, when all my youthful thought
    Besides the Muse, was Jacobinic fame,
How fair it flourisheth and changeth not,
    Alone enduring, when the Monarch's name,
And Conqueror's too, depend upon one's quill;
And 'twixt ourselves, perhaps I think so still.

The *Examiner*'s parody of stanzas nine and ten strangely anticipates Byron's *ottava rima* in *Don Juan*:

Yea, in this now, is foretaste given my lips
    Of that fine meed, (spite of malicious joker);
Here I enjoy, amidst my haws and hips,
    The friendship of *wise* Grosvenor and *good* Croker:—

[36] *Critical Heritage* (above, n. 20) 225–30.

The battles of the Kings and Priests I fought ye 'em,
And so at last they've crowned my *caput mortuum*.

That wreath which Spenser, my dear master, wore,
    (At least I chuse to say it,—so am right),
Which Drayton, just about as much too, bore,
    And Jonson really did, and Daniel might,—
(That fellow's laugh there isn't to be borne!)
By glorious hand 'twas given, by glorious head 'tis worn.

Both Southey's *Lay of the Laureate* and *The Poet's Pilgrimage to Waterloo*, published a few months before *The Lay of the Laureate*, were written in *sesta rima*, a six-line stanza, a quatrain and a couplet. With the addition of two more lines at the beginning, the stanza would be Byron's *ottava rima*. The *Examiner's* parody anticipates many of the characteristics of Byron's use of *ottava rima*: the double and triple rimes; the asides, digressions, and flippant commentary; and the linguistic frolic through many levels of language. "The Laureate Laid Double" is particularly adept at the use of slang: "haws," a form of stammering; "hips," a hypochondriac ill-temper; and *caput mortuum*, not only the *momento mori* of serious moralizing, but in the eighteenth century also the residue of something once living, but now defunct and a curious addition to the lengthening list of satires on Southey's head. The *Examiner's* parody gives Southey a witty voice he does not have, which is compounded of his earlier Jacobinism, his present cynical monetary motives, and his pride and duplicity. While Hunt's gift of a voice and signature to Southey unmasks him, it also places his caricature within Regency society, a caricature that speaks the language of that society, when the real Southey cannot. Byron, by speaking in his own voice in *Don Juan*, silences Southey and places himself in that society. Southey, as proud poet laureate and Bottom the Weaver, is thus both in and out of place.

William Keach has reviewed the sources of Byron's *ottava rima* in the poetry and adaptations of Frere, Merivale, and Rose.[37] Byron said that Frere was the source for *Beppo* (1818), his first experiment in *ottava rima*: "*Berni* is the Original of *all.—Whistlecraft* was *my* immediate *model*. Rose's *Animali*—I never saw till a few days ago" (*BLJ* 6: 24). Merivale's *Orlando* was published in 1814. Byron read and admired it, but Merivale's verse is a somewhat sober rendering of Pulci's language, without much of the verbal play in Byron's use of the stanza. Nor is there much of Byron's verbal exuberance in Frere, whose "Prospectus and Specimen of an Intended National Work," popularly known as "Monks and Giants," was published in 1817, after Hunt printed "The Laureate Laid Double." William Stuart Rose's adaptation of Casti's *Animali Parlanti* contains much of the verbal play

---

[37] William Keach, "Political Inflection in Byron's *Ottava Rima*," *SIR* 27 (1988) 551–62.

found in Hunt and Byron but was published later in 1819. Byron read Casti in 1816, and as Peter Vassallo has argued, the style may have come from Byron's reading of Casti.[38] Hunt's parody may be the first English use of the full possibilities of *sesta rima* for burlesque and may be a source for Byron's *ottava rima*. No one would mistake Hunt's stanzas for Byron's. Byron has a cosmopolitan wit, and Hunt, a metropolitan humor. But they do contain more of the characteristics of the style of *Don Juan* than do the other English works in *ottava rima* often cited as sources of *Don Juan*: the violation of all rules of decorum in language. There is only a small possibility that Byron would have known "The Laureate Laid Double," since he left England before it was printed and even slighter evidence that Byron experimented with *ottava rima* as early as 1813 in his verses on Southey, which Hunt may have known. One cannot be sure that Byron's source was in fact "The Laureate Laid Double." However, in the public discourse the affinity between *Don Juan* and the *Examiner*'s satire makes *ottava rima* an appropriate form to satirize Southey's laureate poetry in *sesta rima*. The joke of the Dedication and canto I of *Don Juan* is that it parodies Southey's laureate verse.

Jeffrey's review of *The Lay of the Laureate* in the *Edinburgh Review* of June 1816 was unsparing:

> The laurel which the King gives, we are credibly informed, has nothing at all in common with that which is bestowed by the Muses; and the Prince Regent's warrant is absolutely of no authority in the court of Apollo. If this be the case, however, it follows, that a poet-laureate has no sort of precedency among poets,—whatever may be his place among pages and clerks of the kitchen;— and that he has no more pretensions as an author, than if his appointment had been to the mastership of the staghounds.

Jeffrey defines Southey by his location, by his titles and title pages; his title is that of a page. To Jeffrey, Southey's place as poet-laureate is that of menials and domestics of the royal household, a place from which Southey takes "an air of prodigious confidence and assumption." Southey's works are "disfigured with the most abominable egotism, conceit and dogmatism, that we ever met with in any thing intended for the public eye."[39] The second half of Byron's opening antithesis, "representative of all the race," as bitter as it is deceptively simple, alludes to Southey's extreme vanity, which Byron's readers at Murray's would have recognized immediately. They would have understood that Southey's pride was in an unworthy place, so that in the second half of the antithesis rests another antithesis.

---

[38] Peter Vassallo, *Byron: The Italian Literary Influence* (New York: St. Martin's Press, 1984) 43–81.
[39] Rev. of *The Lay of the Laureate*, *Critical Heritage* (above, n. 20) 216–17.

Southey's *Lay of the Laureate*, in which an excessively vain poet laureate, a member of the Royal Spanish Academy and the Royal Spanish Academy of History, who has forsaken his earlier identity as "young Robert" and "natural Bob," celebrates both himself and the marriage of a princess, is parodied in *Don Juan* by the history of a young Spanish Don, a natural man, whose adventures disrupt one marriage and unveil the hypocrisy of marriage in *ottava rima* that parodies Southey's laureate *sesta rima*. The frequent digressions in *Don Juan* parody Southey's self-portraiture in his laureate verse. While *Don Juan* is a portrait of Byron's failed marriage, young Juan is a "young Robert," a "natural Bob."[40] Byron's references to his own marriage were obvious to *Don Juan's* first readers. Frere, along with others, recognized that Byron intended Juan's sexual adventures to carry a political meaning, since he mentioned to Moore that he thought it strange that Byron thought "there was any connection between patriotism & profligacy—if we had a very puritan court indeed, one can understand *then* profligacy being adopted as a badge of opposition to it, but the reverse being the case, there is not even that excuse for connecting dissoluteness with patriotism."[41] Frere seems not to have taken into account that along with the Dedication, canto I was a satire on Southey's moral self-righteousness, not the profligacy of the court. Although one of Byron's purposes is to mock Southey's *Lay of the Laureate* and politics, he is seriously entering his "claim to praise." In competition with Southey's *Lay of the Laureate*, he is offering his rattle of the first minstrel.

Although Byron frequently disclaimed any plan or outline for *Don Juan*, he may well have planned from the very beginning to bring Juan to England. Peter Graham has explained that much of *Don Juan* answered Southey's *Letters From England*, and from the very beginning Byron may have intended *Don Juan* as a parody of Southey's Don Manuel Alvarez Espriella.[42] Since young Juan changed from a rebel and libertine to one who was "Proud with the proud, yet courteously proud, / So as to make them feel he knew his station / And theirs" (15: 117–19), his career parodies Southey's. Perhaps had Byron continued the English cantos, some of his original satirical intention would have been played out in Juan's apostasy. The well-accommodated Juan in England might have been Byron's parody of the older Southey.

[40] Leslie Marchand mentions that Byron began a novel that Hobhouse mentioned in his diary for January 4, 1818, saying that Byron "adumbrates himself Don Julian" with Lady Byron as Donna Josepha (*Byron: A Biography* [New York: Alfred A, Knopf, 1957] 2: 720). See Nicholson (above, n. 23) 77–78, 346–48 and *BLJ* 6: 96.

[41] *The Journal of Thomas Moore*, ed. Wilfred S. Dowden (Newark: University of Delaware Press, 1983) 1: 140.

[42] Peter W. Graham, Don Juan *and Regency England* (Charlottesville Va.: University Press of Virginia, 1990).

"WAT TYLER" (1817) AND EPIC RUNAGATES

Byron was in England when Southey became poet laureate and would have known Hunt's and Jeffrey's earlier attacks on him. In 1817 the pirated publication of Southey's radical drama *Wat Tyler*, written in 1794, was the occasion for Southey's first public ridicule as a renegade and for Byron to call him an "epic renegade." By this time Byron was in Italy, although he did read *Wat Tyler*. Southey tried to prevent publication, but Lord Eldon, the Lord Chief Justice, denied Southey's motion on the grounds that no one could claim rights over seditious writing. On March 14, 1817, William Smith, a Unitarian M.P. from Norwich, spoke in the House of Commons during a debate on the Seditious Meetings Bill, which would have limited free speech. He read from the *Quarterly Review*, in which Southey had attacked the liberal press:

> When the man of free opinions commences professor of moral and political philosophy for the benefit of the public, the fables of old credulity are then verified; his very breath becomes venomous, and every page which he sends abroad carries with it poison to the unsuspicious reader. . . . The dangers arising from such a state of things are now fully apparent, and the designs of the incendiaries, which have for some years been proclaimed so plainly, that they ought, long ere this, to have been prevented, are now manifested by overt acts.[43]

The "overt acts" were the Spa Fields riots of the previous December, which followed the public meetings led by Orator Hunt. William Smith, however, would not accept such reprimands from a former radical: "What he most detested, what most filled him with disgust, was the settled, determined malignity of a renegade,"[44] a phrase that was reprinted in William Hone's edition of *Wat Tyler* issued in 1817 with a preface stating that "we object to his calling on the Legislature to crush principles which he once contributed to propagate; in short, we do not object to the weakness of the man, but to the intolerance of the proselyte, and 'the malignity of the Renegado.'"[45] This public opinion, which Byron echoed in his letters, was nearly unanimous. Even before the publication of *Wat Tyler*, the *Examiner*'s quarrel with Southey was "not upon the ground of a mere change of opinion" but "for his indecent violence of language respecting those who differ with

---

[43] "Parliamentary Reform," *Quarterly Review* (Oct. 1816): 227, reprinted in *Life and Correspondence* 4: 367–68 and quoted from Hansard's *Parliamentary Debates From the Year 1803* 35: 1090–91. See also Southey's "Rise and Progress of Popular Disaffection" *Quarterly Review* (Jan. 1817).

[44] Smith may have read Letter LXXV of Southey's *Letters from England: by Don Manuel Alvarez Espriella*, which contains the brief story of "An English Renegado," who leaves England to join the Turks (*Letters from England*, ed. Jack Simmons [London: Cresset, 1951] 463–64).

[45] *Wat Tyler* (above, n. 32) xiv.

him, after his running from one extreme to another" (Sept. 26, 1813). When *Wat Tyler* was published, Byron echoed similar views of Southey: "I hate all intolerance—but most the intolerance of Apostasy—& the wretched vehemence with which a miserable creature who has contradicted himself—lies to his own heart— & endeavours to establish his sincerity by proving himself a rascal—*not* for changing his opinions—but for persecuting those who are of less malleable matter" (*BLJ* 5: 220).

Smith then read a speech by John Ball, a priest and rebel, from *Wat Tyler*:

> My brethren, these are truths, and weighty ones:
> Ye are all equal; Nature made ye so.
> Equality is your birth-right; when I gaze
> On the proud palace, and behold one man,
> In the blood-purpled robes of royalty,
> Feasting at ease, and lording over millions;
> Then turn me to the hut of poverty,
> And see the wretched labourer, worn with toil,
> Divide his scanty morsel with his infants;
> I sicken, and, indignant at the sight,
> Blush for the patience of humanity.[46]

He then expressed astonishment that the author of *Wat Tyler* was not prosecuted for seditious writing.

Smith's use of the word *renegade* provoked Southey to reply with a letter in the *Courier* on March 17 and provoked Coleridge, too, to respond with letters to the *Courier*,[47] which excused *Wat Tyler* on the grounds of Southey's youth and referred to the Jacobin Southey as "the stripling bard," an unfortunate echo of Southey's early poem on his own miniature picture, to which Hazlitt responded. Shortly afterward Southey issued a forty-eight-page quarto pamphlet entitled *Letter to William Smith, Esq., M.P. from Robert Southey, Esq*.[48] The insult that most bothered Southey was Smith's use of the term *renegade*. A review of Southey's letter in the Unitarian *Monthly Repository* (May 1817) explains some of the nuances of the word in 1817: "Renegade may be a term of Spanish origin, and Mr. Southey, as a master of that language, may be able to affix to it a very malignant signification; still, we have no notion that it is never used in any other sense, or was indeed on this occasion; but was merely meant to convey the charge of a change of opinion, or associates, without any charge of moral turpitude."[49]

---

[46] *Wat Tyler* (above, n. 32) 31; *Life and Correspondence* (above, n. 7) 4: 368.

[47] Coleridge wrote four letters in defense of Southey: March 17, 18, 27 and April 2 (*EOT* 2: 449–60, 466–78). For the title of his response, Hazlitt borrowed Coleridge's phrase "the stripling bard" (*EOT* 3: 277–79).

[48] Reprinted in *Life and Correspondence* (above, n. 7) 4: 370–90.

[49] *Monthly Repository* (May 1817) 275. The review was signed "A.R."

The *Monthly Repository* was a bit disingenuous, because the primary meaning of *renegade* in the public discourse, as Coleridge explained in his fourth *Courier* letter, defines a Christian who "has been tempted or tortured into a renunciation of his baptismal faith by Turks or Moors" (*EOT* 2: 473). Southey had reason to think that he had been charged with a moral failure, political apostasy, and a change of religious faith, as someone who had forsaken Christian Europe and Catholic Spain for Moorish Africa, a world of eunuchs and sultans. *Renegade* is pun on *runagate*, "someone who deserts, or runs away, a fugitive," a word Coleridge used about 1807 in a marginal annotation to *Fears in Solitude* to describe the accusations that he left his wife and child and went to Germany in 1797. The geography and Geography of the Dedication are quite precise. Byron displaces Southey from London to Spain to Algeria.

Southey's *Letter to William Smith* responded to the term *renegado*, because it carried, as the *Monthly Repository* hinted, the implication of a moral failure, a malicious intent, an infidelity, a weakness of character, a purely mercenary motive, and an unwarranted vanity: "But when the Member for Norwich asserts . . . that I impute evil motives to men merely for holding now the same doctrines which I myself formerly professed, and when he charges me . . . with the malignity and baseness of a renegade, the assertion and the charge are as *false* as the language in which they are conveyed is coarse and insulting."[50] At the end of *A Letter to William Smith*, Southey concluded with a self-portrait, which provoked further complaints about his vanity:

> How far the writings of Mr. Southey may be found to deserve a favourable acceptance from after ages, time will decide: but a name which, whether worthily or not, has been conspicuous in the literary history of its age, will certainly not perish. Some account of his life will always be prefixed to his works, and transferred to literary histories and to the biographical dictionaries, not only of this but other countries. There it will be related that he lived in the bosom of his family, in absolute retirement; that in all his writings there breathed the same abhorrence of oppression and immorality, the same spirit of devotion, and the same ardent wishes for the amelioration of mankind. . . . It will be said of him, that in an age of personality he abstained from satire, and that during the course of his literary life, often as he was assailed, the only occasion on which he ever condescended to reply, was when a certain Mr. William Smith insulted him in Parliament with the appellation of a renegade.[51]

Southey claims his permanent place in literary history and implicitly suggests that a "certain" William Smith should be as uncertain of his position and fame as Southey is certain of his own.

[50] *Life and Correspondence* (above, n. 7) 4: 373.
[51] Ibid. 4: 389–90.

In the review of the *Letter to Smith*, the *Monthly Repository* asks what Byron's Dedication asks: "Mr. Southey's unparalleled self-sufficiency provokes the inquiry, Who is he?" The *Monthly Repository*'s answer is that Smith's name will live longer than Southey's, because Smith is the consistent friend of humanity who has worked for the "abolition of the slave traffic, the relief of conscience, the preservation and extension of civil rights and the removal of mitigation of the crimes and horrors of war."[52] Byron's answer is that he is "Bob Southey" and the poet laureate, who is an "epic renegade." In the Dedication, when Byron asks, "What are ye at," he echoes the *Edinburgh Review*'s question in its review of Southey's *Letter to William Smith*: "What would the worthy Laureate be at?"[53] Southey is in place, because he is poet laureate, but he is out of place because it is a servile place and because he has no just claim to be the first poet of the age. Hazlitt is bothered by the same question. In his review of the *Letter to William Smith*, Hazlitt quoted Southey's statement that he had never before responded to criticism, and on this occasion, "he vindicated himself, *as it became him to do*." Hazlitt responded on May 18, 1817: "How so? Mr. Southey is only a literary man, and neither a commoner nor a peer of the realm" (Howe 7: 208). Hazlitt uses the word *commoner* in the narrow sense of a member of the House of Commons, implying that Southey is not a member of Parliament and no equal to William Smith. Since Southey represents no one, he speaks for no one. In spite of his titles and title pages, he has no real place; his title pages assume titles that have no currency.

While the *Monthly Repository* was decorously indignant over Southey's calls for silencing the radical press, the *Examiner* was deliriously satirical over his *Letter to William Smith*. Leigh Hunt quickly published an article on April 13, 1817, entitled "Death and Funeral of the Late Mr. Southey":

> On Thursday se'nnight, according to a notice in the *Courier* from the pen of his friend and physician the celebrated Dr. Paracelsus Broadhum Coleridge, departed this life the better portion of Robert Southey, Esquire, formerly "Man of Humanity" and Independent Poet, latterly Poet Laureat and Member of the Royal Spanish Academy. Mr. Southey's numerous works, remarkable for their impartial argument *for* and *against* despotism, and their equally impartial satire upon the writers on the two sides of the question are well known.

Southey was described as both a Nimrod, the hunter of men, or rather reformers, and a Don Quixote, who rode forth with the perplexing cries of "King and no King! Here come two of us," and "Charity and Persecution for ever! Principle and Apostacy ditto." Hunt quotes the *Lay of the Laure-*

[52] *Monthly Repository* (May 1817) 301.
[53] *Edinburgh Review* (March 1817) 166.

ate to describe Southey's quixotic charges against "the objects of his pursuit, who in the mean while did not stir a foot, but stood pitying him and laughing by turns." Southey rode forth crying "with a hideous grimace—'Grin, Envy!' " repeating words from the Proem of *The Lay of the Laureate*, attempted an attack on his enemies but tumbled "head and heals." When Southey died from wounds suffered in his political battles, the funeral cortege was composed of Murray and the *Quarterly* reviewers; "Jacobins with their coats turned"; "A Deputation from the Royal Spanish Academy, / Ditto from the Inquisition, holding thumb-screws," words that recall Byron's manuscript annotation to "Ode from the French"; "Dr. Paracelsus Broadhum Coleridge, / Holding an enormous white handkerchief to his eyes, / and supported by two Bottle-holders"; and, as pall-bearers, "Renegadoes from Algiers." Coleridge along with Southey is located among the company of impoverished Catholics, Spaniards, and irritable reviewers, and as his final resting place, the company of renegadoes, sultans, and eunuchs. In an introduction to Burke's *Reflections on the Revolution in France*, L. G. Mitchell has explained that after publication of the *Reflections*, Burke was caricatured in cartoons as Don Quixote: "If not sorrowing for the fate of the Catholic Church, Burke is shown as Don Quixote or 'Don Dismallo,' a broken-down knight errant pursuing the Dulcinea of Marie Antoinette and tilting at imaginary windmills." Mitchell adds later: "Again and again, Burke is given the character of Don Quixote. In pamphlets and cartoons, he is shown as an elderly, broken-down knight errant, whose enfeebled mind leads him to charge windmills."[54] Hunt's description of Southey in "Death and Funeral of the Late Mr. Southey" suggests that he may have seen the cartoon "The Knight of the Wo[e]ful Countenance Going to Extirpate the National Assembly," attributed to Frederick George Byron. If Mitchell is correct, then Southey as a Don Quixote is another Burke who, like Burke, has forsaken a sympathy with revolution for reactionary principles. In his review of Southey's *Letter to William Smith*, Hazlitt says Burke was "an apostate, 'a malignant renegado' like Mr. Southey" (Howe 7: 186). *Don Juan* is thus also a satire on Burke.

In the second stanza of the Dedication, Byron groups Coleridge with Southey and relies on the Regency reader's knowledge that Coleridge defended Southey in the controversies over *Wat Tyler*. The *Examiner* had associated Southey with Coleridge from the early months when Southey became poet laureate, but Byron's source for the attacks on Coleridge is not the *Examiner*. He relies on reviews of the *Biographia Literaria* in the Whig

---

[54] *RRF* 17, 25. Some of the cartoons are reproduced in Nicholas K. Robinson, *Edmund Burke: A Life in Caricature* (New Haven: Yale University Press, 1996) and in David Duff, *Romance and Revolution: Shelley and the Politics of a Genre* (Cambridge: Cambridge University Press, 1994). Duff suggests that Paine's ridicule of Burke's "Quixote . . . nonsense" began the comparisons of Burke and Don Quixote (24). See also *RRF* 58.

Edinburgh Review and Tory *Blackwood's*, probably sent to him in Italy by Murray, to form the image of the "hawk encumbered with its hood." In the *Edinburgh Review*, Hazlitt portrays Coleridge as someone who soars and sinks, thus suggesting the trope of rising and falling, one of the organizing tropes of *Don Juan*:

> Mr. Coleridge has . . . from the combined forces of poetic levity and metaphysic bathos, been trying to fly, not in the air, but under ground—playing at hawk and buzzard between sense and nonsense,—floating or sinking in fine Kantean categories . . . going up in an air balloon filled with fetid gas from the writings of Jacob Behmen and the mystics, and coming down in a parachute made of the soiled and fashionable leaves of the Morning Post.[55]

Byron's figure of the "hawk encumbered with his hood" is completed with a figure from John Wilson's review of the *Biographia* in *Blackwood's*: "while he darkens what was dark before into tenfold obscurity, he so treats the most ordinary common-places as to give them the air of mysteries, till we no longer know the faces of our old acquaintances beneath their cowl and hood."[56] Wilson may have borrowed the figure of the hood from Hazlitt's review of *A Lay-Sermon on the Distresses of the Country* in the *Examiner* for September 8, 1816, in which Coleridge's true self is encased in "his shroud and surplice."

Hazlitt's review of the *Letter to William Smith* in the *Examiner* claimed that Southey shows "himself to be a base and malignant Renegade, by defending all the rotten, and undermining all the sound parts of the system to which he professes to be a convert. . . . This is as natural in a Renegado as it would be unaccountable in any one else" (Howe 7: 196). He also comments on Southey's moral rectitude, which one would love to be able to prove that Byron saw in 1817 or early 1818: "We hope Mr. Southey, when he was in town, went to see *Don Giovanni*, and heard him sing that fine song, 'Women and wine are the sustainers and glory of life.' We do not wish to see Mr. Southey quite a *Don Giovanni* (that would be as great a change in his moral, as to see him Poet-laureate, is in his political character) but if he had fewer pretensions to virtue, he would, perhaps, be a better man" (Howe 7: 202). Hunt had anticipated Hazlitt's association by calling Southey a Don Quixote so that Byron was not the first to connect Southey with Spain.

Copies of the *Examiner* that contained Hazlitt's review of early May 1817 may have reached Byron through Shelley, although the evidence is not conclusive. In a letter to Byron from England on December 17, 1817, Shelley promised to send "a parcel of books . . . and if I find that they will escape the embargo, I will enclose some newspapers."[57] Since Shelley became in-

---

[55] Rev. of *Biographia Literaria* in *The Edinburgh Review* (Aug. 1817) 491.

[56] "Observations on Coleridge's 'Biographia Literaria,' " *Blackwood's Magazine* (Oct. 1817) 5.

[57] *The Letters of Percy Bysshe Shelley*, ed. Frederick L. Jones (Oxford: Clarendon Press, 1964) 1: 584.

creasingly friendly with Hunt and since Hunt stayed with the Shelleys at Marlow beginning in April 1817, it is most likely that Shelley intended to send copies of the *Examiner*. The parcel was not sent, but Shelley did bring some books for Byron when he went to Italy in the spring of 1818. When Shelley wrote to Byron on April 28 from Milan, he told Byron, "You will receive your packet of books. Hunt sends you one he has lately published," most likely *Foliage*.[58] From Italy, Shelley had requested that Peacock send him copies of the *Examiner*, and Peacock replied to Shelley on July 5, 1818, that he "sent off a small box directed to Mr. Gisborne for you, containing the 'Cobbetts' and 'Examiners' from your departure to the present time . . . ,"[59] so Shelley, at least, was eager to receive all the *Examiner*s since he left England. Byron wrote to Moore on June 1 that Hunt "sent out his 'Foliage' by Percy Shelley," so Byron received the packet of books before he began work on *Don Juan*, although there is no specific mention of either the *Examiner* or newspapers in general (*BLJ* 6: 46).

If Byron did not see the Hazlitt's review, he certainly did read Coleridge's analysis of Don Juan's character in the *Biographia*:

> Rank, fortune, wit, talent, acquired knowledge, and liberal accomplishments, with beauty of person, vigorous health, and constitutional hardihood,—all these advantages, elevated by the habits and sympathies of noble birth and national character, are supposed to have combined in *Don Juan*, so as to give him the means of carrying into all its *practical* consequences the doctrine of a godless nature, as the sole ground and efficient cause not only of all things, events, and appearances, but likewise of all our thoughts, sensations, impulses, and actions. Obedience to nature is the only virtue.[60]

Even if Byron did not see Hazlitt's review of *A Letter to William Smith*, there was enough in the public press to suggest to Byron the connection between Southey, Spain, and Don Quixote. Byron's choice of Don Juan for his hero must have been an obvious one considering Southey's memberships in the Royal Spanish Academy and the Royal Spanish Academy of History. The Dedication and canto I, sent to Murray before canto II was written—as though it were a separate work, like the different cantos of *Childe Harold*—are Byron's answer to Southey's *Lay of the Laureate*. The manuscripts sent to Murray in November begin with an apostrophe to Southey and end with a quotation from *Lay of the Laureate*:

> 'Go, little book, from this my solitude!
>   I cast thee on the waters, go thy ways!
>   And if, as I believe, thy vein be good,

---

[58] Ibid. 2: 13.
[59] Ibid. 2: 24n.
[60] *BL* 2: 213. M. K. Joseph calls attention to this passage in the *Biographia* (163).

> The world will find thee after many days,'
> When Southey's read, and Wordsworth understood,
>   I can't help putting in my claim to praise—
> The four first rhymes are Southey's every line:
> For God's sake, reader! take them not for mine.
>
> (1: 1769–76)

Jeffrey quoted this final stanza and described it as the "very soul of silliness and self-complacency," and Byron's quoting Southey's stanza suggests that he saw Jeffrey's review in the *Edinburgh Review* for June 1816.

When Byron used the phrase "epic renegade" in 1818, there was nothing original about it; its significance had been created by the public disputes. When Byron attacked Southey, he was one among many who attacked Southey for exactly the same reasons. Byron must have known that *renegade* was the one word that would hurt Southey the most. Southey is an "epic renegade" in many senses. He is a renegade of epic proportions. At the same time, he is excessively proud of his epic poetry. He is an "epic renegade" in that his poetry has supported the position, as Leigh Hunt put it, of "King and No King." The earlier drafts of the Dedication call Southey both an "epic Convert" and a "loyal Convert."[61] Byron's revised phrase indicates that Southey is a political and moral renegade, who stakes his fame on his own epic poetry and his laureateship, solemnly assured that the fame of poets is grander than that of statesmen and monarchs. The first stanza of the Dedication argues that Southey is a nobody or no-thing because he is two contrary things. His is a "common case," not only in that both Wordsworth and Coleridge share the malady, but because his uncommon pride is common for a commoner who is not a member of the House of Commons, a person who is in place where he does not belong, where he represents nothing. To be somewhere is to be representative. Antithesis is stretched to the breaking point; Southey in Byron's apostrophe is, like Dryden's Zimri or Pope's Sporus, a "vile antithesis," an impossible object.

Contradictions multiply upon Southey's head. Byron begins the seventh stanza with an ironic allusion to Southey's pride: "Your bays may hide the baldness of your brows." The figure of Southey's baldness in the public press is long and complex. The radicals in "New Morality" wave their "cropp'd heads in sign of worship" of Lépeaux (*PAJ* 235). Leigh Hunt registered his astonishment at Southey's appointment as poet-laureate in the *Examiner* with the long sentence that ended with the "court-laurel" being "planted on the primitive head of Mr. Robert Southey." "The Laureate Laid Double" commented on his *caput mortuum*. Later, Hazlitt picked up the figure in his unforgiving review of Southey's *Letter to William Smith*: "He lays open his character to the scalping knife, guides the philosophic hand in its

---

[61] *BP* 5: 3; *Don Juan Variorum* (above, n. 18) 2: 9.

painful researches, and on the bald crown of our *petit tondu*, in vain con-
cealed under withered bay-leaves and a few contemptible gray hairs, you
see the organ of vanity triumphant—sleek, smooth, round, perfect, polished, horned, and shining, as it were in a transparency"(Howe 7: 187).
Hazlitt's description may owe something to Milton's "Animadversions upon
the Remonstrants Defense against Smectymnuus" where Milton proclaims,
"O what a death it is to the Prelates to be thus un-visarded, thus uncas'd, to
have the Periwigs pluk't off that cover your baldnesse, your inside naked-
nesse thrown open to publick view."[62]

Hazlitt's phrase *petit tondu* literally means the "little shaved one," or "the
shaveling." Coleridge's defense of Southey as the "stripling bard," and Hazlitt's criticism of the "*petit tondu*" combine to denude Southey's figure, to
make him a truly unaccommodated man, with no vestiges of his offices and
no public signs of his pride but withered bays on a bald head. The primary
figurative sense of "bald" in the eighteenth century was "bare or destitute
of meaning," "lacking in pregnant import," or "meagre, trivial, paltry," and
the later figurative sense of "explicit" or "nonrhetorical" became primary
later in the nineteenth century. Southey's poetry is "bald" not only in the
sense that it is literal and lacking in figurative power, but also in the sense
that it is virtually meaningless. "Le Petit Tondu," however, is Napoleon, a
challenging phrase to Byron who later would claim to be the "grand
Napoleon of the realms of rhyme" (11: 440). To complicate the portrait of
Southey by suggesting that he aspires to be the Napoleon of literature and
succeeds only in being a "petit tondu," only in baring the sign of a conqueror, is to see him as a fruitless contradiction, as a stripling who is not
only out of place but unnaturally out of season. In addition, *tondu* suggests
tonsure, a sign of priestly vows and authority, which itself may have been
suggested by Hunt's description of Southey's "primitive head." While *primitive* obviously means "rude" or "simple," it also alludes to the Primitive
Methodist Connexion, a group under Hugh Bourne that split from the
Methodists in 1810 to return to earlier practices. Southey's 1810 article in
the *Quarterly*, "On Evangelical Sects," established his connection with religious self-righteousness. Thus "baldness" exposes Southey's political and
religious aspirations as well as his vanity. The misprint of "boldness" for
"baldness" in the 1833 edition is a canny error.

Throughout his review, which extends over several issues of the *Examiner*, Hazlitt poses again and again the question, "Who is Southey?" and
contrasts him with political figures, who are representatives of their race.
Here the implicit comparison is between Napoleon, whom Hazlitt always
admired, and Southey, whom Hazlitt describes as "neither a commoner
nor peer of the realm" (Howe 7: 208) but a mere literary figure. Thus

---

[62] *The Works of John Milton*, Vol. III, Part 1, ed. Harry Morgan Ayres (New York: Columbia University Press, 1931) 112.

when Byron makes a personal reference to Southey's baldness, he is drawing on published and public criticism of Southey's ambition and vanity.
When he claims to envy neither Southey's "fruit nor boughs," he is con-
trasting his ironic praise with Hunt's reference to the "court-laurel" as a
"sapless and shapeless nonentity" and Hazlitt's reference to the "withered
bay-leaves."

MILTON AND MEDIATION

Although Byron politely admits that the Lake poets have their "fruits" and
"boughs," his comment upon the "baldness of your brows" applies to Coleridge and Wordsworth as well as Southey. While Southey and Coleridge,
commonly satirized together, were easy targets, the case of Wordsworth is
much more complicated. The first reference to him in the fourth stanza
is commonplace enough, but when Byron invokes Milton as the poet who
is faithful to his republican principles, he inevitably alludes to Wordsworth's
similar invocation of Milton in his sonnets of 1802. The fourth stanza on
Wordsworth comes almost word for word from the first few pages of Jeffrey's review of *The Excursion* in the *Edinburgh Review*. Jeffrey complained
that "it fairly fills four hundred and twenty good quarto pages," and Byron
remarks parenthetically, "I think the quarto holds five hundred pages." Jeffrey complained about Wordsworth's "peculiar system. His former poems
were intended to recommend that system, and to bespeak favour for it by
their individual merit;—but this, we suspect, must be recommended by the
system." Byron complains of "his new system." Jeffrey attributes the
strangeness of Wordsworth's system to "long habits of seclusion, and an excessive ambition of originality,"[63] and Byron similarly complains that
Southey's, Coleridge's, and Wordsworth's ambition comes "by dint of long
seclusion / From better company," the company in which Byron locates
himself. Here, as before, Byron's originality is not the issue. He agrees with
Jeffrey that literature is a social matter, and that solitude is inimical to literature. His words are Jeffrey's words; he quotes almost directly. There
would be no point in transforming Jeffrey's words or disguising his repetitions. These quotations depend on their being recognized as common opinion of the literary world, not on their being original, or eccentric, or sple-
netically personal. If Byron can claim his legitimate place, he must not speak
with a unique voice, or from personal motives. He speaks a public language;
he must assert his place and prove that Southey is out of place.

---

[63] *Edinburgh Review* (Nov. 1814) 1–3. The final paragraph of Wordsworth's Preface to *The
Excursion* referred to his system: "It is not the Author's intention formally to announce a system: it was more animating to him to proceed in a different course; and if he shall succeed in
conveying to the mind clear thoughts, lively images, and strong feelings, the Reader will have
no difficulty in extracting the system for himself" (*WP* 5: 2).

In stanza 10, Byron invokes Milton by quoting the beginning of Book VII of *Paradise Lost*:

> If fallen in evil days on evil tongues,
>   Milton appeal'd to the Avenger, Time,
> If Time, the avenger, execrates his wrongs,
>   And makes the word "*Miltonic*" mean "*sublime*,"
> *He* design'd not to belie his soul in songs,
>   Nor turn his very talent to a crime—
> *He* did not loathe the sire to laud the son,
> But closed the tyrant-hater he begun.
>
> Think'st thou, could he, the blind Old Man, arise
>   Like Samuel from the grave, to freeze once more
> The blood of monarchs with his prophecies,
>   Or be alive again—again all hoar
> With time and trials, and those helpless eyes
>   And heartless daughters, worn, and pale, and poor,
> Would *he* adore a sultan? *he* obey
> The intellectual eunuch Castlereagh?
>
> (73–88)

At the beginning of Book VII of *Paradise Lost*, Milton descends from heaven to earth to describe the creation, but the descent brings with it Milton's consciousness of his own dangerous position after the Restoration:

> More safe I Sing with mortal voice, unchang'd
> To hoarse or mute, though fall'n on evil days,
> On evil days though fall'n, and evil tongues;
> In darkness, and with dangers compast round,
> And solitude. . . .
>
> (*PL* VII, 24–28)

He prays to be delivered from that "barbarous dissonance," which might silence his poetic voice by its "savage clamor" (*PL* VII: 32, 36). Byron invokes the Milton who remains faithful to his political principles and defies those who have shifted their political allegiances, a Milton who is less concerned with heavenly matters than with earthly ones. Milton's prophetic sublime becomes Byron's political sublime. Book VII begins with a petition to Urania to descend to common earth:

> Up led by thee
> Into the Heav'n of Heav'ns I have presum'd,
> An Earthly Guest, and drawn Empyreal Air,
> Thy temp'ring; with like safety guided down
> Return me to my Native Element:

> Lest from this flying Steed unrein'd, (as once
> *Bellerophon*, though from a lower Clime)
> Dismounted, on th'*Aleian* Field I fall
> Erroneous there to wander and forlorn.
> Half yet remains unsung, but narrower bound
> Within the visible Diurnal Sphere;
> Standing on Earth, not rapt above the Pole. . . .
>
> (*PL* VII, 12–23)

Byron's Milton, "the blind Old Man," stands in sharp contrast to the Lake poets and particularly to "young Robert," the "stripling bard," who has forsaken his youthful republicanism. Byron's contrast between Southey and Milton is a stark admonishment to a poet who invokes Spenser as his master. Southey is representative of the race of place holders and poets laureate, not of prophetic outcasts. If the allusions to Milton are read in the context of a literary history that reads only its grand landmarks, the allusions to Milton are uncomplicated and direct. If, however, Byron's allusions to Milton are read in the context of the public discourse, the invocation of Milton becomes much more complicated because it is mediated. It may even be that no invocation of a great literary past can escape such mediation. After all, whose Milton is being invoked? In this instance it is both Leigh Hunt's and, ironically enough, Wordsworth's.

On February 18, 1816, just before Byron left England, Hunt published an article in the *Examiner* entitled "Heaven Made a Party to Earthly Disputes—Mr. Wordsworth's Sonnets on Waterloo," a criticism of poems originally printed in the *Champion* February 4: two sonnets now titled "Occasioned by the Battle of Waterloo" ("Intrepid Sons of Albion" and "The Bard, Whose Soul Is Meek") and the "Siege of Vienna Raised by John Sobieski" (*WP* 3: 149–50). Although Hunt admired Wordsworth's poetry, ranking him far above Southey and Scott, he deplored the Holy Alliance of kings and the unholy alliance between poets and monarchs. He did not, however, oppose the use of poetry for political subjects: "Poetry has often been made the direct vehicle of politics. . . . Milton, besides his political sonnets, took an opportunity in his *Paradise Lost* of insinuating some lessons to Kings, which it might not be amiss to recollect now-a-days." Hunt quoted Book I: "It is well known that the *Licenser* under King Charles the 2d hesitated at that noble simile about the eclipse which 'with fear of change / Perplexes Monarchs'" (*PL* I, 598–99), a citation that may have suggested Byron's invocation to Milton to return to "freeze once more / The blood of monarchs with his prophecies."

Wordsworth's second sonnet, "The Bard, Whose Soul Is Meek as Dawning Day," describes Waterloo as "this victory sublime," "which the blest angels, from their peaceful clime / Beholding, welcomed with a choral shout." Wordsworth assumes a prophetic detachment:

He whose experienc'd eye can pierce the array
Of past events,—to whom, in vision clear,
The aspiring heads of future things appear,
Like mountain-tops whence mists have roll'd away:
Assoiled from all encumbrance of our time. . . .

Wordsworth adds a note identifying Spenser as the origin of the word *assoiled*: "And, hanging up his arms and warlike spoil, / From all this world's encumbrance did himself assoil."[64] Hunt, who had placed Spenser in an Italian tradition to replace the Tory influence of Pope and the French school of poetry, protests "the enlistments of Heaven in earthly quarrels. It is something worse than begging the question, especially when we know all that the Allied Sovereigns have done in France, in Italy, Poland, Spain, &c &c." He similarly protests Wordsworth's portrait of the visionary poet who considers himself liberated from the historical moment: "For our parts, we certainly do not pretend to be 'meek as dawning day,' nor 'assoiled from all the time's encumbrance'; and so, it seems, we must not pretend to comprehend '*this* victory sublime.'" Hunt's complaint is not merely that Wordsworth invokes heaven to justify political acts, but that Wordsworth claims a Miltonic vision of heaven, aloof from politics, that enables him to ignore history. Wordsworth's sublimity rests on his heavenly vision of the angel's "choral shout."

Earlier in his career Wordsworth had passed "unalarmed" by the "choir / Of shouting angels" in "Home at Grasmere," used in the Preface to *The Excursion* (1814). Hunt was alert to the difference since he refers to Wordsworth's earlier praise of Milton, "whose tone of thinking, . . . comes out very singularly sometimes among these panegyrics on modern princes and the restoration of discarded dynasties. Mr. Wordsworth, we should think, must feel some strange qualms on that point, especially as in one of his sonnets he expressly said, that Milton ought to 'be living at that hour,' and that the times 'had need of him.'" Hunt concludes his article with a wish that Wordsworth's poetry forsake the heavenly sublime, removed from his times yet at the same time invoked as a justification for the restoration of monarchy, and return to the political sublime of the republican Milton: "We hope to see many more of Mr. Wordsworth's sonnets, but shall be glad to find them, like his best ones, less Miltonic in one respect, and much more so in another." When Byron defines the word *Miltonic* to mean "sublime," his context signifies the political sublime that Hunt defines in direct opposition to the sublimity of invoking heaven in earthly disputes, a sublime that is not an elevation but a descent, that is located in its historical moment, and that evokes its terror by both freezing "the blood of monarchs" and suf-

---

[64] *Faerie Queene* VI, v, 37 in *Poetical Works of Edmund Spenser*, ed. J. C. Smith and E. de Selincourt (Oxford: Oxford University Press, 1912).

fering the dangers of blind isolation. Byron's selection of the invocation from Book VII confirms the political sublime.

Of course, Hunt was correct to hear Miltonic echoes in these sonnets and to recall Wordsworth's earlier invocation of Milton in "Sonnets Dedicated to Liberty" published in *Poems in Two Volumes* (1807). David Erdman has remarked that those who have described Wordsworth's shift away from the principles of the French Revolution "have been inclined to overlook the evidence that it was the English Commonwealth writers—-Harrington, Milton, Sidney—who inspired the French as well as the British *in Paris* during the Revolution."[65] Wordsworth's "London 1802" invokes that tradition:

> Milton! thou should'st be living at this hour:
> England hath need of thee: she is a fen
> Of stagnant waters: altar, sword, and pen,
> Fireside, the heroic wealth of hall and bower,
> Have forfeited their ancient English dower
> Of inward happiness. We are selfish men;
> Oh! raise us up, return to us again;
> And give us manners, virtue, freedom, power.
> Thy soul was like a Star and dwelt apart:
> Thou hadst a voice whose sound was like the sea;
> Pure as the naked heavens, majestic, free,
> So didst thou travel on life's common way.
> In chearful godliness; and yet thy heart
> The lowliest duties on itself did lay.[66]

Byron speculates that if Milton could "arise / Like Samuel from the grave," he would not "adore a sultan," as Southey adores the Prince Regent and Castlereagh, would not be a runagate to Algiers. The prophetic Samuel arose to warn Saul that God had forsaken him because "thou obeyedst not the voice of the Lord, nor executedst his fierce wrath upon Amalek" (I Sam. 28: 18), but Samuel also warned against monarchy: "And ye shall cry out in that day because of your king which ye shall have chosen you; and the Lord will not hear you in that day. Nevertheless the people refused to obey the voice of Samuel; and they said, Nay; but we will have a king over us. (I Sam. 8: 18–19). Byron's invocation of Milton echoes Wordsworth's invocation: "return to us again." Wordsworth invokes Milton as both the celestial traveler and the poet of "life's common way," and his sonnet follows the descent described at the beginning of Book VII from heavenly poetry to earthly duties. Byron and Hunt are concerned less with the heavenly poet and more

[65] David V. Erdman, "Milton! Thou Shouldst Be Living," *The Wordsworth Circle* 19 (Winter 1988): 3. Erdman argues that Wordsworth was a Whig humanist.

[66] *'Poems in Two Volumes' and other Poems, 1800–1807*, ed. Jared Curtis (Ithaca: Cornell University Press, 1983) 165.

with the earthly poet. Byron's reference to the "pedestrian Muses" had as much do with his attempt to align himself with a Milton who has returned to earth than it does with questions of the genres of epic and satire. Byron rejects the "winged steed" of heavenly poetry, not because it aspires to divine vision and lapses into unintelligibility, but because Byron's "winged Steed" is Milton's "flying steed."

In his sonnets on Waterloo, Wordsworth had invoked prophetic heavenly vision to justify the restoration of monarchy. Byron's pedestrian muse is not simply the *musa pedestris*, the muse of instruction, but the muse who rejects the politics of paradise, the muse who leads Milton and Byron in political opposition that intends to disrupt legitimacy and established order by the elevating energy of a descent to earthly conflicts. For Hunt and Byron the pedestrian is the sublime. Categories are switched. The word *Miltonic*, which Byron equates with sublimity, is precisely the sublimity of political engagement, the designation of Byron's own public signature, which bears the traces of both Hunt and Wordsworth. Byron's purpose is to replace Southey as the first poet of the age by telling him to get off his high horse.

Jerome McGann has argued that the style of the Dedication is modeled on Horace and Juvenal and that "the 'Dedication' is as republican in its literary theory as it is in its politics, and sets forth one of *Don Juan*'s most important ideas: that the more one tries to 'soar' beyond the actual variety and experience of the world into coherent mentalistic ranges, the lower one falls, the narrower and more restricted one becomes." But the style and politics of the Dedication cannot be completely explained by reference to the classics, and the rejection of sublimity is less of a choice of an empirical (or material) and social reality over visionary intoxication than a redefinition of the political sublime on Miltonic terms as Hunt defined them. Elsewhere McGann observes that "*Don Juan* . . . is an impeccable rendering of aristocratic conversational idiom," and citing prose from Byron's letters, he states that "this is also a prose which finds its poetical equivalent in the *musa pedestris* of *Don Juan*."[67] It is difficult to ignore the aristocratic idiom of Byron's style in *Don Juan* and the appeal that it had for the circle at Murray's, and at the same time it is difficult to ignore the sublimities of his pedestrian muse.

By alluding to the public discourse, Byron ridicules Southey by alluding to previous attacks upon him, which portray the youthful Southey as the "stripling bard," as the worshiper of his own miniature portrait taken at two

---

[67] Don Juan *in Context* (above, n. 4) 110–11; "The *Biographia Literaria* and the Contentions of English Romanticism," *Coleridge's Biographia Literaria: Text and Meaning*, ed. Frederick Burwick (Columbus, Ohio: Ohio State University Press, 1989) 253. For an account of Byron as a Whig in politics, see Malcolm Kelsall, *Byron's Politics* (Sussex: Harvester Press, 1987), and for an account of Byron as "The Poet of the Revolution," see Michael Foot, *The Politics of Paradise: A Vindication of Byron* (London: Collins, 1988).

years of age, and as poet whose egotism is unbounded, but when he invokes Milton as a prophetic Samuel, he invokes Wordsworth's similar invocation. Although Wordsworth in 1816 praises alliances that Byron thought unholy, the Wordsworth of 1802 is not the object of ridicule that the Southey of 1797 is. Byron's invocation of Milton intends to banish Southey, but the early republican Wordsworth is not as easily dismissed. His voice remains present, and Byron's is an echo of Wordsworth's.

Byron's assertion that Milton would not "adore a sultan," would not "obey / The intellectual eunuch Castlereagh" completes the figure of Southey's apostasy, his migration, and places Southey as a Moor adoring a sultan. Byron invokes Wordsworth's Milton to shame Castlereagh's impotence as well as Southey's apostasy. Byron questions not only the quality of Castlereagh's mind, but also his masculinity, a particularly sensitive issue considering his later suicide. Castlereagh's reputation as a poor speaker and a childless man was openly discussed, not something whispered in private. Early in the morning of January 23, 1799, in a heated debate in the Irish Parliament over Union with England, William Plunket followed Castlereagh's speech supporting Union with a bitter denunciation of the proposed Union and of Castlereagh personally:

> The example of the Prime Minister of England [Pitt] inimitable in its vices may have deceived the noble lord. The Minister of England has many faults. He abandoned in his later years the principle of reform by professing which he had attained the early confidence of the people of England, and in the whole of his political conduct he has shown himself haughty and untractable. But it must be admitted that he is endowed by nature with a towering and transcendent intellect, and that the vastness of his resources keeps pace with the magnificence and unboundedness of his projects. I thank God that it is much more easy for the noble lord to transfer the minister's apostasy and his insolence than his comprehension and his sagacity; and I feel the safety of my country in the wretched feebleness of her enemy. *I cannot fear that the Constitution which has been founded by the wisdom of sages and cemented by the blood of patriots and heroes is to be smitten by such a green and sapless twig as this.*

As M. H. Hyde points out, Lady Castlereagh's "childlessness had frequently been a subject for gossip."[68] While Plunket compares Pitt's apostasy with Castlereagh's, he contrasts Pitt's genius with Castlereagh's mental weakness and implies that Castlereagh is precisely what Byron called him, "an intellectual eunuch." In the words of the Dedication, Castlereagh

---

[68] M. H. Hyde, *The Rise of Castlereagh* (London: Macmillan, 1933) 298. Plunket's speech may be found in *The Life, Letters and Speeches of Lord Plunket*, ed. The Hon. David Plunket (London, 1867). For details on Castlereagh's suicide, see Louis Crompton, *Byron and Greek Love: Homophobia in Nineteenth-Century England* (Berkeley: University of California Press, 1985) 301–11. Byron mentioned Castlereagh's childlessness in 1813 (*BP* 3: 90).

has "just enough of talent, and no more." The word *eunuch* has a secondary meaning as an officer of a state, as Byron's association of Castlereagh with Eutropius suggests. Gibbon explains that during the reign of Arcadius,

> Eutropius, one of the principle eunuchs of the palace of Constantinople, succeeded the haughty minister whose ruin he had accomplished, and whose vices he soon imitated. Every order of the state bowed to the new favourite; and their tame and obsequious submission encouraged him to insult the laws, and, what is still more difficult and dangerous, the manners, of his country. . . . Eutropius was the first of his artificial sex, who dared assume the character of a Roman magistrate and general.[69]

Behind Byron's phrase is Plunket's figure of the "green and sapless twig" and Leigh Hunt's phrase on the laureateship as a "sapless and shapeless nonentity." If Southey had actually seen a copy of the original Dedication that included the Castlereagh stanzas, he would have seen that Byron was making more comparisons between him and Castlereagh than the accidental fact that they were "the two Roberts." In Byron's eyes both were apostates, vain, ambitious, and weak-minded. Southey was figuratively as fruitless as Castlereagh was literally fruitless. The "dry Bob" joke applied to both.

The debates in the Irish Parliament were not the only public location of Castlereagh criticism which Byron would have known. When Leigh Hunt was in prison, Thomas Barnes began a series of parliamentary profiles in the *Examiner*. His article on Castlereagh on August 29, 1813 verifies Byron's lines on Castlereagh's oratory:

> An orator of such set trash of phrase
>   Ineffably, legitimately vile,
> That even its grossest flatterers dare not praise,
>   Nor foes—all nations—condescend to smile:
> Not even a *sprightly* blunder's spark can blaze
>   From that Ixion grindstone's ceaseless toil,
> That turns and turns, to give the world a notion
> Of endless torments, and perpetual motion.
>
> (97–104)

Castlereagh's "ideas are few and puny, but his words, the symbols or phantoms of his ideas, are extended to a supernatural expansion, so that the signifier and the thing signified bear the same proportion which one sometimes observes between a small heavy stone and its alarming shadow, elongated to the distance of many a rood." For Barnes, even Castlereagh's in-

---

[69] Edward Gibbon, *The History of the Decline and Fall of the Roman Empire*, ed. David Womersley (London: Penguin, 1994) 2: 239.

tellectual life is without energy: "One puerile affectation may be forgiven
him, because it seems to arouse all his energies, and really stirs him into a
sort of warmth: a military subject is to him what Galvanism is to a dead frog:
he jumps about with symptoms of life, which might deceive a common observer, till on looking for the animating soul, you find that all these exertions were merely accidental." The "trash" of Castlereagh's public oratory
is neither a violent vulgarity nor a handbook of platitudes. His speeches lack
wit and understanding and, as Barnes points out and Byron emphasizes, his
oratory is labored and disconnected. His lack of literary and oratorical skill
made him a common butt of jokes and placed him with Southey outside the
boundaries of Regency wit and intelligence, out of place.

In ridiculing Castlereagh, Byron repeats the common opinion and common gossip of his day. His opinions on Castlereagh were well formed before he left England. Byron does not raise new issues because he does not
need to raise them. Castlereagh was publicly accused of being both a eunuch and an "intellectual eunuch." Such were the implications of William
Plunket's attack on him in the Irish Parliament in 1799. Such sensational
accusations are not easily forgotten. Byron knew Plunket as early as 1813
when he heard Plunket in the House of Commons deliver "the best speech
I ever heard" (*BLJ* 3: 22). If Byron did not get information on Castlereagh
directly from Plunket, one can safely assume, I think, that the report of
Plunket's speech would have reached Byron through Thomas Moore, who
was at school in Dublin when Plunket spoke. In 1828 he reminisced with a
supporter of Castlegreagh "about the events of 98 in Ireland, when . . . I
was a young sucking Rebel at college."[70] Moore was friendly with Robert
Emmet and opposed to Castlereagh in 1798. Although one would not expect him to have deep sympathy with Plunket, who proved his nationalism
by citing his part in the suppression of the 1798 rebellion, Moore may have
known and remembered Plunket's attack on Castlereagh.

RECEPTION AT MURRAY'S

Although the reviews of *Don Juan* were predictable, the poem elicited from
some readers exactly the response that Byron intended by his choice of
style, his attacks on Southey as "representative of all the race," and his
"claim to praise" in the final stanza of canto I. On January 5, 1819, Hobhouse wrote Byron to persuade him not to publish the poem. The circle at
Murray's realized that the references to Byron's failed marriage, the personal attack on Castlereagh, and the parody of the Ten Commandments
were offensive, but they were personally much less offended by the moral
tone. They recommended that the work be suppressed primarily because it

---

[70] *Journal of Thomas Moore* (above, n. 41) 3: 1161.

would offend the general public, not the readers at Murray's.[71] Even considering that a recommendation not to publish would have to be handled with extreme tact, Hobhouse's letter repeats, again and again, the judgment at Murray's that Byron is the first poet of the age, thus granting Byron a literary legitimacy. Hobhouse first read the manuscript in company with Scrope Davies. They both admired "the genius, wit, poetry, satire, and so forth, which made us both also at the same time declare that you were as superior in the burlesque as in the heroic to all competitors and even perhaps had found your real forte in this singular style." Hobhouse also consulted John Hookham Frere, who "is one of your warmest admirers and the greatest part of his arguments were drawn from the admitted acknowledgment that you had and deserved to have by far the greatest reputation of any poet of the day." Byron's parody of the Ten Commandments, Hobhouse thought, was "indefensible even by the first poet of the age." The argument against publishing a satire on Southey, Wordsworth, and Coleridge was, in Frere's words, that "Lord Byron is too great a man to descend into the arena against such wretched antagonists and however clever the satire may be the world will recollect that he has suppressed one Satire and will say that he may suppress this also at some future day." Hobhouse added that "neither Southey, Wordsworth nor Coleridge have any character except with their own crazy proselytes some fifty perhaps in number: so what harm can you do them and what good can you do the world by your criticism?"[72]

Lockhart echoed the opinions at Murray's. In 1821 he published anonymously *A Letter to the Right Hon. Lord Byron by John Bull* in which he advised Byron to quit his romantic poetry as so much humbug, but to continue in the style of *Don Juan*. He divided the literary kingdom between Sir Walter Scott, the baronet, and Byron, the baron:

> Scotland, therefore, is and will remain Sir Walter's. And what, you will say, is mine? I will tell you, Lord Byron: England is yours, if you choose to make it so.—I do not speak of the England of days past, or of the England of days to come, but of the England of the day that now is, with which, if you be not contented, you are about as difficult to please as a Buonaparte. There is nobody but yourself who has any chance of conveying to posterity a true idea of the *spirit* of England in the days of his Majesty George IV. Mr. Wordsworth may

---

[71] Leslie Marchand remarked that "it was the feeling of Byron's friends that he had been out of England so long that he was unaware of the growing moral temper of the bulk of the reading public, a development that was in part a general reaction to the profligacy of the court under the Regent and the moral laxness of the upper classes that Byron had chiefly known during his years of fame in London" (2: 765). E.D.H. Johnson remarks that Byron's readers at Murray's were "too worldly themselves to object to the freedom of tone" in *Don Juan* ("*Don Juan* in England," *English Literary History*, 11 [1944]: 151).

[72] *Byron's Bulldog* (above, n. 10) 256–60. Byron suppressed "English Bards and Scotch Reviewers."

write fifty years about his "dalesmen"; if he paints them truly it is very well; if untruly, it is no matter: but you know what neither Mr. Wordsworth nor any Cumberland stamp-master ever can know. You know the society of England,—you know what English gentlemen are made of, and you know very well what English ladies are made of; and, I promise you, that *knowledge* is a much more precious thing, whatever you at present may think or say.

Lockhart echoes the opinions that Byron held of Southey, Coleridge, and Wordsworth as early as 1814:

> They know nothing of the world; and what is poetry, but the reflection of the world? . . . Look at their beastly vulgarity, when they wish to be homely; and their exquisite stuff, when they clap on sail, and aim at fancy. Coleridge is the best of the trio—but bad is the best. Southey should have been a parish-clerk, and Wordsworth a man-midwife—both in darkness. I doubt if either of them ever got drunk, and I am of the old creed of Homer the wine-bibber. (*BLJ* 4: 85)

Byron was obviously pleased with the *A Letter to . . . Lord Byron*: "it is diabolically *well* written—& full of fun and ferocity.—I must forgive the dog whoever he is" (*BLJ* 8: 145).

For Lockhart, England is London and London is St. James's, the world of Lockhart's English gentlemen and ladies, "for as to the London east of Temple Bar, God knows there are enough of rhymesters, and prosers too . . . for no gentleman ought to know more of the polite Cockneys than may be learnt from reading one number of the Examiner."[73] Lockhart's letter is as bold in its admiration for *Don Juan*, when it was reviled elsewhere, as it is hopeful in its attempt to reclaim Byron from the influence of the *Examiner* and the Cockneys, whom Lockhart had been ridiculing in *Blackwood's* since 1817. Lockhart reports that *Don Juan* was received with great pleasure at Murray's. "Old Gifford's brow relaxed as he gloated over it; Mr. Croker chuckled; Dr. Whitaker smirked; Mr. Milman sighed; Mr. Coleridge (I mean not the madman, but the madman's idiot nephew) took it to his bed with him. The whole band of the Quarterly were delighted" (82–83). Cockneys and dalesmen were simply of no interest; they were not England, nor, Lockhart implies, did they occupy any place within the English society. For Lockhart they did not constitute a significant public. He locates Byron as the first poet of English society; for him Byron is in his natural place and has his public.

J. W. Croker agreed with the liberal Hobhouse and the conservative Lockhart on Byron's place in society and in the contemporary hierarchy of poets: "I have acquaintance none, or next to none, with him, and of course no interest beyond what we must all take in a poet who, on the whole, is the

---

[73] *John Bull's Letter to Lord Byron*, ed. Alan Lang Strout (Norman, Oklahoma: University of Oklahoma Press, 1947) 95–96.

one of the first, if not the very first, of our age." Having read cantos three and four, he found little offensive in *Don Juan* except an occasional phrase, but like Lockhart, he wished to move Byron away from political extremes. He encouraged Murray to persuade Byron to revise "some phrases in his poem which in reality disparage it more than its imputed looseness of principle; I mean some expressions of political and personal feelings which, I believe, he, in fact, never felt, and threw in wantonly and *de gaieté de coeur*, and which he would have omitted, advisedly and *de bonté de coeur*, if he had not been goaded by indiscreet, contradictory, and urgent *criticisms*, which in some cases, were dark enough to be called *calumnies*."[74] Croker seriously misjudged Byron's hatred of Southey and Castlereagh, which Byron expressed in private letters and conversations, but Croker's concern is to remove the attacks on his political allies. Otherwise Byron's style, inoffensive to the readers at Murray's, places him as the first poet of the age.

The language of polite life, the language of Regency society, does not depend totally on class or political affiliation. Leigh Hunt explained in his *Autobiography* that the *Examiner* "was named after the *Examiner* of Swift and his brother Tories. I did not think of their politics. I thought only of their wit and fine writing, which, in my youthful confidence, I proposed to myself to emulate; and I could find no previous political journal equally qualified to be its godfather."[75] Hunt also borrowed from the *Anti-Jacobin* for his parodies of Southey, an allusive strategy that provided him with both a satirical style and a not-so-subtle reminder that Southey's current political friends were those who abused him in 1797 and 1798, Canning and Frere. While Byron takes the majority, but by no means all, of his parody from the radical and Whig opposition press, the readers who class him as the first poet in the age are supporters of the Tory government, particularly Croker, Lockhart, and Frere. Byron's immediate audience and public convenes at Murray's, the Houses of Parliament, and the great and little houses of England. It is circumscribed by the traces of the private circulation that includes Southey at its periphery. Southey is in place, finally, because he is addressed, but he is also out of place by being so addressed.

Canning and Frere were, of course, the principle authors of parodies of the *Anti-Jacobin* and, for many, the models of political poets in the tradition of Pope and Swift since the late 1790s, a fact that William Hone was quick to point out during his first trial for blasphemy on December 18, 1817.[76]

---

[74] *Murray Memoirs* (above, n. 13) 1: 414–5.

[75] *The Autobiography of Leigh Hunt*, ed. J. E. Morpurgo (London: Cresset, 1949) 173.

[76] See Wood for Hone's use of the conventions of religious literature, advertising, and newspapers for satire and parody. See also Frederick William Hackwood, *William Hone: His Life and Times* (New York: Augustus M. Kelley, 1912) 154–73. Olivia Smith discusses the Hone trials as Tests of the distinction between elegant English and "vulgarity" (*The Politics of Language* [Oxford: Clarendon Press, 1984] 154–201).

For Hone, the source and authority for his parodies were the parodies of the *Anti-Jacobin*. Hone was tried before Mr. Justice Abbott for publishing "The Late John Wilkes's Catechism of a Ministerial Member," which was "to be learned by every person before he be brought to be confirmed a Placeman" and listed as its first article: "I believe in George, the Regent Almighty, Maker of New Streets, and Knights of the Bath." Hone conducted his own defense by reading great works of literature containing parodies of religious writing, including Martin Luther's parodies of psalms, and many others. Hone "alluded to the celebrated parody of Mr. Canning—yes, of Mr. Canning, who ought, at that moment, to be standing in his place, but who had been raised to the rank of a Cabinet Minister." Hone's use of "New Morality" in his defense illustrates the primacy of location in cultural criticism. In the hands of the ministerial party, "New Morality" is an attack on the Jacobins; in Hone's hands, the poem is an attack on the legitimacy of the ministerial party. Hone held aloft a copy of *The Poetry of the Anti-Jacobin*, published, as he argued, with financial support from Pitt, Canning, and other ministers, and read selections from "New Morality," which parodied scripture.[77] One selection parodied Psalm 148:

> Pr—tl—y and W—f—ld, humble holy men,
> Give praises to his name with tongue and pen!
>
> Th—lw—l, and ye that lecture as ye go,
> And for your pains get pelted, praise Lepaux!
>
> Praise him each Jacobin, or fool, or knave,
> And your cropp'd heads in sign of worship wave!
>
> All creeping creatures, venomous and low,
> Paine, W-ll-ms, G-dw-n, H-lcr-ft, praise Lepaux!

Hone also read sections of "New Morality" that parodied Genesis (I: 21):

> ———— and ———— with ———— join'd.
> And every other beast after his kind.

> (*PAJ* 235–36)

Hone was acquitted amidst much laughter, and his defense illustrates the significant point that while parody was used by radical writers from the mid 1790s, it was also the primary mode of the Tory satirists who resided at the center of political power. To parody scripture, or any other writing, for that matter, was not necessarily a sign of radicalism; it was also a sign of authority, a matter that William Hone raised by publishing *Don John, or Don Juan Unmasked*, which attacks John Murray for publishing "a Parody on the Ten Commandments of God, whilst this prosecution is pending . . . for Par-

---

[77] *The First Trial of William Hone* (1818) 7, 32.

ody on the Litany, which is an entirely human composition. . . . Why did
not Mr. Murray suppress Lord Byron's Parody on the Ten Commandments? . . . Because it contains nothing in ridicule of Ministers, and therefore nothing that they could suppose would be to the displeasure of
Almighty God?"[78] The difference, as Godwin and Burke could have anticipated, was that the government feared dissemination of seditious writing
to the general public far more than it feared the writing itself. If parody of
scripture supported established power, it was permitted. Byron's style in
Don Juan cannot be assigned a simple ideological position in the public discourse. It is irreverent and oppositional, yet at the same time it was the style
used by the Tory satirists and admired by the *Quarterly* circle at Murray's.
Byron's style cannot be described in Bakhtinian terms because there is no
simple opposition between an authoritative monologic voice issuing from
St. James's and another dialogic and parodic voice coming from the public
square.

The allusiveness of Byron's style in the Dedication is astonishingly complex. Hobhouse, Croker, Frere, and Lockhart agreed that it made Byron
the first poet of the age, the poet who knew more about English society than
any other poet, the society that constituted for Lockhart and the others
their public sphere. Within their compass the public sphere existed, yet
Byron regularly transgressed its boundaries. Style made Byron the first poet
of the age and made Southey a ridiculous figure, out of place, except, as
Hobhouse explained, with his "own crazy proselytes some fifty perhaps in
number." Yet while Lockhart and Croker correctly perceived Byron's politics becoming more radical, his style, as defined by its use in the public discourse, remained the language of those with power. The language of Regency society, of polite life, determines the allusive significance of style and
legitimates Byron's claims for priority and place.

The contemporary locations of satire are much more important in determining its social and ideological implications than genre theory, literary
history, or the dialogic nature of its verbal play. The hierarchy of genres implies that satire is merely a pedestrian style, but by taking at once the low
road of raillery and the high road of the political sublime Byron claims the
highest class of poetic and social standing. The style of *Don Juan* is best explained, not with reference to its origins in Pope or Dryden, but with reference to the public press and private conversations of Byron's day. The
satirical implications of allusion and quotation are quite lost if Byron is read
in the exclusively literary context, instead of the political context of Hunt,
Hazlitt, Jeffrey, Wilson, Steevens, Barnes, Plunket, and others. *Don Juan* is
discursive in that it speaks directly to specific works and words of the day.

[78] Wilfred S. Dowden, "A Jacobin Journal's View of Lord Byron," *Studies in Philology* 48
(1951): 58.

The significant context is a contest for authority and literary legitimacy. While *Don Juan* alludes to Milton, or Pope, or Dryden, it does not speak to them. Although it may invoke them, it does not challenge them or their authority, even though allusions to them, or to the classics, are wedged in between smutty schoolboy double entendres and nursery rhymes.

Chapter Six

KEATS'S "LEAF-FRINGED LEGEND"

IN SEPTEMBER 1820 *Blackwood's* published an anonymous satirical poem by John Gibson Lockhart and William Maginn,[1] called "The Building of the Palace of the Lamp," subtitled "Or, as it might be rendered, of the Illuminati," a secret society in Germany blamed in several multivolume books in the 1790s for conspiring to begin the French Revolution. Genii are building the palace, and two of them report in dactylics, the meter of some of Southey's early radical verse and an echo of Hunt's languid meter in *Rimini*:

> We, in the shape of reviewers went rooting,
> And here have brought up, from the modern Parnassus,
> The principal flowers of its principal asses;
> False figures, false tropes, false language, false reason,
> True venom, true blasphemy, very true treason,
> Mixed with true affectation, true *mimini pimini*,
> In fact, what you find in Endymion and Rimini.
>
> (676)

Lockhart's poem lacks the wit of the earlier *Anti-Jacobin* satirists and displays the fierce prejudice that the writers in *Blackwood's* mistook for spirited playfulness, but its criticisms are not idle, and its denunciations are prompted by more than their mean spirit. Each phrase of the poem has its precise significance in what Lockhart saw as subversive tendencies in literature. His accusations cannot be dismissed as thoughtless railing. In the terms of Addison's essay on true and false wit,[2] the figures of Cockney poetry are false because they are constructed on the resemblance of words and not ideas. Modern poetry is void of thought, counterfeits truth, and represents nothing; its language is merely self-generating and self-contained, and its rhetoric violates established decorum. Modern poetry is treasonous and blasphemous because its esthetics unapologetically oppose established religion and morals, its figures are false, and its classical subject matter is associated with Jacobinism, paganism, and sensuality. When Keats published

---

[1] A. L. Strout, *A Bibliography of Articles in Blackwood's 1817–25* (Lubbock: Library of Texas Technical College, 1959) 71.

[2] May 11, 1711. *The Spectator*, ed. Donald F. Bond (Oxford: Clarendon Press, 1965) 1: 263–70.

"On a Grecian Urn," its title in the *Annals of the Fine Arts* in 1819, Grecian subjects were highly suspect because in the public press Greek myths and art were linked with atheism, skepticism, and liberty.[3] With some exasperation Lockhart asks in "Mr. Wastle's Diary," in the same number of *Blackwood's*, "What in the name of wonder tempts all these fellows to write on *Greek* fables?" (665).

Keats and his critics in the late twentieth century have bequeathed to us an "Ode on a Grecian Urn" that is no more political than Tillyard's or Woodring's "Ancient Mariner." Keats's poem does not contain one word of politics. Perhaps more than Coleridge's and Wordsworth's lyrics, it has been the archetypal Romantic lyric for our age and has become a model for an esthetic that claims autonomy for literature. Cleanth Brooks described it as "history without footnotes," and with few exceptions critics have accepted such judgments. Autonomy, however, has its costs by implying a rhetoric that must be read within its esthetic borders. The bound autonomy of allegory or symbol in "Ode on a Grecian Urn" cannot articulate a social vision or location, but in the public discourse literary language alludes to that discourse. Poetry's figures frequently cross the local borders of its paratext. The bound autonomous poem in the late twentieth century cannot hear its allusive echoes and cannot know itself or its historical origin. To hear the poem's allusive richness, one must read the public discourse.

In the context of the disputes over taste at the end of the eighteenth century and in the heat of the debates over the merits and value of the Elgin Marbles, Keats's "On a Grecian Urn," in the *Annals of the Fine Arts*, occupies a location within a radical movement that rejects the ideals and esthetics of the Royal Academy, a pillar of established order and what Hazlitt called legitimacy. Although often disagreeing among themselves and arguing for widely diverse causes, many voices constructed a public discourse on Greek art that questioned the notion of an ideal art. An advocate of Greek art, Richard Payne Knight was highly skeptical of art's ability to represent Platonic ideals and the immutable truths of Christianity. William Hazlitt, Benjamin Robert Haydon, and many other practicing artists challenged Sir Joshua Reynolds's ideal of art by championing the Elgin Marbles, a more concrete and empirical imitation of nature, a more accurate representation of the human body, and not an abstract ideal. The *Annals of the Fine Arts* was playfully, and at times belligerently, anti-idealistic. As read by many of

---

[3] See Marilyn Butler's chapter "The Cult of the South," *Romantics, Rebels, and Reactionaries: English Literature and Its Background, 1760–1830* (Oxford: Oxford University Press, 1981) 113–37. Robert M. Ryan traces the influence of Hunt's skepticism and Bailey's religion on Keats (*Keats: The Religious Sense* [Princeton: Princeton University Press, 1976]). Ronald A. Sharp argues that Keats's views were largely skeptical (*Keats, Skepticism, and the Religion of Beauty* [Athens: University of Georgia Press, 1979]). For the political implications of Keats's interests in Greek mythology, see Ryan's "The Politics of Greek Religion," *Critical Essays on John Keats*, ed. Hermionie de Almeida (Boston: G. K. Hall, 1990) 261–79.

its contemporary reviewers, Keats's poetry expresses nothing beyond its own esthetic construction; it has no referential value, represents only itself, and defies reference to an ideology outside itself. The paradox of the poem's claim for autonomy in 1820 is that standing apart from politics defies a conservative social order that condemns its esthetics and demands a political, specifically nationalistic significance to literature based on a system of patronage. The anti-idealistic esthetics of sensation in the *Annals* was read by opponents as nonsense. An irony of literary history is that Keats's first critics were not those of the left who accused him of escaping from social consciousness but conservatives who found his esthetics subversive. Criticism since Keats's day has appropriated his poem for an ideology opposite that of the *Annals of the Fine Arts*, for an esthetics more Coleridgean than radical, more ideal than empirical.[4] The practice of reading the urn as an idealized object persists in the late twentieth century among both Keats's defenders and his critics, who wish to preserve its idealism for a critique that finds its esthetics full of contradictions.[5] The strange fate of the "Ode on a Grecian Urn" is to have become an idealized object, when its original context strongly denied the existence of that ideal. In the *Annals* the poem rejects an idealism that would appropriate empirical reality for service to a class flattered by Sir Joshua Reynolds's portraits.

In my mapping of that location, I will be reading not simply the poem, nor the poem as a reflection of Keats's consciousness, but the public sites of its presentation, several significant contributors to the dialogue of art criticism, and the local resonances of their language, all of which give Keats's poem a discursive significance. Contradictory as it may seem, a reading of Keats's esthetics must take place at the level of contextualization, not of the isolated work.[6] Otherwise, the art object itself becomes a mirror of a criti-

---

[4] See Terry Eagleton's *The Ideology of the Aesthetic* (Oxford: Blackwell, 1990): "After the work of Blake and Shelley, myth and symbol in English literature becomes increasingly a preserve of the political right" (61). Eagleton contrasts the ideological opposition between the esthetic, the affective, and the physical body and the cognitive, the rational, and the theoretical.

[5] See for examples Jerome McGann's influential essay "Keats and the Historical Method in Literary Criticism," *Modern Language Notes* 94 (1979): 988–1032, reprinted in *The Beauty of Inflections* (Oxford: Clarendon Press, 1985) 17–65: Keats's urn presents "both a real concrete object" and "an ideal," the "perfect and complete embodiment of a perfect and complete idea of The Beautiful" (44); and Nancy M. Goslee, "Phidian Lore: Sculpture and Personification in Keats's Odes": "from Winckelmann through Reynolds to Flaxman, the ideal and abstract qualities of classical sculpture make this art appropriate for the illustration of concepts thought to be universal and permanent." (*SIR* 21 [1982]: 75–76).

[6] Paul Hamilton's "Keats and Critique," *Rethinking Historicism*, ed. Marjorie Levinson et al. (Oxford: Blackwell, 1989) is an example of the complex contextualization of esthetics in Keats's day and economics in ours. He reads the contradiction in Keats's esthetics: "Art educates us in wanting to realize the fulfilled humanity we can experience only esthetically, without being inhibited by the need to observe the autonomy of art, which enabled us to intuit such emancipation in the first place" (113).

cal sensibility already shaped by its own exclusionary practices. A final purpose of such a reading here, as elsewhere in this book, is to map a sharp contrast between a located historical reading that illuminates the centers of public Romanticism and the received readings that we have inherited in the late twentieth century, a contrast that teaches us how we read literature and culture.

The urn in itself is an object of simple outline, an "Attic shape" and "fair attitude," but it is framed with a series of paratexts, the most extended of which is the discourse that it enters in the *Annals of the Fine Arts*. That location frames a paratext in the poem, the ghostly legend that "haunts about thy shape," not clearly either on or merely near the "Attic shape" but hovering uncertainly between inscription and mythical legend of interpretation. In turn, the legend frames the utterance of the urn that "Beauty is Truth, Truth Beauty—that is all / Ye know on Earth and all ye need to know,"[7] which in turn reads the "Attic shape" with the figures worked upon it. The importance of one of the frames is that it determines the significance of the others at the same time that it forms the cultural crossroads from poem to public discourse. In contrast to *Don Juan*, in which the Dedication stands as a paratextual threshold to a long poem that ends only with the death of the author, Keats's "On a Grecian Urn" is almost all paratext, all entrances that are also exits. Rather than begin with the paratextual inscriptions and legends that haunt the urn, I begin with the larger paratext of the discourse on literature, art, and esthetics that the poem's location in the *Annals of the Fine Art* implies and then turn to a reading of the public location in the *Annals* and the poem itself. Keats is Romanticism's most intense paratextual reader.

KEATS'S STYLE AND "LEGITIMATE ORIGINALITY"

Perhaps prompted by Leigh Hunt's article on the new poets, Keats, Shelley, and John Hamilton Reynolds, in the *Examiner* on December 1, 1816, *Blackwood's* began its attacks on the *Examiner* writers in October 1817. Lockhart, writing under the pseudonym of Z, began a series of reviews on what he called the Cockney School of poetry. Lockhart's primary target was Leigh Hunt and the incest in the *Story of Rimini*, but he included Keats as well as Haydon and Hazlitt.[8] In the first article Lockhart wrote that "all the great poets of our country have been men of some rank in society, and there is no vulgarity in any of their writings." Lockhart remarks that "the two great elements of all dignified poetry, religious feeling, and patriotic feel-

---

[7] I quote "On a Grecian Urn" from *AFA* 4: 638–39.

[8] The first essay "On the Cockney School of Poetry" was published in Oct. 1817; other essays appeared in Nov. 1817, July 1818, Aug. 1818 (a review of Keats's poetry), April 1819, and Oct. 1819. Letters from Z to Leigh Hunt appeared in Jan. 1818 and May 1818.

ing, have no place in his writings." He reads Hunt's poetry as unbounded pretension and bad taste, which transparently reveals its own commonness:

> One feels the same disgust at the idea of opening Rimini, that impresses itself on the mind of a man of fashion, when he is invited to enter, for a second time, the gilded drawing room of a little mincing boarding-school mistress, who would fain have an *At Home* in her house. Every thing is pretence, affectation, finery, and gaudiness. The beaux are attorneys' apprentices, with chapeau bras and Limerick gloves—fiddlers, harp-teachers, and clerks of genius: the belles are faded fan-twinkling spinsters, prurient vulgar misses from school, and enormous citizens' wives.

In January 1818 after the second essay on the Cockney poets, Lockhart responded to Hunt's challenges in the *Examiner* with a "Letter from Z to Mr. Leigh Hunt," which indicted Hunt on eight counts:[9]

> 1. The want and the pretence of scholarship; 2. A vulgar style in writing; 3. A want of respect for the Christian religion; 4. A contempt for kingly power, and an indecent mode of attacking the government of your country; 5. Extravagant admiration of yourself, the Round Table, and your own poems; 6. Affectation; 7. A partiality for indecent subjects, and an immoral manner of writing concerning the crime of incest, in your poem of Rimini; 8. I have asserted that you are a poet vastly inferior to Wordsworth, Byron, and Moore!

The serious indictments are, of course, atheism, immorality, and sedition, but they are joined to matters of taste, education, vulgarity, affectation, pretension, and extravagance. Offences against taste are involved with those against government. In the first article on the Cockney Poets, Lockhart attacks Hunt's pretensions in appropriating classical subjects: "He is a man of little education. He knows absolutely nothing of Greek," and "almost nothing of Latin." The fourth reviews Keats's poetry and accuses him of the same ignorance:

> His Endymion is not a Greek shepherd, loved by a Grecian goddess; he is merely a young Cockney rhymester, dreaming a phantastic dream at the full of the moon. Costume, were it worth while to notice such a trifle, is violated in every page of this goodly octavo. From his prototype Hunt, John Keats has

---

[9] On Nov. 2, 1817, Hunt challenged Z: "The Writer of the Article signed Z, in *Blackwood's Edinburgh Magazine* for October 1817, is invited to send his address to the Printer of the *Examiner*, in order that justice may be executed on the proper person." On Nov. 16 Hunt quoted lines from Z's essay that were deleted in later editions. Hunt reprinted his challenge on Nov. 23, and on Dec. 14 he expressed thanks to the author of a sixty-page pamphlet, *A Review of Blackwood's Edinburgh Magazine for October 1817* (Edinburgh 1817), who thought *Blackwood's* to be "loathsome, repulsive, and disgusting" (9). The pamphlet also contains a defense of Wordsworth and Coleridge, whose *Biographia Literaria* was reviewed in the same issue of *Blackwood's*.

acquired a sort of vague idea, that the Greeks were a most tasteful people, and
that no mythology can be so finely adapted for the purposes of poetry as theirs.
It is amusing to see what a hand the two Cockneys make of this mythology;
the one confesses that he never read the Greek Tragedians, and the other
knows Homer only from Chapman; and both write about Apollo, Pan,
Nymphs, Muses, and Mysteries, as might be expected from persons of their
education.[10]

Lockhart's almost parenthetical comment about costume is as canny as it is
petty. He knows that location defines and that costume or decoration is the
frame of public character. In the discourse of art criticism, location and
drapery serve the same function to define both characters and authors, and
Lockhart was not the first to use the tactic. Earlier, it had been one of Haydon's primary rhetorical strategies in attacking the Royal Academy in the
Annals of the Fine Arts.

In his "Preface, including Cursory Observations on Poetry and Cheer-
fulness" in *Foliage* (1818), Hunt combined a defiant defense of *Rimini* with
a prospectus of the volume, which expressed "a love of sociality, of the country, and of the fine imagination of the Greeks" (18). The moral of *Rimini*,
Hunt proclaimed, was "tolerant and reconciling, recommending men's
minds to the consideration of *first* causes in misfortunes," and "the danger
of confounding forms with justice, of setting authorized selfishness above
the most natural impulses, and making guilt by mistaking innocence" (17).
Of Hunt's description of Polyphemus, Lockhart says in the sixth essay on
the Cockneys (Oct. 1819) that "instead of breathing 'of the fine imagination of the Greeks,' it is nothing more than a copy in words of a picture in
oil. Mr. Hunt used to be a great lounger in picture-dealers' shops, and was
a sad bore among the artists. . . . Whenever you meet with a vivid image in
his verses, you are sure that it is taken from a picture." Lockhart's portrayal
of Hunt's and Keats's ignorance of Greek is more than a sniffing dismissal
of their class associations. The falseness of their depiction is a failure of accurate representation, in Lockhart's mind, which is the failure of representation altogether.

Lockhart concluded his review of Keats's poetry in August 1818 with a
note that "we had almost forgot to mention, that Keats belongs to the
Cockney School of Politics, as well as the Cockney School of Poetry. It is
fit that he who holds Rimini to be the first poem, should believe the Examiner to be the first politician of the day. We admire consistency, even in
folly. Hear how their bantling has already learned to lisp sedition." Lockhart then quotes the first twenty-two lines of Book III of *Endymion*, which

[10] Martin Aske's survey of the eighteenth-century views of Greek arts and mythology makes
it clear that Lockhart's understanding of Grecian subjects was as tendentious as Hunt's and
Keats's (*Keats and Hellenism: An Essay*. [Cambridge: Cambridge University Press, 1985]).

ridicule those who "lord it o'er their fellow-men / With most prevailing tinsel." Keats's "tinsel" is not simply a sign of his Cockney knowledge and values. It is rather another in a long series of comments in the public debates over the decoration that adorns aristocratic portraits, the displays of rank that value the trivial. For example, Hazlitt described Thomas Moore's poetry in similar terms: it was "verbal tinsel," a "*cosmetic art*," a "patch-work style," and, finally, "*mimminee-pimminee*" (Howe 11: 170–74). Lockhart was not the only reviewer to see *Endymion* as seditious. In June 1818 the *British Critic* called these lines "a jacobinical apostrophe to 'crowns, turbans, and tiptop nothings.'" In September 1819 Lockhart wrote a short article in *Blackwood's*, "Cockney Poetry and Cockney Politics: Bristol Hunt and Hampstead Hunt," which noted surprise at Leigh Hunt's disdain for Henry "Orator" Hunt: "The Cockney School of Politics . . . is so intimately connected with the Cockney School of Poetry, that it is almost impossible to describe the one without using many expressions equally applicable to the other. They are twin establishments erected about the same time, supported by the same dupes, and enlightened by the same quacks." Lockhart is amused at the thought of Leigh Hunt's worrying "that the nation might think the House of Hunt were sticking too much together, and were plotting their own rise on the ruins of the House of Hanover; and he adopts this unnatural style of severity in order to relieve our fears. Surely never was adjective more happily connected with substantive than in Mr Johnny Keats's favourite phrase of 'kind Hunt.'"

Josiah Conder's review of *Lamia* in the nonconformist *Eclectic Review* for September 1820 repeats Lockhart's characterizations of Hunt and Keats without his class distinctions. Conder is more representative of Keats's critics than Lockhart. Conder's major criticism is that Keats has dedicated himself to poetry for its own sake: "The exclusive cultivation of the imagination is always attended by a dwindling or contraction of the other powers of the mind." He repeats his earlier strictures on Keats's poetry from his review of *Poems* (1817) in the *Eclectic Review* for September 1817 where he scolded Keats and other modern poets for the utter lack of thought: "On what ground, then, does the notion rest, that poetry is a something so sublime, or that so inherent a charm resides in words and syllables arranged in the form of verse, that the value of the composition is in any degree independent of the meaning which links together the sentences?" When poetry declines into empty artfulness, thought is lost, and the only possible product is mere novelty: "We know of no path to legitimate originality, but one, and that is, by restoring poetry to its true dignity as a vehicle for noble thoughts and generous feelings, instead of rendering meaning the mere accident of verse." In a belated age that regards poetry as mere imitation of earlier works of art, poetry degenerates into artifice divorced from thought: "Mind cannot be imitated; art can be: and when imitative skill has brought

an art the nearest to perfection, it is then that its cultivation is the least allied to mind; its original purpose, as a mode of expression, becomes wholly
lost in the artificial object,—the display of skill." The efforts at reaching
originality produce only "the effect of novelties," a word that implied an indifference to all established order. In *Reflections on the Revolution in France*,
Burke identified a "literary cabal" whose purpose was the destruction of
Christianity: "These writers, like the propagators of all novelties, pretended
to a great zeal for the poor, and the lower orders, whilst in their satires they
rendered hateful, by every exaggeration, the faults of courts, of nobility, and
of priesthood" (*RRF* 162). Hunt defended Keats against such strictures in
his review of *Lamia* in the *Indicator* (Aug. 2, 1820), where he fears that *Lamia*
will give credence to the commonplace that poetry must give place to math-
ematical certainty: "Even if there were nothing new to be created,—if philosophy, with its line and rule, could even score the ground, and say to poetry 'Thou shalt go no further,' she would look back to the old world, and
still find it inexhaustible. The crops from its fertility are endless. But these
alarms are altogether idle. The essence of poetical enjoyment does not con-
sist in belief, but in a voluntary power to imagine."

The result of single-minded devotion to poetry is, Conder wrote in his
review of 1820, "the true source of affectation and eccentricity":

> In no other way can we account for the imbecility of judgement, the want of
> sober calculation, the intense enthusiasm about mean or trivial objects, the real
> emptiness of mind, which are sometimes found connected with distinguishing
> talents. Poetry, after all, if pursued as an end, is but child's play; and no won-
> der that those who seem not to have any higher object than to be poets, should
> sometimes be very childish. What better name can we bestow on the nonsense
> that Mr. Keats, and Mr. Leigh Hunt, and Mr. Percy Bysshe Shelley, and some
> other poets about town, have been talking of "the beautiful mythology of
> Greece?" To some persons, although we would by no means place Mr. Keats
> among the number, that mythology comes recommended chiefly by its gross-
> ness—its alliance to the sensitive pleasures which belong to the animal. With
> our Author, this fondness for it proceeds, we very believe, from nothing worse
> than a school boy taste for the stories of the Pantheon and Ovid's Metamor-
> phoses, and the fascination of the word *classical*.[11]

Conder attributes Keats's style to his lack of a classical education and his inability to use classical allusions with propriety. While Lockhart honors classical literature and finds the Cockneys wanting in knowledge of it, Conder
is suspicious of its paganism. Classical allusions "please in proportion to
their slightness and remoteness: it is as illustrations, sometimes highly pic-

---

[11] Conder quotes the Preface to *Endymion*: "I hope I have not in too late a day touched the
beautiful mythology of Greece, and dulled its brightness" (*KP* 64).

turesque illustrations of the subject, not as distinct objects of thought,—it is as metaphor, never in the broad and palpable shape of simile, that they please." Conder distinguishes between metaphor as a remote illustration of a subject and simile as similarity or likeness, which is inappropriate for serious poetry because it confuses pagan grossness and modern morality. A poet may use classical myth as illustration, but not for its own sake; it must be kept at a distance. Allusion must be remote and should not imply a similarity between a modern subject and a classical myth. As an uneducated devotee of pure poetry, Keats errs in choosing classical subjects rather than a modern patriotism or a universal Christianity:

> Mr. Keats, seemingly, can think or write of scarcely any thing else than the "happy pieties" of Paganism. A Grecian Urn throws him into an ecstasy: its "silent form," he says, "doth tease us out of thought as doth Eternity,"—a very happy description of the bewildering effect which such subjects have at least had upon his own mind; and his fancy having thus got the better of his reason, we are the less surprised at the oracle which the Urn is made to utter:
>
> > '"Beauty is truth, truth beauty," —that is all
> > Ye know on earth, and all ye need to know.'
>
> That is, all that Mr. Keats knows or cares to know.—But till he knows much more than this, he will never write verses fit to live.

The "Ode on a Grecian Urn" is a poem of unknowing, written by a poet who knows nothing. To Conder, what must be known is either Christianity or patriotism. All else is unknowing because the classics, as Conder viewed them, offer an inappropriate paganism. To Lockhart, the classics are the measure of excellence; to Conder, they are morally dangerous.

Francis Jeffrey agreed with the characterization of Keats's style but disagreed that Keats's single-minded dedication to imagination was a flaw. Perhaps prompted by Hazlitt, he defended Keats against the attacks in *Blackwood's*. The difference between Keats and his great predecessors is that "imagination in them is subordinate to reason and judgment, while, with him, it is paramount and supreme—that their ornaments and images are employed to embellish and recommend just sentiments, engaging incidents, and natural characters, while his are poured out without measure or restraint, and with no apparent design but to unburden the breast of the author, and give vent to the overflowing vein of his fancy." Jeffrey's comments may have originated in Hazlitt's *Lectures on the English Poets*, delivered at the Surrey Institute in early 1818 and published in the same year, lectures that were ridiculed in Lockhart's essays on the Cockney Poets. Hazlitt commented on Spenser that "the love of beauty, however, and not of truth, is the moving principle of his mind; and he is guided in his fantastic delineations by no rule but the impulse of an inexhaustible imagination. He lux-

uriates equally in scenes of Eastern magnificence; or the still solitude of a
hermit's cell—in the extremes of sensuality or refinement" (Howe 5: 35).
Jeffrey then offers an account of Keats's writing as a process of a self-
generating, but wandering and errant, figuration:

> It seems as if the author had ventured everything that occurred to him in the
> shape of a glittering image or striking expression—taken the first word that pre-
> sented itself to make up the rhyme, and then made that word the germ of a new
> cluster of images—a hint for a new excursion of the fancy—and so wandered
> on, equally forgetful whence he came, and heedless of whither he was going,
> till he had covered his pages with an interminable arabesque of connected and
> incongruous figures, that multiplied as they extended, and were only harmo-
> nized by the brightness of their tints, and the graces of their forms.[12]

Jeffrey acknowledges the accuracy of charges made against Keats's poetry. Benjamin Bailey reported to Keats's publisher John Taylor on August
29, 1818, that "I fear Endymion will be dreadfully cut up in the Edinburgh
Magazine (*Blackwood's*). I met a man in Scotland who is concerned in that
publication, & who abused poor Keats in a way that, although it was at the
Bishop's table, I could hardly keep my temper. . . . The objections he stated
were frivolous in the extreme. They chiefly respected the *rhymes*" (*KC* 1:
34). Criticism of the rhymes was, however, more explicit in Croker's response in the *Quarterly Review* (April 1818), in which he read the narrative
sequence determined by nothing more than "*bouts-rimés*" in which there is
no meaning:

> He seems to us to write a line at random, and then he follows not the thought
> excited by this line, but that suggested by the *rhyme* with which it concludes.
> There is hardly a complete couplet inclosing a complete idea in the whole
> book. He wanders from one subject to another, from the association, not of
> ideas but of sounds, and the work is composed of hemistiches which, it is quite
> evident, have forced themselves upon the author by the mere force of the
> catchwords on which they turn. (205–6)

The problem with Keats's figures, then, is that their only referents are the
preceding figures that generated them. They are constructed upon "false
figures," false wit, as "The Building of the Palace of the Lamp" noted. With
the possible exceptions of Hunt's enthusiasm and Hazlitt's tolerance, the
public was not yet ready to read literature aptly characterized as the play of
signifiers. For Keats, poetic imitation became mannerism, and beauty me-
andered in luxurious rhymes. Keats offended against legitimate reference

---

[12] *Edinburgh Review* (August 1820). William Keach cites Jeffrey's analysis and asks whether
Keats's "arbitrary phonetic and semantic convergences" present "an issue with political implications, amenable to historical and political understanding" ("Cockney Couplets: Keats and
the Politics of Style," *SIR* 25 [1986]: 191).

and intellectual coherence, a legitimacy that Conder saw as mapped so as to restrict symbol to national boundaries and to alienate geographical distance and rhetorical illustration. There is an extravagance in Keats's poetry as dangerous, perhaps, as that of Coleridge's mariner.

RICHARD PAYNE KNIGHT AND "MELTING WHALES"

Keats's poetry of sensation was read as nonsense. Conder, Hazlitt, Jeffrey, and Croker, whom I take to be more representative of public opinion than Lockhart, read Keats's poetry as nonsense, rather than as parody of a legitimate poetry.[13] While reviewers regarded Keats's poetry as meaningless, self-generated, and a random collection of disconnected fragments, his affection for Greek subjects implied to his contemporary readers a cluster of subversive themes, all of which challenged reigning legitimacy. The genial coincidence between Christianity and Greek philosophy that other ages found comforting, did not predominate in Keats's day. The explicit themes of the public discourse on Greek art are sexuality and sensuality, the relation of art to patronage and the court, and the skeptical view of an ideal in art or of an ideal art. While Keats's poetry may appear to be a collection of classical fragments that reveal his class orientation and aspiration, if read in the context of writing on Greek art, his poetry is less bourgeois and acquisitive and more politically oppositional. His poetry, although read by Lockhart as a useless collection of classical souvenirs cluttering a Cockney mantle, represents a social and political interest more determined to liberate itself from legitimacy than to arrange and display the signs of a class it wished to ape, as Lockhart suggested, or of an art that it wished to parody, as later critics have suggested. Art may mean nothing, may be autonomous, may even deceptively present itself as isolated, but its connections are more important that its deceptions. Its allusions betray its illusions of autonomy.

In the controversies over the Elgin Marbles, Benjamin Robert Haydon and Richard Payne Knight, the leader of the Dilettanti society,[14] were bitter antagonists. Both, however, belonged in the opposition camp, both held radical opinions, and both promoted an esthetics of classical art that outraged the conservative social order. In advocating the Elgin Marbles as the

---

[13] Following Marjorie Levinson (*Keats's Life of Allegory* [Oxford: Blackwell, 1988]), Paul Hamilton explicates Lockhart's reaction to *Endymion*: "Keats's supposed vulgarity was not a subversive *parody* of high art, precisely because it shared the same founding assumptions of the prevailing idealistic esthetic. The deflection of criticism of the poem into criticism of the poet's Cockney presumption is what turns the poem into a parody" (118).

[14] For information on Knight see Frank J. Messman, *Richard Payne Knight: the Twilight of Virtuosity* (The Hague: Mouton, 1974) and *The Arrogant Connoisseur: Richard Payne Knight, 1751–1824*, ed. Michael Clarke and Nicholas Penny (Manchester: Manchester University Press, 1982). William St. Clair includes a useful summary of Knight's career in *Lord Elgin and His Marbles* (New York: Oxford University Press, 1967, 1983).

models of excellence in art, Haydon, along with Hazlitt, challenged Sir Joshua Reynolds's ideal of art. As an advocate of historical painting, Haydon spared no efforts to ridicule the Royal Academy, whose members prospered on painting portraits of aristocrats. Haydon held strong religious convictions, but Knight was charged with atheism, sensuality, and immorality. I will not argue that Knight was a direct influence on Keats's poetry, although his influence in the period was stronger than the almost total disregard of his work in the twentieth century would suggest, particularly on Peacock and perhaps Shelley. He is, however, representative of the writers on Greek art and culture associated with liberal causes and with the fascination with what Conder called "grossness—-its alliance to the sensitive pleasures which belong to the animal." He represents the views of Greek art attacked in much of the public press.

Knight was an M.P., a follower of Fox, and a wealthy connoisseur, who traveled to Italy to collect antiquities, particularly bronzes, coins, and jewels. As a member of the Dilettanti Society he sponsored the publication of elegant books illustrating ancient art and financed expeditions to recover and record it. His first published work, amply illustrated, *The Worship of Priapus* (1786), described the origins of fertility cults and their symbolism. The book's circulation was restricted and later suppressed, but the themes of sexuality, paganism, and a strong anti-clerical bias, along with a deep skepticism on the truths of Christianity, remain throughout his later works. Although he avoided most references to orgiastic sexuality in his later works, the theme remained and became a delicate subject in much writing about Greek art. For example, Henry Moses commented in *A Collection of Antique Vases* (1814) that vases contained information about "the sacred and solemn mysteries of the Greeks," and "the frantic orgies of Bacchus" (6). James Christie's *Disquisitions upon the Painted Greek Vases, and Their Probable Connection with the Shows of the Eleusinian and other Mysteries* (1825) concluded its description of Greek religious mysteries with the comment that "to have exposed more of what I have discovered than has been submitted, would have only been to stir a filthy pool. The grossness of paganism we may be pardoned for omitting" (107): "A veil seems to have been kindly drawn by Providence, for ages past, over the disgusting errors of paganism" (108). To depict mythological subjects on vases was to run the risk, in 1820, of presenting sexual practices that might shock a Regency dandy. To pursue a scholarly and historical inquiry into the representations of Greek art was to invite the possibility of an unpublishable knowledge and at the same time to introduce the representation of the human body concretely into esthetics to challenge the reigning ideology.[15] A professed innocence of the sex-

---

[15] See G. S. Rousseau, "The Sorrows of Priapus: Anticlericalism, Homosocial Desire, and Richard Payne Knight," *Sexual Underworlds of the Enlightenment*, ed. G. S. Rousseau and Roy Porter (Chapel Hill: University of North Carolina Press, 1988) 101–53.

ual meanings of Greek art was truly disingenuous. Philip Fisher has keenly remarked that Keats's poem is a museum that contains the urn, a work of art that represents a pastoral world, but a representation of pastoral is itself a literary convention, neither an accurate representation of any historical period nor an accurate account of what, in the inquiring eyes of Keats's contemporaries, those figures may actually have represented.[16] To describe country matters as conventional pastoral is as much an idealizing reconstruction as a tendency among other critics to see all Greek art as ideal.

In 1796 Knight published *The Progress of Civil Society: A Didactic Poem in Six Books*, which was parodied by the *Anti-Jacobin* as *The Progress of Man*. Knight's Preface apologizes for the "historian or antiquary, who endeavours to trace the symbolical or mystical use, which has been made of these parts of the body, in any particular system of religion or philosophy, though it may be equally void of any thing inflammatory or lascivious." He claimed to be "totally free from any of that *criminal obscenity*" (xix). His persistent explanation, throughout his writings, that the artifacts he describes and illustrated are to be read symbolically, did not convince even those who might be sympathetic. In the *Champion* of February 25, 1816, John Scott ridiculed Knight's connoisseurship and said that the controversy over the Elgin Marbles "reduces the learned commentator on the scriptures and symbols of the God of Obscenity, to even an inferiority of pretension, as a judge of art, beneath the humble but enthusiastic student of the refinement and talent of the great masters." Hazlitt, also, commented on "The Elgin Marbles" in the *Examiner* of June 16, 1816, that "we lay somewhat more stress on the value of the Fine Arts than Mr. Payne Knight, who considers them (we know not for what reason) as an elegant antithesis to morality." Although Hazlitt thought art and morality related, his explanation of the relationship offers no comfort to the conservative cause:

> All morality seems to be little more than keeping people out of mischief, as we send children to school; and the Fine Arts are in that respect a school of morality. They bribe the senses into the service of the understanding; they kill Time, the great enemy of man; they employ the mind usefully—about nothing; and by preventing *ennui*, promote the chief ends of virtue. A taste for the Fine Arts also, in periods of luxury and refinement, not ill supplies the place of religious enthusiasm. . . . (Howe 18: 101)

In the Preface, Knight responds to the charge of atheism with an equivocation. Claiming that the word *Christian* has "not only had a different signification in every age and country, but in the mouth of almost every individual who has ever used it, I will not pretend to it, till its meaning is so far

---

[16] "A Museum with One Work Inside: Keats and the Finality of Art," *Keats-Shelley Journal* 33 (1984): 85–102.

determined, that I may know whether I can justly pretend to it or not. . . .
I am not certain that I can thereby claim the title of a *good Christian*" (xvii-
xviii).

The Progress of Civil Society itself attributed man's transition from the state
of nature, which was perpetual warfare, to a social state to sexual love:

> Each jarring element in concord joins,
> And sensual joy with social bliss refines;
> In softer notes bids Libyan lions roar,
> And warms the whale on Zembla's frozen shore;
>
> . . . .
>
> From the same source the attractive power began,
> And changed the wandering brute to social man.
>
> (I, 95–98, 129–30)

The *Anti-Jacobin*'s parody marks:

> How Lybian tigers' chawdrons love assails,
> And warms, midst seas of ice, the melting whales;—
> Cools the crimpt cod, fierce pangs to perch imparts,
> Shrinks shrivell'd shrimps, but opens oysters' hearts;—
> Then say, how all these things together tend
> To one great truth, prime object and good end?
>
> (*PAJ* 75)

Knight complains of the restrictions of marriage:

> But when in bands indissoluble join'd,
> Securely torpid sleeps the sated mind;
> No anxious hopes or fears arise, to move
> The flagging wings, or stir the fires of love:
>
> (III, 160–63)

The *Anti-Jacobin*'s parody replies in what its Argument defines as "Influence of Sexual Appetite":

> Of WHIST or CRIBBAGE mark th'amusing game—
> The Partners *changing*, but the SPORT the *same*
> Else would the Gamester's anxious ardour cool,
> Dull every deal, and stagnant every pool.
> —Yet must *one** Man, with one unceasing Wife,
> Play the LONG RUBBER of connubial life.

A note reads, "The word *one* here, means all the inhabitants of Europe (ex-
cepting the French, who have remedied this inconvenience), not any particular individual. The Author begs leave to disclaim every allusion that can

be construed as personal" (*PAJ* 102). Benjamin Bailey saw a similar tendency in *Endymion*, which, as he remarked to Taylor, had two faults:

> The first must offend *every* one of proper feelings; and indelicacy is not to be borne; & I greatly reproach myself that I did not represent this very strongly to him before it was sent to the Press. . . . The second fault I allude to I think we have noticed—The approaching inclination it has to that abominable principle of *Shelley's*—that *Sensual Love* is the principal of *things.*" (*KC* 1: 34–35)

Knight's *Analytical Inquiry into the Principles of Taste* (1805)[17] was remarkable for nothing so much as its skepticism. Knight quotes Hume that "beauty is no quality in things themselves"[18] but is merely a subjective quality: "The word Beauty is a general term of approbation, of the most vague and extensive meaning, applied indiscriminately to almost every thing that is pleasing" (9). The confusion about taste comes, Knight argues, because we confuse the simple sensation of taste, which is purely subjective, with ideas or ideals: "wandering clouds of confusion and perplexity seem to have arisen from employing the Greek word *idea*, sometimes in its proper sense to signify a mental image or vision, and sometimes in others the most adverse and remote, to signify *perception, remembrance, notion, knowledge* and almost every other operation, or result of operation, of which the mind is capable" (40). Knight is perfectly skeptical of Platonic ideas or ideals: "When men once renounce the evidence of their senses, either in believing or doubting, there is nothing which they may not believe or doubt with perfect consistency. . . . Scepticism has never attempted to make proselytes by fire or sword, and is therefore at least an innocent absurdity compared with its antagonist bigotry" (39–40). Knight summarizes, "I could therefore wish to drop or modify the use of the word *idea*" (41). Knight was one of many students of classical art in the early nineteenth century who wished to dissociate the works of art from any notion of their ideal nature. A strong reaction to Reynolds's notion of ideal art was under way, to culminate in the heated debates over the value of the Elgin Marbles, when Haydon and Hazlitt rejected Reynolds's ideal art in favor of a natural art. Although Knight disagreed with Haydon and Hazlitt and considered the Elgin Marbles inferior to the Apollo Belvedere, he retained his empiricist theories of beauty, which he shared with Haydon and Hazlitt. To those who advocated the

---

[17] For Coleridge's and Wordsworth's views of Knight's *Inquiry*, see Coleridge's *Lectures 1808–1819, On Literature*, ed. R. A. Foakes (Princeton: Princeton University Press, 1987) 1: 31–34; his "Principles of Genial Criticism" in *Shorter Works and Fragments*, ed. H. J. and J. R. de J. Jackson (Princeton: Princeton Univeristy Press, 1995) 1: 355, 363n.; and *Margin.* 3: 400–13.

[18] I quote from Knight, *Analytical Inquiry*, 3d ed. (1806) 16. Knight quotes Hume's "Of the Standard of Taste." See Hume's *Essays Moral, Political, and Literary*, ed. Eugene F. Miller (Indianapolis: Liberty Classics, 1985) 230.

Marbles, their excellence rested in their truth to nature, not in their ideal qualities. The esthetic climate of classical art in the charged political context of the early nineteenth century made it extremely difficult to see that art as either ideal or transcendent. To both liberals and conservatives, it embodied all forms of liberty, including sensuality.

Knight concludes his *Inquiry* with a section on novelty, which offers both a Paterian justification of fine art and a justification for collecting and connoisseurship:

> Even without confinement, were we doomed to spend our lives with one set of unchanging objects, which could afford no new varieties, either of sensations, images, or ideas; nor produce any new modifications or dispositions in those previously felt or acquired, all around us would soon have the tiresome sameness of the walls of a cell. . . . Thus, if we suppose the world and its inhabitants to be fixed in one unchangeable state for ever, deprived of all variations of seasons, and of every kind of progressive or successive growth, decay, or reproduction, how perfect soever we may suppose that fixed state to be, we should soon become so tired of it, were it realized, that we should eagerly covet any change.

Our genuine happiness

> consists in the *means* and not the *end*:—in *acquisition*, and not *possession*. The source and principle of it is, therefore, *novelty*: the attainment of new ideas; the formation of new trains of thought; the renewal and extension of affections and attachments . . . and, above all, the unlimited power of fancy in multiplying and varying the objects, the results, and the gratifications of our pursuits beyond the bounds of reality, or the probable duration of existence. (471–72)

Such a continuous change cannot be anchored in any certainty of an ideal or a transcendent: "So absurd and presumptuous is it in us to attempt to form any ideas of the beatitude of superior beings, whose faculties and modes of intelligence have, perhaps, nothing in common with our own" (473).

When Knight applied these esthetic principles to practical art criticism, the political implications became clearer. In 1809 he wrote a "Preliminary Dissertation on the Rise, Progress, and Decline of Antient Sculpture" for the first volume of *Specimens of Antient Sculpture, Ægyptian, Etruscan, Greek, and Roman: Selected from Different Collections in Great Britain, by the Society of Dilettanti*, where, on the subject of Egyptian art, he makes it clear that he was describing a Britain ruled by Burke's principles.[19] He explained the

---

[19] London, 1809. Noting the connections between the fallen gods and Egyptian sculpture in *Hyperion*, Alan Bewell reads the conflict of the Titans and the Olympians as "less as a theogony within a single culture than as an international event, a confrontation between the gods of Europe and those of the Orient" ("The Political Implication of Keats's Classicist Aes-

Egyptian impersonal style of art that continued unchanged for centuries in terms of the rigid social structure based on hierarchy and inheritance:

> This torpid state, in which the art of sculpture continued during so many ages in Ægypt, is not so much to be attributed to the genius of the people, as to the constitution of their government, both civil and ecclesiastical. All trades and professions being hereditary, the way of life of each individual was predestined, and the boundaries of his ambition circumscribed even before his birth. The jealous temper of the hierarchy, too, dreading every innovation, as not knowing where it might stop when once suffered to begin, limited the exertions of art to given forms of the rudest and most ungraceful kind; so that taste and invention were wholly excluded; and all the excellence by which the artist could hope to gratify his ambition, confined to the finishing of detached parts, without any reference to their general effect in the whole composition. (iv)

In such a state, humans "become, like the plants in a shorn hedge, each fashioned to his station and moulded to his place" (v). A similar description of the artisan as a slave comes in Book IV of *The Progress of Civil Society*:

> And Egypt's sons, in frigid method bound,
> Still onward move their dull mechanic round;
> Race after race arise, and pass away;—
> Unvaried live, and uniform decay;
> Each class its destined task alone pursue,—
> Content to learn just what their fathers knew:
> Rank within rank hereditary pent,
> In peaceful drudgery still onward went;—
> Drawl'd on through life, as mystic priestcraft taught;
> And, only as directed, moved and thought;—
>
> (IV, 417–26)

Although Knight does not complete the comparison between Egyptian tyranny and Grecian liberty as Haydon and James Elmes were to do later in the *Annals of the Fine Arts*, Knight attributes the superiority of the Greeks to commonly cited characteristics: climate, language, their love of sport, and, most important to Knight, liberal patronage. He gives highest praise, however, to Greek literature and Homer, whom he describes in terms usually reserved for the Christian God: "The effulgence of his mind still bursts upon us like the rays of the sun, which traverse the immensity of space with undiminished brightness, and diffuse life and motion through the universe, though we know not the nature of the body, which emits them, nor the regions of inanity, through which they pass" (xiii).

---

thetics," *SIR* 25 [1986]: 224). For a discussion of Keats's knowledge of Egypt, see Helen Darbishire, "Keats and Egypt," *Review of English Studies* 3 (1927): 1–11; and Barbara Garlitz, "Egypt and *Hyperion*," *Philological Quarterly* 34 (1955): 189–96.

The Elgin Marbles and Systematic Art

Knight collected bronze sculpture and consistently belittled the Elgin Marbles. Perhaps jealous over Elgin's possession of them, he complained that they were merely architectural decoration, carved by workmen of varying skills, to be seen at a height of over forty feet, and carved in such shallow relief as "to produce an effect like that of the simplest kind of monochromatic painting."[20] Knight further thought that they were of little value because they were merely stone, a material inferior to gold, ivory, and bronze and were broken and corroded, lacking the finely polished surfaces of ideal art. Haydon records in his *Autobiography* that Knight ridiculed the Marbles publicly: "At the first dinner-party at which Lord Elgin met him, he cried out in a loud voice, 'You have lost your labour, my Lord Elgin; your marbles are overrated; they are not Greek, they are Roman of the time of Hadrian.' Lord Elgin, totally unprepared for such an assault, did not reply, for he did not know what to say" (Haydon 244). The attacks on the Marbles continued through 1815, when Haydon came to their defense, because he was "astonished at hearing from various quarters that their beauty, truth, and originality were questioned by a great authority in matters of art" (Haydon 241). Haydon campaigned for the Marbles because he saw that their naturalness and empirical truth were superior to the artificial ideal recommended by Sir Joshua Reynolds. They were not formal, symmetrical, systematic, mannered, and theatrical like the Apollo Belvedere, the standard by which sculpture was measured. To call into question that ideal was not only to question the metaphysics of the ideal, as Knight had done, but also to challenge the Royal Academy that had supported it and the system of patronage that in turn supported the Royal Academy. Haydon and others praised the Elgin Marbles as casts taken from nature, the antithesis of ideal abstract art. Although the sensuality of Greek art was not a question with the Marbles, the senses and the physical body were. Those who advocated the Marbles praised them as exemplary of an esthetics of the senses rather than of the ideal. A reading of Keats's poetry that places the Marbles in the tradition of ideal art described by Winckelmann and Reynolds is a misreading both of art history and literature. Keats's "On a Grecian Urn" supports Haydon's and Hazlitt's view of the Marbles and of art at the same time that it implies an oppositional politics.

Haydon first saw the Marbles in 1808 and immediately recognized their truth to nature. He saw that the muscles of all the figures were sculpted exactly as they existed in nature, not after the model of an ideal in which muscles were displayed in unnatural positions, such as those on the Belvedere torso. In the Theseus he remarked "that the two sides of his back varied,

---

[20] *Specimens of Antient Sculpture*, xxxix.

one side stretched from the shoulder-blade being pulled forward, and the other side compressed from the shoulder blade being pushed close to the spine as he rested on his elbow, with the belly flat because the bowels fell into the pelvis as he sat." The Marbles represented a new excellence in sculpture—an art that expresses, not a vague idea in the artist's mind, but an image that precisely imitated the motions of the human body: "I foretold that they would prove themselves the finest things on earth, that they would overturn the false beau-ideal, where nature was nothing, and would establish the true beau-ideal, of which nature alone is the basis" (Haydon 77–78). What was the most heroic was, for Haydon, at the same time, the most true to nature. The Elgin marbles would replace the ideal art of the Apollo Belvedere, the Belvedere Torso, and the Laocoön as models of excellence.

In 1815, when the government was considering the purchase of the Marbles, and when Knight belittled them, Haydon came to their defense. The following year he published "On the judgment of Connoisseurs being preferred to that of Professional Men—The Elgin Marbles" in both the *Champion* and the *Examiner.*[21] Haydon defended the judgment of professional artists against the judgment of mere connoisseurs by arguing that the fragments were not merely pieces of a ruined ideal but possessed life in themselves: "The great principles of life can be proved to exist in the most broken fragment as well as in the most perfect figure. Is not life as palpable in the last joint of your forefinger as in the centre of your heart? On the same principle, break off a toe from any fragment of the Elgin Marbles, and there I will prove the great consequences of vitality, acting externally, to be" (Haydon 275). Canova agreed. In a widely circulated letter to Lord Elgin supporting the Marbles, Canova wrote, "I admire in them the truth of nature united to the choice of finest forms. Every thing here breathes life, with a veracity, with an exquisite knowledge of art, but without the least ostentation or parade of it."[22] It is possible, Haydon argues, to infer an idea or intention, in the movement of the bones, muscles, and sinews:

> It is this union of nature with ideal beauty,—the probabilities and accidents of bone, flesh, and tendon, from extension, flexion, compression, gravitation, action, or repose, that rank at once the Elgin Marbles above all other works of art in the world. The finest form that man ever imagined, or God ever created, must have been formed on these eternal principles. The Elgin Marbles will as completely overthrow the old antique, as ever one system of philosophy overthrew another more enlightened. (Haydon 276–77)

[21] Haydon 274–80. See also *The Diary of Benjamin Robert Haydon*, ed. Willard Bissell Pope, 5 vols. (Cambridge, Mass.: Harvard University Press, 1960–63) 1: 433–42.

[22] House of Commons, "Report from the Select Committee on the Earl of Elgin's Collection of Sculptured Marbles," *Sessional Papers, 1816*, 25 March 1816, vol. 3, p. 68.

Haydon did not view the fragments as the ruins of a former and greater world; on the contrary, they were models to revitalize a moribund British art. Haydon constructed a new standard of art based on empirical reality. He defined beauty not by transcendence, abstraction, or generalization—it was not Sir Joshua Reynolds's ideal or noble art—but by the "probabilities and accidents" of the posture of the human body whose depiction depended upon an idea in the artist's eye and mind. Grant Scott has pointed out that while those who admired the ideal art of the Apollo Belvedere praise the smoothly finished surfaces of sculpture, Haydon and other advocates of the Elgin Marbles tended to ignore the surface corrosion for the truth of the interior body motions, the bones, muscles, and veins.[23] Haydon explains in detail that the artist's job is to represent the human body acted upon by a great passion or idea:

> We know not how an intention acts by the will on the frame, any more than we know what vitality is; we only know it by its consequences, and the business of the artist is to represent the consequences of an idea acting on the form and feature, on the parts which it does influence, and the parts which it does not, so truly, as to excite in the mind of the spectator the exact associations of the feeling intended to be conveyed. (275–76)

For Haydon, the truth of the Elgin Marbles is truth to the interior of the human frame, to a concrete, physical reality, not an imaginary ideal nor a smoothly polished surface.

In early 1816 a Select Committee of the House of Commons met to consider purchase of the Elgin Marbles.[24] They inquired of the leading artists, connoisseurs, and dealers about the legal authority by which Elgin had purchased them, their artistic merit, and their monetary value. The newspapers and reviews widely reported their deliberations. The Committee concluded:

> The testimony of several of the most eminent Artists in this kingdom, who have been examined, rates these Marbles in the very first class of ancient art,

[23] "Beautiful Ruins: The Elgin Marbles Sonnet in its Historical and Generic Contexts," *Keats-Shelley Journal* 39 (1990): 128; see also Scott's *The Sculpted Word: Keats, Ekphrasis, and the Visual Arts* (Hanover: University Press of New England, 1994) 45–67. Along with William St. Clair, Scott is one of the few critics who has noted the significant difference between ideal art and the Elgin Marbles. For a contrary view, see Theresa M. Kelley "Keats, Ekphrasis, and History," in *Keats and History*, ed. Nicholas Roe (Cambridge: Cambridge University Press, 1995) 212–37. A. W. Phinney notes some of the differences between the ideal art as expressed by Winckelmann, Reynolds, and Flaxman and the Elgin Marbles, but is primarily interested in historicizing the differences between the sculptures as ideal and their historical origins ("Keats in the Museum: Between Aesthetics and History," *Journal of English and Germanic Philology*, 90 [1991]: 208–29).

[24] For the history of the purchase of the Marbles, see St Clair (above, n. 14).

some placing them a little above, and others but very little below the Apollo Belvidere [sic], the Laocoon, and the Torso of the Belvidere. . . . It is surprising to observe in the best of these Marbles in how great a degree the close imitation of Nature is combined with grandeur of Style, while the exact details of the former in no degree detract from the effect and predominance of the latter. . . . The two finest single figures of this collection differ materially in this respect from the Apollo Belvidere, which may be selected as the highest and most sublime representation of ideal form, and beauty, which Sculpture has ever embodied, and turned to shape.[25]

The Committee asked each witness whether the Elgin Marbles were better examples of excellence in art than the Apollo Belvidere. Knight and Flaxman took the conservative position that the ideal art of the Apollo was superior to the Elgin Marbles. Sir Thomas Lawrence thought the Elgin Marbles superior: "I consider that there is in them an union of fine composition, and very grand form, with a more true and natural expression of the effect of action upon the human frame, than there is in the Apollo" (3: 38). Francis Chauntry agreed with Lawrence. When asked "Are they not more according to common, but beautiful nature, than the Apollo?" Chauntry responded, "Certainly; I mean nature in the grand style, not the simplicity of the composition visible in every part; but simplicity and grandeur are so nearly allied, it is almost impossible to make a distinction" (3: 36). For Lawrence and Chauntry the simple and the common were equated with the grand style. Alexander Day was asked, "Do you mean they conform more to general nature, and give a more exact imitation of it?" He judged the Elgin Marbles greatly superior to the Apollo and explained that "they conform more to what the artists call Sublimated Nature, not common nature, but nature in its highest perfection" (3: 54). Day, too, admired the sublime nature of the common rather than the ideal of the Apollo.

Benjamin West could not attend the Committee meetings but responded to a set of written questions in which he valued the Elgin Marbles over the ideal of the Apollo, or what he called systematic art. He had seen the marbles as early as 1808, and Farington recorded in his diary that West said that at age 70 he would begin his studies of art anew: "There was to be seen the perfection of art, where nature predominated everywhere,—and was not resolved into & made obedient to a system."[26] The Committee asked West, "In what class of Art do you rank the best of these Marbles?" and he responded, "In the first of dignified art, brought out of nature upon unerring truths, and not on mechanical principles, to form systematic characters and systematic art." He was also asked, "Can you compare, in money value, Lord Elgin's Marbles, or any part of them, with the money value of the Phy-

[25] *Sessional Papers* (above, n. 22) 3: 6–7.
[26] *The Farington Diary*, ed. James Greig (London: Hutchinson, 1925) 5: 68.

galian, or the Townley collection?" and he responded, "I judge the Elgin Marbles, from their purity and pre-eminence in art over all others I have ever seen, and from their truth and intellectual power; and I give them the preference to the Phygalian and Townley collection, most of which is systematic art." To the question, "Have you seen and examined Mr. Knight's collection of Bronzes, and in what class does their character materially differ from the best of Lord Elgin's Marbles?" West responded "I have seen them, and they are of the first class, as Bronzes. They, as most bronzes, are of systematic art" (3: 58–60).

The arrival of the Elgin Marbles effected a revolution in the appreciation of art that challenged the dominance of Reynolds's notion of the ideal. Haydon was an important influence—whatever his achievement as an artist or as a public antagonist—but even though the Select Committee excluded him from testifying, the decision would have been the same with or without Haydon. In other words challenges to ideal art were not restricted to Haydon and the *Examiner* circle, who questioned reigning legitimacy and used the change of taste to their political advantage. To West, Canova, Haydon, and others the Elgin Marbles exemplified the highest excellence in an art that they variously described as natural, true, and common, yet purified or sublimated into grandeur and into what West called dignified art, which opposed what he called systematic art or what Knight and Flaxman continued to uphold as ideal art in the tradition of Sir Joshua Reynolds. The sublimation praised by advocates of the Elgin Marbles is strikingly similar to Keats's declaration to Benjamin Bailey in the letter of November 22, 1817, that "what the imagination seizes as Beauty must be truth—whether it existed before or not." Keats's speculations echo the esthetic theory that sees the excellence of the Marbles in their precise sublimation of the physical body: "We shall enjoy ourselves here after by having what we called happiness on Earth repeated in a finer tone and so repeated—. . . . Imagination and its empyreal reflection is the same as human Life and its spiritual repetition."[27] In this context Keats's speculations on the repetition of sensation "in a finer tone" imply the denial of the abstract ideal and the noble for the common.

Hazlitt reviewed the Select Committee Report in the *Examiner* beginning June 16, 1816, and agreed with the judgments of Haydon, West, and the others:[28]

---

[27] *The Letters of John Keats, 1814–1821*, ed. Hyder Edward Rollins (Cambridge: Harvard University Press, 1958) 1: 184–85.

[28] Herschel Baker explains that Hazlitt repeated Haydon's views of the Elgin Marbles (*William Hazlitt* [Cambridge, Mass.: Harvard University Press, 1962]) 239–41. For Hazlitt's disagreements with Reynolds, see David Bromwich, *Hazlitt: The Mind of a Critic* (New York: Oxford University Press, 1983) 205–17. See also John Barrell's *The Political Theory of Painting from Reynolds to Hazlitt* (New Haven: Yale University Press, 1986), in which he traces Reynolds's

The Elgin Marbles are the best answer to Sir Joshua Reynolds' Discourses. Considered in that point of view, they are invaluable: in any other, they are not worth so much as has been said. Nothing remains of them but their style; but that is everything, for it is the style of nature. Art is the imitation of nature; and the Elgin Marbles are in their essence and their perfection casts from nature,—from fine nature, it is true, but from real, living, moving nature; from objects in nature, answering to an idea in the artist's mind, not from an idea in the artist's mind abstracted from all objects in nature. (Howe 18: 100)

Hazlitt's enthusiasm for the Marbles is tempered by a skepticism that cannot ignore their ruined state and that must historicize what remains as merely style; for him nothing else remains, which was precisely Josiah Conder's complaint about Keats's poetry. It knows nothing. Art survives only as style because time has ruined or obscured its other claims to truth. Hazlitt implies that the Marbles' origin is lost and that they are alienated from their origin by being brought into England. He is skeptical of Elgin's claims to legal possession of the Marbles and keenly aware of the nationalism involved in removing art works during the Napoleonic wars, when the Louvre could boast possession of the Apollo, the Laocoön, the Dying Gladiator, among many other treasures "where the triumphs of human liberty had been, there were the triumphs of human genius," a just rebuke to "the worshippers of hereditary power and native imbecility" (Howe 18: 102).

Hazlitt makes a similar point on style in his review of Schlegel's *Lectures on Dramatic Literature* in the *Edinburgh Review* for February 1816. Classical art is self-contained form in contrast to modern literature, which always points beyond itself to imponderable meanings. Following Schlegel, Hazlitt distinguishes classical literature and art as describing "things as they are interesting in themselves" from modern literature, which describes things "for the sake of the associations of ideas connected with them": "the one dwells more on the immediate impressions of objects on the senses—the other on the ideas which they suggest to the imagination" (Howe 16: 63). "The Pagan system reduced the Gods to the human form, and elevated the powers of inanimate nature to the same standard. . . . The Christian religion, on the contrary, is essentially spiritual and abstract; it is 'the evidence of things unseen.' In the Heathen mythology, form is everywhere predominant; in the Christian, we find only unlimited, undefined power."[29] Hazlitt then turns from Christianity as the agent that separates the moderns from knowledge of the classical, to history as the creator of the modern sensibility:

---

adaptation of the ideal of civic humanism to an abstract, ideal imagining of "representative images, whose function is . . . to enable us to grasp what we each have in common with others" (86). Barrell also traces Hazlitt's reaction to Reynolds in a separation of the republic of taste from the political republic.

[29] Howe 16: 65–66. Howe identifies the quotation from Hebrews 11:1.

History, as well as religion, has contributed to enlarge the bounds of imagination; and both together, by showing past and future objects at an interminable distance, have accustomed the mind to contemplate and take an interest in the obscure and shadowy. . . . The mere lapse of time then, aided by the art of printing, has served to accumulate for us an endless mass of mixed and contradictory materials; and, by extending our knowledge to a greater number of things, has made our particular ideas less perfect and distinct. . . . We are lost in wonder at what has been done, and dare not think of emulating it. (Howe 16: 66)

Because of the "lapse of time," classical art is exclusively an esthetic object for Hazlitt, with nothing remaining but style. History reinforces the esthetic in a way that renders Greek art a shadowy wonder for modern speculation. It is not the case, for Hazlitt and Keats, that Greek art represents an ideal now lost or ruined, an ideal that nevertheless exists through time and is available to imagination; it is, rather, that the historical condition, the "lapse," compels moderns to view a Greek art or read a classical literature that is beset by "an endless mass of mixed and contradictory materials," which, as Hazlitt implies, will never yield clear meaning. Thus the sestet of Keats's "On Seeing the Elgin Marbles" remarks less on a grand but inaccessible ideal than upon the confusion or uncertainties of their significance and the lapse of history. The Marbles' sublimity rests, not in a transcendent and unreachable ideal, but in imponderables created by historical distance. Hazlitt, like Keats, is a belated viewer of classical art, distant from art's origin and unsettled by too much conflicting information. They know both too little and too much and are "lost in wonder":

> Such dim-conceived glories of the brain
>   Bring round the heart an undescribable feud;
> So do these wonders a most dizzy pain,
>   That mingles Grecian grandeur with the rude
> Wasting of old time—with a billowy main—
>   A sun—a shadow of a magnitude.
>
> (*KP* 58)

To Hazlitt, as to Haydon, the style of the marbles was the style of nature, not Reynolds's ideal. Hazlitt wrote in an article on the "Fine Arts" in the *Encyclopedia Britannica* in 1817 that "the *ideal* is not the preference of that which exists only in the mind, to that which exists in nature; but the preference of that which is fine in nature to that which is less so" (Howe 18: 113). The appropriate ideal in art is the preference for the reality of physical nature—of a cast taken from nature—rather than "*ideal* creations, borrowed from the skies," as he expressed it in an article "On the Elgin Marbles" in the *London Magazine* for February 1822 (Howe 18: 147), which in a continuation of the article in May he called "suspended in the regions of thought alone" (Howe 18: 150). Keats's final phrase in the Elgin marbles sonnet, "a shadow of a magnitude," may be a play on Hazlitt's scorn for the fashionable collectors, who maintained the eighteenth-century ideal when Hazlitt suggested that to the connoisseurs classical art was the mere "shadow of a shade" (Howe 18: 101). The Elgin Marbles possess "no alliteration or antithesis . . . , no setness, squareness, affectation or formality of appearance. The different muscles do not present a succession of *tumuli*, each heaving with big throes to rival the other. If one is raised, the other falls quietly into its place. Neither do the different parts of the body answer to one another, like shoulder knots on a lacquey's coat or the different ornaments of a building" (Howe 18: 148). The Elgin Marbles are not, in West's words, systematic art, which Hazlitt reads in terms of theatricality and paratextual decoration.

Many newspapers and journals published the deliberations and decisions of the Select Committee. In "Lord Elgin's *Collection of Sculptured Marbles*," the *Quarterly Review* (January 1816) admitted the excellence of the Marbles and aptly summarized the terms of the debate: those who testified before the Select Committee "all consider the Apollo as the finest specimen of what is called the *beau ideal*, and the Theseus and Ilissus as the finest specimens of *natural beauty*; and the only difference of opinion is on the abstract point, whether the beau ideal or the exact imitation of fine nature is the more valuable of the art" (530). The *Quarterly* admired the Panathenaic Procession more than the individual statues. The procession was

> the highest intellectual delight—that festival of the metropolis of the civilized world, connected with all the delicious remembrances of Athenian history . . . and exhibiting on the marble which we may *now* call ETERNAL, the noblest moral recollections with the most exquisite forms of natural beauty;—who is there, we say, who can look at this admirable work without feeling that expansion of the heart, that exaltation of the mind, which it is the first and proudest office of the fine arts to create! (544)

The *Quarterly* read the procession as an example of patriotic pride, moral grandeur, and noble dignity but thought the individual statues of the Theseus and Ilissus without any grandeur: "As mere works of art, these are, doubtless, superior even to the Procession; but they are not in the same degree connected with moral associations, and though they fill the eye perhaps more perfectly, they convey less gratification to the mind." The figures that the artists, especially Haydon, most admired, possessed no meaning because to the *Quarterly*, they had no moral character. The *Quarterly* much preferred the Apollo, not because of its *"natural form,"* but because of its *natural emotion*; the consistency of character, the mingled grace and dignity which pervade the whole from the forehead to the foot, and which delight us as a fine theatrical exhibition of the same high qualities, by some excellent actor, would do. It is this which, in their present state, the Theseus and the Ilissus want. . . . Superior, then, as the Theseus is to the Apollo as a model and school for artists, it never, from its want of character, can be a mere object of mental gratification, equal to the exalted divinity of the Vatican. (544–45)

Undoubtedly the *Quarterly* viewed the Apollo through Reynolds's adaptations. Hazlitt was perfectly correct about these statues: nothing was left but their style, yet the *Quarterly* associated the procession with the universal nobility of patriotic pride and read the Apollo's posed and poised theatricality as its aristocratic dignity. No wonder Keats saw the Marbles as both a sun and as a shadow.

"THE ANNALS OF THE FINE ARTS"

If the location of a poem's first publication determines its historical significance, Keats's "Ode to the Nightingale," its title in the *Annals*, and "Ode on a Grecian Urn" should be read in their first printed versions, where they were printed at Haydon's request in 1819 (*KC* 2: 142). The "Ode to the Nightingale" was published in the second number of the year for July 1819, and the "Grecian Urn," in the final number. The *Annals of the Fine Arts* was edited by James Elmes, an architect and friend and supporter of Haydon. Ian Jack offers a succinct account of its purposes and allegiances.[30] Its first issue was dedicated to the Select Committee of the House of Commons that recommended purchase of the Elgin Marbles. Throughout its five years of publication it promoted the study of the Marbles as models of excellence in art, ridiculed the Royal Academy of Art, and promoted Haydon's career. In his *Autobiography* Haydon described Elmes as a generous supporter but "extremely thoughtless, full of imagination, always scheming and very likely to bring himself and his friends into scrapes. I cared nothing for his peculiarities. I hated the Academy, and was very glad of the use of a publication where I had unlimited control" (292). He boasted, with some reason, that his attacks ruined the authority of the Academy: "I laid open the pretences of a set of men who were masking their real views by the grossest hypocrisy, and prepared the people and the Government for what was their duty, if they wished the country to take its proper rank" (295).

---

[30] Ian Jack, *Keats and the Mirror of Art* (Oxford: Clarendon Press, 1967). See the description of *AFA* in *British Literary Magazines. The Romantic Age, 1789–1836*, ed. Alvin Sullivan (Westport, Ct.: Greenwood Press, 1983).

The second volume of the *Annals* printed three letters from the "Ghost of Barry," who had been expelled from the Royal Academy.[31] In another letter published in that volume, Haydon specifically denied that he was the author of the letters (2: 507), but they reflected both his criticism and his recklessness. "The Ghost of Barry" might well be Haydon's public signature. Haydon had several reasons to attack the Academy, particularly the members' practice of painting aristocratic portraits rather than historical painting that Haydon promoted. The "Ghost of Barry" railed about "the unnatural love for the pretty, over the sublime, in art; and hence the little influence that the grandioso style has yet acquired" and complained that the members of the Academy "encourage brilliant little works, pretty portraits, dull domestic scenery, flowers and still-life, instead of noble, instructive history, and sublime imagery" and preferred "Chinese baubles and whim-whams, instead of noble architecture" (2: 296–97). By ridiculing the Academy in such terms, the "Ghost of Barry" uses the rhetoric of belittlement that Lockhart used several years later to ridicule the Cockneys. The members of the Academy flatter themselves while flattering others and take an air of inflated self-esteem from laboring on the trivial. Lockhart's rhetoric in the essays "On the Cockney School" imitates that of his adversaries. His style was neither unique to him nor, in the second decade of the nineteenth century, unique to his class. Lockhart portrayed the Cockneys as petty tradesman just as Haydon and Elmes had portrayed the members of the Academy as trivial craftsmen. Members of the Academy were, to Elmes and Haydon, guilty of the same presumption and affectation that Lockhart saw in the Cockneys. The products of the academicians were merely "foolish faces and tailors' patterns—of coats, of waistcoats, and of diamond rings." Their art was mere adornment that aimed at flattery but earned them only that status of tailors or pattern makers. The corruption of taste, as it appeared to Haydon and Elmes, led to "the commerce of mutual considerations and advantages. Patronage! ! the exchange of money for money's-worth patronage! !" (2: 302–3):

> Art, Sir, has never flourished, nor ever can it flourish, as a useless foppery, and appendage to luxury, whatever the depicters of scarlet coats and embroidered pelisses may think or assert. On the contrary: worthlessness, imbecility and destruction, have always been the consequences of its passing into that state; and the vulgar error of supposing otherwise, can only have arisen from inattention, want of feeling and the absurdity, not to say mean adulation, of magnifying its accidental, casual connection with patronage, into something staminal and essential to its growth and perfection. (2: 301–2)

[31] Letters "To the Dilettanti Society" (2: 129–45), "To the Prince Regent" (2: 295–305), and "To . . . the Marquis of Stafford, Deputy President and Director of the British Institution for promoting the Fine Arts" (2: 447–61).

The letter of the "Ghost of Barry" had some sting to it, because it was possible to view some of Reynolds's full-length portraits as modeled on the Apollo Belvedere. It would have been easy for Haydon and Elmes to view Reynolds as someone who merely draped the Apollo with elegant robes, or as Keats expressed it at the beginning of Book III of *Endymion*, with "prevailing tinsel." As examples one could cite Reynolds's *The Honourable Augustus Keppel* or *Lord Middleton*, modeled on a Van Dyck portrait, but strongly reminiscent of the Apollo. Aileen Ribeiro describes Lord Middleton's coat: "a superb brocaded silk (probably French), trimmed with silver thread lace, gold thread, tinsel and sequins."[32]

The "Ghost of Barry" concludes this letter to the Prince Regent saying that patronage "is a term . . .the most impertinent and ill-applied that ever was used, as is abundantly evident in the history of art, where, unhappily, we too often find its vigour and growth stinted, and liable to blight, when the great, and *their patronage*, came unluckily to interfere and tamper with it" (2: 303). The fifth volume of the *Annals* included "An Essay on the Superiority of the Ancient Greeks in the Fine Arts . . . ," which repeats the themes that have run through all the numbers: "The noble ardour of genius is restrained when the imagination is to be racked for flattering allegories to compliment one whose life has never supplied an action worthy of the admiration of posterity. Gaudiness and littleness usurp the places of simplicity and grandeur" (5: 45).

There is surely a political point to Elmes's republishing Hazlitt's essay "On Gusto" in the fourth volume of the *Annals*, in the same number in which "On a Grecian Urn" appeared.[33] Gusto, defined as the "power or passion defining any object" (4: 543) is contrasted with trivial and characterless abstraction, the ideal of academic painting. To argue that the academic ideal of painting lacks gusto is to attack the Academy and its system of patronage. As first printed in the *Examiner* and reprinted in the *Annals*, the essay claimed that "perhaps the Greek Statues want gusto," but when printed in Hazlitt's *Round Table*, it claimed "the gusto in the Greek statues is of a very singular kind" (Howe 4: 79). In the *Annals* the essay continues: "The sense of perfect form occupies the whole mind, and hardly suffers it to dwell on any other feeling. It seems enough for them *to be* without acting or suffering. Their forms are ideal, spiritual. Their beauty is power" (4:

---

[32] Quoted in Nicholas Penny, ed., *Paintings by Reynolds with Prints after his Works* (New York: Abrams, 1986) 210. The Academy did encourage historical painting. Aileen Ward has pointed out to me that all the Gold Medals for painting and sculpture awarded by the Academy between 1770 and 1829 were for historical subjects.

[33] Howe 4: 77–80, 377. "On Gusto" first appeared in the *Examiner* (May 26, 1816) and was reprinted in *The Round Table* (1817). Howe did not note its appearance in *AFA*, but Hazlitt's contributions to *AFA* were noted by Clarke Olney, "William Hazlitt and Benjamin Robert Haydon," *Notes & Queries*, 169 (1935): 256.

548). Hazlitt argues that idealized Greek statues possess "perfect form," not the expression of an individual passion or character. In literary criticism, as well as art criticism, he uses the Greek statues as examples of passionless, expressionless art. His introductory lecture in *Lectures on the English Poets*, "On Poetry in General," describes the statues as though they were the very aristocrats for whom the Apollo stood as a model in Reynolds's portraits. The statues, for Hazlitt, have a noble indifference:

> The Greek statues are little else than specious forms. They are marble to the touch and to the heart. They have not an informing principle within them. In their faultless excellence they appear sufficient to themselves. By their beauty they are raised above the frailties of passion or suffering. By their beauty they are deified. But they are not objects of religious faith to us, and their forms are a reproach to common humanity. They seem to have no sympathy with us, and not to want our admiration. (Howe 5: 11)

Hazlitt's definition of ideal Greek art that is aloof and indifferent to human life is formed from the Apollo Belvedere: "What has given rise to the common notion of the *ideal*, as something quite distinct from *actual* nature, is probably the perfection of the Greek statues" (Howe 18: 112). Yet, for Hazlitt, the Elgin Marbles "are opposed to the fashionable and fastidious theory of the ideal" (Howe 18: 147). As David Bromwich has ably demonstrated, Keats's poem embodies Hazlitt's attitude toward Greek art,[34] but, like Haydon, Hazlitt had two attitudes toward Greek statues—one of the ideal Apollo and the second of the natural Elgin Marbles. Keats's poem, in the *Annals*, reflects the entire public debate over Grecian art and the attitudes of his immediate circle toward earlier ideals of art, and their rejection of those ideals certainly had political implications.

The political implications of these attacks are obvious. Haydon was included in Lockhart's attack on the Cockney School. With a flair for self-dramatization, Haydon inflates his importance to the cultural scene, but the social implications of his position are unmistakable:

> War is war; and if you carry it on you must not complain of its inconveniences; but I considered it hard, because I proved a nest of portrait painters were ruining public taste, to be accused of designs against the throne and the altar. All this, however, I ought to have foreseen. The Academy was a royal institution, one of the institutions of the country, and so imbedded in the habits and weaknesses and pleasures of people of fashion, that it would have been foolish to expect that every effort would not be made to support the institution and to blacken the characters of its enemies. Touch a link of the chain from the people to the Crown, and you risk destroying the equilibrium of both. (Haydon 312–13)

---

[34] *Hazlitt* (above, n. 28) 362–409.

The "Ghost of Barry" complains in his first letter that the Academy refused to make available to their students the greatest models of art for study: "When I pointed out these omissions and these errors in the Academy, a slight amendment of which, has been wrung from their unwilling hands, I was hooted at as a democrat and a factious railer, stigmatized to our gracious Monarch as a leveller and as an incendiary, expelled from my situation as teacher of painting, disgraced in the eyes of my pupils, my academical diploma torn from me" (2: 135–36). To attack the Royal Academy for trivializing art, for painting stylish clothing instead of character, for emptying art of its heroic content, is to attack it for depicting no-things, the signs of social significance without their content. Nobles who demand such expenditures in return for their patronage receive a coinage without value, a medium of exchange that changes as fashion changes. More important, however, is the attack upon the system of patronage itself. To strike at patronage is to strike at the heart of the social and economic system and to try to liberate art from the imperatives of subservience, from the demands to reduce human passion and character to the cut of a coat. To strike at systematic art is to strike at the system.

Haydon's boast that he rattled the social order is verified by William Paulet Carey's attack on articles in numbers 8 and 10 of the *Annals* (*AFA* 3: 79–90, 507–12). Carey had written a pamphlet praising West's *Death on a Pale Horse* and called West not only the best but the only historical painter in England. Haydon took offense and answered Carey in the *Annals* with an attack on patronage. Carey's response to Haydon's attack on him was the pamphlet *Desultory Exposition of an Anti-British System of Incendiary Publication*.[35] The purpose of the *Annals*, or the *Liber Falsitatis* as Carey called it, was to "defame the Royal Academy" (ix). Carey's response was primarily a personal attack published by Carey himself, and it expressed outrage at Haydon's contempt for "the exchange of money for money's-worth patronage" (*AFA* 2: 302–3): "This contemptible cavil on the word '*patronage*,'" was "a malicious fling at the Nobility and Gentry, the Great and their Patronage, who are associated for the patronage and encouragement of British Art. . . . But the Anti-academical principle, however disguised, is an absolute and inveterate *Unitarianism*, altogether *Anti-British* . . ." (181). "Unitarianism" in Carey's invective means simply that Haydon considered himself the only worthy historical painter in England, but the word retains its connotations of political and theological dissent that threatened English institutions: "Individuality, or Unitarianism; the monopoly of praise for

---

[35] Its full title was *Desultory Exposition of an Anti-British System of Incendiary Publication, &c. Intended to Sacrifice the Honour and Interests of the British Institution, the Royal Academy, and the Whole Body of the British Artists and Their Patrons, to the Passions, Quackeries and Falsehoods of Certain Disappointed Candidates for Prizes at the British Gallery and Admission as Associates into the Royal Society* (London, 1819).

only one, is the rock, upon which all great public interests split" (24). Carey understood Haydon's criticism of the Royal Academy as an attack on royalty, patronage, and the British public:

> The habit of arrogant disrespect for rank and dignity of the highest order, and of base ingratitude to the Benefactors and Patrons is inculcated. Public Institutions and Personages the most exalted, are, alike, calumniated and blackened. The Royal Academy is held up as perverted and hostile to the Fine Arts, ever since it refused to elect Mr. Haydon an associate. (186)

The liberal allegiances of the *Annals* were clear on the first title page, which quoted from James Thomson's *Liberty*:

> OH GREECE! thou sapient Nurse of FINER ARTS;
> Which to bright Science blooming Fancy bore,
> Be this thy Praise, that Thou, and Thou alone
> In These hast led the Way, in These excelled,
> Crowned with the Laurel of assenting Time.[36]

The first number contained an "Analysis of the Poem called 'Liberty.' By James Thomson, Author of the 'Seasons,'" which lamented that

> A very extraordinary degree of apathy and neglect has been the fate of one of the most elegant descriptive poems in the English Language, the "Liberty" of Thomson. Dr. Johnson, whose bigotted Toryism, and confined views of polity, tinctured all his actions, hated the very name of Liberty, and confounding the philosophical poetical visions of the poet, with the political party he associated with, conceived it was only an apology for licentiousness, or in praise of that which every one knew full well how to value. The contempt with which this truly great critic has treated this poem, has contributed in a very great degree, if not totally, to the little acquaintance of the public with its beauties.[37]

Elmes and Haydon admired Thomson's poem, for it promoted the same views of Greek art that they had used to argue the superiority of the Elgin Marbles: "And every muscle swelled, as nature taught" (II, 308), but while

---

[36] James Thomson, *Liberty, The Castle of Indolence, and Other Poems*, ed. James Sambrook (Oxford: Clarendon Press, 1986). The quotation is from Book II, 252–56.

[37] *AFA* 1: 49. In the "Life of Thomson" (*The Lives of the English Poets*, ed. George Birkbeck Hill [Oxford: Clarendon Press, 1905]) Johnson wrote that

> a long course of opposition to Sir Robert Walpole had filled the nation with clamours for liberty, of which no man felt the want, and with care for liberty, which was not in danger. Thomson, in his travels on the continent, found or fancied so many evils arising from the tyranny of other governments, that he resolved to write a very long poem, in five parts, upon *Liberty*. . . . *Liberty* called in vain upon her votaries to read her praises, and reward her encomiast: her praises were condemned to harbour spiders, and to gather dust: none of Thomson's performances were so little regarded. 3: 289.

its esthetics were admirable, it also was primarily a political poem. Thomson's poem traces the progress of liberty from Greece to eighteenth-century Britain and rejoices that perfect liberty was established in 1688 with government power balanced among the monarch, aristocrats, and commoners. His exhortation was that liberty must be maintained by public virtue. *Liberty* was completed in 1736, but when it was read in 1816, "liberty" had a vastly different significance. Although the praise of the poem in the *Annals* could be read as an acceptable form of Whig oppositional rhetoric, to many it implied revolutionary liberty. John Barrell points out that lines from *Liberty* were read in court in defense of Thomas Hardy in the 1794 treason trials and had been quoted by the London Corresponding Society, with purposes quite different than those Thomson intended. The significance of *Liberty* in 1816 was mediated by the London Corresponding Society and the treason trials.[38] To deplore the corruption of taste is to deplore a social and economic system that was by nature corrupt, and to contrast Grecian liberty with the tyrannies of Egypt and Rome and its successors, is to re-locate the present British government in Egypt.

Thomson's *Liberty* anticipated Richard Payne Knight's description in *Specimens of Antient Sculpture*, of the "torpid state" of Egyptian art that resulted from its government and system of hereditary trades. The Goddess of Liberty granted art to Egypt but

> Then *Tyrant Power* the righteous Scourge unloos'd:
> For yielded Reason speaks the Soul a Slave.
> Instead of useful Works, like Nature's great,
> Enormous cruel Wonders crush'd the Land;
> And round a Tyrant's Tomb, who none deserv'd,
> For one vile Carcass perish'd endless Lives.
>
> (II, 59–64)

Keats's *Hyperion* draws on such discussions for the public nuances of its figures. Thea's face "was large as that of Memphian Sphinx."[39] Hyperion reads the signs of the zodiac as "hieroglyphics old" (I, 277). At the end of Book II, Keats describes him as an Egyptian:

> Golden his hair of short Numidian curl,
> Regal his shape majestic, a vast shade
> In midst of his own brightness, like the bulk
> Of Memnon's image at the set of sun
> To one who travels from the dusking east;
>
> (II, 371–75)

[38] John Barrell, *The Birth of Pandora and the Division of Knowledge* (Philadelphia: University of Pennsylvania Press, 1992) xv.

[39] *Hyperion: A Fragment*, I, 31 in *KP* 248.

These references to despotic Egypt would have been obvious to Keats's readers who also read the discourse of art history. The references cannot be explained merely by the accidents of Keats's visits to the British Museum or by esthetic considerations. Keats's fallen and falling gods were Egyptian tyrants with Greek names, representatives of a passing order to be replaced by Greek liberty.

In the fourth volume of the *Annals*, which contained Keats's odes, Elmes wrote an article entitled "A brief View of the Fine Arts among various Nations of Antiquity." He explained in the terms of Richard Payne Knight that in Egypt "restraints on art, by law, religion and policy, operated to depress it, or keep it from rising above its earlier attempts" and defined Greek art in the terms of Thomson's poem and Knight's explanations: "In Greece, the arts, free as the air the natives breathed, and the liberty those happier sons of a happy soil enjoyed, grew and prospered mightily in all the gay and unrestrained luxuriance of unfettered liberty" (4: 209). Greek religious sentiments were motivated, Elmes wrote, by two motives, "fear and acknowledgment; to implore favours and to acknowledge benefits," and some offerings to the gods were works of art, "for vases of bronze, of silver, or of gold, tripods, crowns, altars, candelabrae, &c. were among the dedications of the great" (4: 210–11). Elmes regarded Greek religious ceremonies as public acknowledgment of and praise of their liberty: "Their government also, the aegis of liberty, was most favourable to the fine arts; and their manners and customs, the aliment of a fine and delicate taste, gave them that purity of style and particular graces, for which the arts of Greece are so preeminent" (4: 210). When a people blessed with "freedom and liberty are fit" for reception of the arts, "they seldom fail to offer such contributions on the shrine of independence" (4: 212). Thus to represent the origins of Greek art is to represent those origins displayed at the shrine of liberty.

Such constructions of Greek art and liberty did not go unchallenged. The *Quarterly Review*'s praise of the procession on the Elgin Marbles did not read the procession as a celebration of liberty but as a ceremony of Tory patriotic pride. In its first number of April 1817, *Blackwood's* evaluated the claim that the superiority of Greek art rested on "influences of climate, of religion, of political liberty, of the facility with which the naked figure was studied, and the recompenses with which their artists were distinguished" (9). Examining these claims and rejecting every one, *Blackwood's* triumphantly concluded that the reason for their excellence is the "favour of the legislature,—and it is to *that favour* alone, however obtained, that they always owe anything which deserves the name of more than a mere temporary triumph. . . . In all climates nature fits men for the enjoyment of the arts; in every climate, and under every form of government, their success is the result of public munificence, and the favour of the laws" (15–16). Excellence can come only from a system of benevolent patronage.

While Elmes and Haydon provided the social and political tone of the *Annals*, Hazlitt provided the esthetic tone of the fourth volume, in which Keats's odes were printed. The first three numbers for 1819 reprinted Hazlitt's "An Account of Sir Joshua Reynolds' Discourses" originally printed in the *Champion* from November 1814 to January 1815. The essay was originally in four parts. The first two parts, "Introduction" and "On Genius and Originality," were reprinted in the first number of the *Annals* for 1819. The third part, "On the Imitation of Nature," was reprinted as the first essay in the second number, which contained "Ode to the Nightingale." The final part, entitled in the *Champion* "On the Ideal" and in the *Annals* "On the Discourses of Sir Joshua Reynolds: III," was reprinted in the third number.[40] Hazlitt's essay was perfectly consistent with his later pronouncements on esthetics and his support for the Elgin Marbles. It contained a severe critique of Reynolds's formulation of the ideal in art: "There is a fine spun metaphysical theory, either not very clearly understood, or not very correctly expressed, pervading Sir Joshua's reasoning" (4: 34). The second section of his essay, "On Genius and Originality," ridicules Reynolds's notion that "genius and invention are principally shewn in borrowing the ideas, and imitating the excellences of others." Drawing upon the root meaning of the word *genius* as "individuality," Hazlitt maintains on the contrary that "a work demonstrates genius exactly as it contains what is to be found no where else, or in proportion to what we add to the ideas of others from our own stores, and not to what we receive from them" (4: 37–38). In the third section, "On the Imitation of Nature," Hazlitt dismantles Reynolds's explanation of the general in art: "Sir Joshua's general system may be summed up in two words—'*That the great style in painting consists in avoiding the details and peculiarities of particular objects.*' This sweeping principle he applies almost indiscriminately to portrait, history, and landscape." Hazlitt maintains on the contrary that the highest excellence in art combines "general truth and effect with individual distinctness and accuracy" (4: 165–66). He argues that portrait painting expresses character and that the omission of detail consistent with that character renders a portrait merely abstract and expressionless. Historical portraiture is "representing the individual under one probable, consistent, and striking view; or shewing the different features, muscles, &c. in one action, and modified by one principle. A face, thus painted, is *historical*; that is, it carries its own internal evidence of truth and nature with it; and the number of individual peculiarities, as long as they are true to nature, cannot lessen, but must add to the general strength of the impression" (4: 175).

Hazlitt's attention to the physical details of the muscles in one action parallels Haydon's praise of the postures of the figures in the Elgin Marbles.

---

[40] *AFA* 4: 34–48, 165–78, 385–97. Howe 18: 62–84. Howe did not notice that these essays were reprinted in *AFA*, but they were noted by Olney.

To both the Marbles represent an accurate imitation of the details of the human body, and by that accuracy the figures become properly historical and not abstract or general. Hazlitt implies that a portrait, by becoming individual, becomes historical, that is, true to nature.

The first three parts of Hazlitt's essay lead naturally to the fourth, his severe critique of Reynolds's explanation of the ideal in art, which Hazlitt sees as recommending that the artist

> wander up and down in the empty void of his own imagination, having nothing better to cling to, than certain shadowy middle forms, made up of an abstraction of all others, and containing nothing in themselves. Stripping nature of substance and accident, he is to exhibit a decompounded, disembodied, vague, ideal nature in her stead, seen through the misty veil of metaphysics, and covered with the same fog and haze of confusion. (4:386)

The earlier printing of Hazlitt's essay in the *Champion* of January 8, 1815, is the source of Endymion's lament in Book IV: "I have clung / To nothing, lov'd a nothing, nothing seen / Or felt but a great dream!" (IV, 636–38). Since Keats appropriated Hazlitt's words for *Endymion*, he was intimately acquainted with these essays on Reynolds. To Hazlitt, Reynolds's ideal is a no-thing, "a voluntary fiction of the brain, a fanciful piece of patch-work, a compromise between the defects of nature, or an artificial balance struck between innumerable deformities" (4: 394). Reynolds's ideal is not only a no-thing, it is produced by servile artists who depict an insipid aristocracy. A portrait painter who follows Reynolds's ideal to represent "a Grecian marriage . . . will refine on his favourite principle, till it will be possible to transpose the features of the bridegroom and the bride without the least violation of propriety; all the women will be like all the men; and all like one another, all equally young, blooming, smiling, elegant, and insipid" (4: 388).

As examples of "true nature and true history," Hazlitt cites the Elgin Marbles to refute Reynolds's theories and practice of ideal art:

> The process of fastidious refinement, and flimsy abstraction, is certainly not visible there. The figures have all the ease, the simplicity, and variety of nature, and look more like living men turned to stone than any thing else. Even the details of the subordinate parts, the loose folds in the skin, the veins under the belly or on the sides of the horses, more or less swelled as the animal is more or less in action, are given with a scrupulous exactness. . . . Michael Angelo and the antique may still be cited against us, and we wish to speak on this subject with great diffidence. We confess, they appear to us much more artificial than the others, but we do not think that this is their excellence. For instance, it strikes us that there is something theatrical in the air of the *Apollo*, and in the *Hercules* [Belvedere torso] an ostentatious and overlaboured display of the knowledge of the muscles. Perhaps the fragment of the *Theseus* at Lord Elgin's has more grandeur as well as more nature than either of them. (4: 392–93)

The Urn's Legacy

The "Grecian Urn" was published in the *Annals* at Haydon's suggestion, so that its location is the result of decisions by both Haydon and Keats. One must assume that Haydon sited the poem in the *Annals* because its message, its legend, was compatible with the articles in the volume and opposed to the ideal art of Sir Joshua Reynolds's Royal Academy and to the patronage system that supported its members. Both Keats and Haydon authored the poem's location, and location in the public discourse is prior to significance. Since the articles attacking Reynolds and the Academy in the 1819 volume are by Elmes and Hazlitt, their influence on the poem's significance can be read along with that of Haydon, and they, too, contributed to its collaborative authorship. The poem was not signed, except for an entry in the index that listed "Keats, Mr.," as the author of "Ode to the Nightingale" and "On a Grecian Urn." Since its designation as an ode, which is defined by apostrophe and address, is absent from the title, the title focuses attention on what is "on" the urn, its inscription, its utterance, and the legend that haunts it, rather than the speaker's attitude expressed in his address to it. The title focuses on the urn's paratexts on the "Attic shape." The poem escapes from the confining limits of literary genre, the ode, and enters the public discourse on the value of classical art. The significance of the urn in particular and Greek art in general are at stake in Keats's reading of the urn's legend, frame, or border. The composite public author reformulates and redefines the public significance of Greek art. Keats is the public subject of the poem, not merely its subjective author. Publication changes authorship from a private subjectivity to a public and collaborative act and changes the defining presence in a work to its borders, to its frames.

The *Annals* in general and the 1819 volume in particular provide an extended paratext through which to read the poem: "What leaf-fringed legend haunts about thy shape, / Of Deities, or Mortals, or of both." The "leaf-fringed legend" is both the urn's paratext and text, which designates legends about Greek art and the controversies that the poem reflects. To haunt is to visit regularly, and the legend "haunts about" the shape of the urn as a frequent visitant, a ghostly presence, since its haunting and visiting implies an absence, an inessential or merely decorative aspect on the "Attic shape" of the urn. The legend is "about" the urn both in the sense that it is worked over the urn's surface and in the sense that it concerns the urn as its subject matter, stands apart from the urn, speaks about it, and offers a reading of the urn. Paratext may be both inside and outside, essential and merely decorative. What, after all, is the essential urn? Is it only the "Attic shape, fair attitude," or does it also include its decoration, its "leaf-fringed" legend and sculpture worked over the surface? Does it include the "legends" associated with it, particularly if they suggest Grecian subjects? Except, perhaps, for its shape, the urn is all decoration, all brede, all paratext, or frame. One can only read what is wrought over the urn—not the urn itself, which is pure form. The legend is most literally the inscription or figures on the urn, its readings. The historical nuances of *legend* point to its Latin origins in *legere*, "to read," and to legends of saints' lives and religious readings collected for instruction. But the figures on the urn are pagan, not Christian. *Legend* is also cognate with *law* and *legitimacy* through the Latin *lex, legis*, "law," and *lego, legare*, "to ordain by law" or "to bequeath as a legacy," yet at the same time it retains its more modern meaning of an "inauthentic history," a "probable fiction," and a "ghostly writing" (*Chambers/Murray Latin-English Dictionary*, s.v. "legend"). In "The Eve of St. Agnes" Madeline sleeps in "lap of legends old." In the public discourse, Keats's "legend" resonates with Hazlitt's use of *legitimacy*, his word for the established order of society. What "legend," what reading, the public Mr. Keats inquires, does the simplicity of its "Attic shape" support? Where is its legend and what claims does it make for legitimacy for both gods and men? The public poem, like the other articles in the *Annals*, explores the claims of legends and legitimacy that resonate with the words of the Ghost of Barry, the ghostly interpreter of a haunted aesthesis.

As with other Romantic lyrics, paratexts point both outside the poem and inside. They are the crossroads of discursive significance where private authority meets public legitimacy. The extended paratext of "On a Grecian Urn" combines the volumes of the *Annals* and the legends in the poem. The legend that "haunts about" the shape is the ideal as Reynolds conceived it and as Hazlitt ridiculed it, a no-thing. The abstract ideal of beauty sanctioned by law and promoted by legitimacy "haunts about" the urn as its ghostly interpreter. Keats's poem rejects the legend as a "Cold pastoral," and the rejection parallels Hazlitt's rejection of ideal art. Whether one reads the arguments of Richard Payne Knight, who valued the Apollo Belvedere over the Elgin Marbles, or of Haydon and Hazlitt, who esteemed the Elgin Marbles, one finds a rejection of the ideal as transcendent reality, artistic ideal, or imaginative abstraction. Knight wanted to rid the language of the word *ideal* and base an esthetic on the senses. Hazlitt explicitly, and Haydon implicitly, agreed by rejecting the ideal as mannered abstraction. What Benjamin West called "systematic" art, the elegant theatricality of the Apollo Belvedere, Haydon and Hazlitt regarded as violated nature. Even the *Quarterly Review*, in 1816, in a rare concession to new ideas, judged that "we have great doubts upon the truth of the theory of the '*beau idéal*.'"[41]

One purpose of the *Annals* is to enlist Greek art in what Hazlitt in the *Spirit of the Age* called the struggle of liberty against legitimacy and to construct an origin for liberty in the representations of Greek art. Reynolds's

---

[41] *Quarterly Review* (Jan. 1816) 545.

idealizations of Greek art and his use of it in portraiture had transformed
Greek liberty into British legitimacy. The urn presents itself as a "Silvan
Historian" who recites a legend intended to legitimate idealism. To re-site
classical history is to locate it in the present, but this obscures its associations with liberty that implied republicanism if not democracy, sexual and
artistic freedom, and an esthetic based in the senses. In the instance of the
Annals and "On a Grecian Urn," liberty also implies the freedom from the
domination of an ideal promoted by royal academies and institutions.
Keats's poem challenges the authority that would deny liberty's origins by
idealizing art and making art's idealizations a royal institution.

The obscurity of the urn's legend troubles the urn as historian of the
ideal. The "Sylvan Historian," who speaks a "flowery tale" and recites a
"leaf-fringed legend," must work with contradictions, must mix pastoral
and narrative, inauthentic legend and original form, unravished delight and
sated human passion. As pastoral, the urn's genre is at odds with the gener-
ations that it comforts. What kind of history can idealized pastoral tell, and
how does pastoral speak? How can an authentic history survive such esthetic borders, such entrances, such decoration? If the urn and its legend
constitute a speaking monument, that memorial is an artifact that speaks of
a pastoral history that wants to veil both the country matters amply illustrated by Knight and Christie and the historical distance from its origin that
troubled Hazlitt.

The urn, unbroken from its creation and hence unfallen, memorializes a
lapse, a historical distance from its legendary origin. In Hazlitt's terms, if
the "Sylvan Historian," speaks its legend as history, it narrates its own fall
into a knowledge both too abundant to legitimate and too poor to compensate the imaginative labor of comprehension. Unlike the broken and
corroded Elgin Marbles, the figures on the urn have been preserved in their
original state, but their significance has been lost and their meanings have
been hidden by the veil of time. It is thus no wonder that Hazlitt and Keats
did not read the figures as representing a definable ideal. In 1819 in the *Annals*, "On a Grecian Urn" figures our own ignorance of its legend and context, predicting its future lapses in history and implying that we possess both
too much and too little knowledge to understand its legend. In the late
twentieth century, most of what we think about the poem preserves an ideal
that the poem in the *Annals* nullifies. Our deliberations about the presence
and value of the ideal in the poem are prefigured, not by the urn or poem
itself, but by the disputes over its significance and that of Grecian subjects.
History, in Keats's poem, is lost in the lapses of time and idealized by legends of legitimacy associated with it by the Academy. To the Keats who
reads the legends, that idealized history is a static coldness. To Keats nothing remains but the sensuous apprehension of its form. The discursive public readings of the legend in the second decade of the nineteenth century

constitute an obscure origin for ours. Keats's is a canny urn. It has always known silence is best; it remains still. It allows the public discourse that it generated to construct its genres and engender its origins. As Keats and the circle at the *Annals* knew, in the lapse of history only the shape, the esthetic form remains. All that is left is its immediate appeal to the senses.

History, to Hazlitt and Keats, is a wonder because it is obscure, not that it preserves an ideal. Its legend leaves unspoken the grossness of paganism, that Conder condemned. Keats avoids any suggestion of grossness, yet his poem hints at it while disavowing it. In the *Lamia* volume of 1820 the first stanza ends

> What men or gods are these? What maidens loath?
> What mad pursuit? What struggle to escape?
> What pipes and timbrels? What wild ecstasy?

The words denote an exuberant intoxicated chase, but the tropes of escape and ecstasy, strategically placed at the end of the lines, connote an urge to leave the chase, to escape from its frenzy. Keats frequently turns on the final word in a stanza to turn to the next stanza. The word *pursuit* remains a little vague, so that its primary meaning is sexual pursuit, but it also suggests the more ideal quest in the following stanza. Yet the first stanza in the *Annals* was phrased differently to denote more explicitly sexual pursuit:

> What Gods or Men are these? What Maidens loath?
> What love? What dance? what struggle to escape?
> What Pipes and timbrels? what wild extacy?

With the substitution of the questions "What love? What dance?" the archaic and mystical sense of "extacy" is suppressed for the more modern sense of entrancement. The sensuous is more explicit as Keats gazes on the urn while remembering the public discourse over the grossness of Greek art.

In the *Annals* the second stanza denies the sensual and also risks invoking it. It wants to balance a sublimation of the sensual that does not idealize it or refine it out of physical existence to permanence that can be expressed only in negatives. The piper plays "not to the sensual ear," the lover never can kiss, and the trees will never lose their leaves. The desire of the private and subjective speaker to refine the sensual into permanence conflicts with the words of the public observer who needs to suppress any suggestion of the sensual. Suppressing the senses avoids the public's censure but also limits the sensuous impulse to the esthetic that prompted the utterance in the first place. If the senses are suppressed, the result is a cold and inhuman ideal as indifferent to human passion and suffering as those who advocate the ideal's legitimacy. A "Cold Pastoral" is the result—a phrase that re-writes the "leaf-fringed legend" of the poem's opening. The urn becomes like Hazlitt's description of the Greek statues as "specious forms. They are marble to the touch and to the heart." Having tried the legend of the ideal, Keats finds it inhuman, an abstraction that can only display its aloof detachment. In the *Annals*, "On a Grecian Urn" exposes the aloofness of an ideal legitimacy that "haunts about" a Greek art, which in the public discourse tells Keats another tale, one of sensuous beauty and liberty.

The third stanza is fringed by the word *leaves*. The boughs that "cannot shed" their leaves in the opening lines are those on the trees in the second stanza. They are emblems of idealized pastoral and thus claim a legitimate permanence and a permanent legitimacy. Similarly the melodist, the honey-eyed singer, and the lover are for ever posed in their permanent attitude. The stanza ends, however, with another "leaves" that plays upon the first: a "breathing human passion / That leaves a heart high-sorrowful and cloyed." This second "leaves" denotes a legacy, a bequest of the remainder of human passion. Passion thus becomes a legate supplanting the authority of the idealized urn. The change comes through a turn in the line "All breathing human passion far above," which means that the urn, which is above us in its permanence, embodies the best of all human passion, but which also means its opposite: the urn is above all human passion, which resides below the urn in mutability. Thus the permanent "leaves" of the stanza's opening becomes the residue of human passion. The still permanence of the urn's legend that demands belief in its authority turns to a legacy of human passion. The humanity of the second replaces the aloof perfection of the first, and the urn's claims for legitimacy are replaced with the gift of the human.

The fourth stanza turns from contemplation of private desires to public ceremonies. The turn has been read as echoing the idealizations of the earlier stanzas. Cleanth Brooks, for example, in an essay subtitled "History without Footnotes," remarked that the scene presented in this stanza "emphasizes, not individual aspiration and desire, but communal life. It constitutes another chapter in the history that the 'Sylvan historian' has to tell. And again, names and dates have been omitted. We are not told to what god's altar the procession moves, nor the occasion of the sacrifice." Brooks comments astutely on the town emptied by the procession: "No one in the figured procession will ever be able to go back to the town to break the silence there, not even one to tell the stranger there why the town remains desolate." Brooks considers the confusion of an imaginary and a real town as a "flaw in logic," but logical flaws, in his reading, become tense paradoxes that constitute the unique language of poetry. The paradox echoes the earlier paradox of the "unheard melodies": "the poet, by pretending to take the town as real . . . has suggested in the most powerful way possible its essential reality for him."[42] The figures on the urn who have left the historical town are lost in a labyrinthine funhouse of art. Reading the same stanza, Helen Vendler sees Keats offering

> a new and more adequate hypothesis about the aesthetic experience offered by an artifact, and our aesthetic response. The urn, he suggests, is not just the illustration of a legend or tale about other people; nor is it just a representation, in archetypal and idealized form, of our human aspirations. Rather, it is most truly described as a self-contained anonymous world, complete in itself, which asks from us an empathic identification supremely free both of factual inquiry and of self-interest. . . . Keats, contemplating his third scene—a ritual sacrificial procession—foreign, ancient, remote from anything he has himself known—asks not about an antecedent legend but investigates instead the boundaries of representation.[43]

For Brooks, the value of the stanza rests in its intensification of the pattern of paradoxes that are real to the poet; for Vendler, the value rests in the impersonal esthetic.

Something crucial has happened in the poem. As Brooks says, there is a shift from the individual to the communal, or public festival, and as Vendler insists, there is a change from the deeply personal projection of the speaker's desires to impersonal contemplation. Both, however, read the shift as representing the esthetic and the "boundaries of the representation," which in Vendler's reading can only be the boundaries of the esthetic that offer only a fragmentary view of real life. Yet where are those boundaries? What constitutes them? Is the poem an autonomous artifact that one enters through an entrance that leads to a trance? For Vendler the pathos of the esthetic is that it cannot finally be sustained: "While we are 'within' the urn, we are not outside it; while we are outside reflecting on it, we are not 'within' it. Like the figures on the urn, we cannot be at once in the town where we live and on the urn" (123). For her reading, boundaries of representation, the entrances, can be crossed but they are a deep divide.

My argument is not that these readings are either wrong or inadequate. Both map their own boundaries with brilliant insight and deep human sympathy for our experience of the poem, but they are our boundaries and our representations. As I have argued, however, boundaries can be located but not bound. They are difficult to circumscribe with the clarity that either Brooks or Vendler assume. One can read both inside and outside at the same time, and to do so paratextually is to read a location that does not inquire about the accurate historical origins of the urn. Hazlitt's comment on the

[42] Cleanth Brooks, "Keats's Sylvan Historian: History without Footnotes," *The Well Wrought Urn* (New York: Harcourt, Brace & World, 1947) 160–62.

[43] Helen Vendler, *The Odes of John Keats* (Cambridge: Harvard University Press, 1983) 121.

Elgin Marbles, "nothing remains of them but their style" (Howe 18: 100) sufficiently summarizes common opinion in Keats's day. Mythical representation was simply not a major issue to advocates of the Marbles. To Hazlitt and Haydon the issue of representation, of reality, was their accurate depiction of the human body in action governed by a single idea or character. In the *Annals*, the poem enunciates an esthetic of the senses that speaks of the present rather than a historical past.

While the urn provides only a minute documentary fragment of its Greek origin, the located poem alludes to contemporary readings of communal sacrifice, gifts, and ceremonies, which Keats certainly did know.[44] If the urn's history is inevitably obscure, then it speaks to its audience in 1819 of the present, as perhaps it speaks to us only of our present. As Brooks notes, the fourth stanza moves from the private imagination to the public realm and prompts us ask about the significance of its communal activities. James Elmes's "A Brief View of the Fine Arts," in the same volume of the *Annals* as "On a Grecian Urn," described a sacrifice by a people enjoying "freedom and liberty" as "contributions on the shrine of independence." To the *Quarterly*, public ceremonies worthy of representation are those that represent nobility and moral character, not liberty.

A third commentary on sacrifice available to Keats is Haydon's description of Raphael's cartoon *The Sacrifice at Lystra*, on public exhibition. The *Examiner* published Haydon's analysis on May 2 and 9, 1819, and the *Annals* reprinted it in the fourth volume, which contained Keats's poem.[45] The subject is the story from Acts 14 in which Paul and Barnabas cure a lame man. The public mistakes their miracle, believing Paul and Barnabas to be Jupiter and Mercury. In Raphael's cartoon, the public is about to sacrifice a bull to Paul and Barnabas, while some few in the crowd recognize the obvious displeasure of Paul and Barnabas. Some of the imagery from Haydon's description of the preparation of the bull is found in Keats's description of the sacrifice. The association of this sacrifice and public ceremony with that on the urn is a complex matter, because to Raphael and Haydon there is an undoubted truth of Christianity depicted in the horror of Paul and Barnabas at the pagan rites accorded them. To them the episode represents the public worship of false gods and the clash of Christian and pagan cultures. The errors of pagan worship are clearly condemned, yet also are the errors of the public perception of the miraculous. Only a few in Raphael's crowd perceive the truth of Paul's and Barnabas's displeasure; some more are

---

[44] Discussing the fêtes of the French Revolution, Nicholas Roe says that in the fourth stanza "the questions invite the reader to translate the urn's imagery through historical correspondences and associations while simultaneously resisting that process" (*John Keats and the Culture of Dissent* [Oxford: Clarendon Press, 1997] 86).

[45] *AFA* 4:226–47. J. R. MacGillivray, "Ode on a Crecian Urn," *TLS* 9 (July 1938): 465–66.

struck with simple wonder; the rest carry on the ceremony in pious un-
knowning. The public reaction is mixed and uncertain. Keats's voice in the
fourth stanza echoes that wonder and uncertainty:

> Who are these coming to the sacrifice?
>   To what green Altar, O mysterious Priest!
> Lead'st thou that Heifer lowing at the skies,
>   And all her silken flanks with garlands drest?
> What little town by river or sea shore
>   Or mountain built with peaceful citadel,
>   Is emptied of this folk this pious morn?
> And little Town thy streets for evermore
>   Will silent be; and not a soul to tell
>   Why thou art desolate can e'er return.

The representation of festival, on the urn, empties the town. Those who
join the public ceremony leave the town's streets desolate and silent. Entering the ideal state, as Brooks suggests, leaves ordinary life vacant, since,
in Keats's terms, when one enters the world of art, no return is possible. To
enter an ideal state is to leave human life behind. To enter art, is to leave
life behind, but there is more to the public significance of "On a Grecian
Urn" than the tension between a pained mortal life and a consuming art,
because that art is ideal and therefore noble, the public symbol of the "leaf-
fringed legend" and its pastoral idealism and legitimacy. When the people,
the "folk," join the public procession, the "little town" is "emptied" and the
streets are silent. Ordinary voices are silenced at the sacrifice. When, in
other words, those normally excluded from the public sphere worship at the
shrine of legitimacy in its public display, they become silent and desolate.
What should be a ceremony that Elmes describes, an acknowledgment of
the gift of liberty, has become a silencing of dissent.

In the *Annals* the final paratextual legend, "Beauty is truth, truth beauty"
separates beauty from the "Cold pastoral" of the ideal. Neither truth nor
beauty is found in the haunting legend, the ideal, the moral associations that
the *Quarterly* thought the Apollo possessed of patriotic pride and noble dignity. After all, as the *Examiner* did not cease from pointing out, the public
ceremonies in the days of the *Annals* celebrated the restoration of monar-
chies throughout Europe. No such ideas are associated with the simple
"Attic shape." The titled privilege of noble but theatrical beauty of the
Apollo is countered by the esthetic on the title page of the first number of
the *Annals*. The result is an esthetic that supports the Elgin Marbles over
the Apollo Belvedere, that values a sublimated nature over the shadowy
nothings of an artist's imagination, that clings to naturalness over systematic art,—-above all an esthetic based in the senses and one that is publicly
located. The new legend, "Beauty is truth, truth beauty," in its location in

the *Annals* is a legend without a history, without a narrative, and thus without national boundaries. This new legend replaces the legitimating pastoral history of the opening stanza. Its beauty, defined paratextually by Hazlitt and Haydon, is the beauty of the senses and the exact imitation of nature. Its truth is the truth to physical life. The beauty praised by the urn defies the theatricality that the *Quarterly* praised and insists on the esthetic of the senses that *Blackwood's* distrusted.

INDEX

Abrams, M. H., 39n
Acts of the Apostles, 208
Addison, Joseph, 167
address, 4, 46–53
advertisement, 54–55
allusion, 4, 5, 26, 38, 48, 49, 51–53
Analytical Review, 44, 77, 80, 101, 109
Annals of the Fine Arts, 10, 41, 168–70, 172, 192–204; "Analysis of the Poem called 'Liberty,'" 197–98; "A Brief View of the Fine Arts . . . of Antiquity," 199, 208; "An Essay on the Superiority of the Ancient Greeks," 194; Letters of the "Ghost of Barry," 193–94, 196, 203
Anti-Jacobin, or Weekly Examiner, 22, 41, 41n–42n, 55, 70–77, 80–81, 83–84, 85, 111–12, 122, 124–25, 134, 137, 163–64, 167; "Friend of Humanity and the Knife Grinder," 134; "Inscription for the Door of the Cell," 134; "Loves of the Triangles," 48; "New Morality," 45, 56, 69–70, 77, 83, 84, 164; "The Progress of Man," 48, 179; "The Rovers," 48, 104, 106–8, 134n
Anti-Jacobin Review, 56, 100, 103
apostrophe, 46–53
Aristotle, 98
Aske, Martin, 172n
Aspinall, A., 18n, 22
Austin, J. L., 25

Bailey, Benjamin, 176, 181, 188
Baker, Herschel, 188n
Bakhtin, Mikhail, 25, 111, 123–24, 165
Barbauld, Mrs., 101
Barnes, Thomas, 159–60, 165
Barrell, John, 19, 198
Barruel, Abbé, 99–100
Barthes, Roland, 50
Bate, Jonathan, 51n, 64
Beaty, Frederick, 126n
Beaumont, Sir George, 76
Beauties of the Anti-Jacobin, 41, 42n, 55, 75
Bedford, Grosvenor, 127, 139
Berkley, George, 58, 62, 84, 93
Berni, Francesco, 140

Bewell, Alan, 182n
Bialostoski, Don, 110–11
Binns, John, 73
Blackstone, William, 8
Blackwood's Edinburgh Magazine, 112–13, 125–26, 129n, 148, 162, 171n, 175, 176, 199, 210; "The Building of the Palace of the Lamp," 167–68, 176; "Cockney Poetry and Cockney Politics," 173; "On the Cockney School of Poetry," 47n, 170–73, 195; "Letter from Z to Mr. Leigh Hunt," 171; "Mr. Wastle's Diary," 168
Blair, Hugh, 50
Blake, William, 20, 39, 132, 169n
Bloom, Harold, 52n
Bostetter, Edward, 95
Boulton, James, 13n, 14, 49n
Bourdieu, Pierre, 25–26, 43, 122
Boyd, Elizabeth French, 123n
British Critic, 101, 102, 107, 118, 173
Bromwich, David, 188n, 195
Brooks, Cleanth, 52, 168, 206–7, 208
Brougham, Henry, 43
Burdett, Francis, 20
Bürger, Gottfried, 102
Burke, Edmund, 12, 94, 119; *First Letter on a Regicide Peace*, 15–16, 21, 80, 84, 90, 112, 124–25, 165; *Letter to a Noble Lord*, 47; *Reflections on the Revolution in France*, 13, 14, 17, 49, 72n, 81, 92, 108, 147
Burney, Charles, 96, 102, 111, 112, 118
Butler, Marilyn, 12n, 168n
Byron, Frederick George, 147
Byron, Lord, 47, 76, 171; *Beppo*, 140; *Childe Harold*, 28, 49, 149; *Don Juan*, 9, 14, 25, 53, 78, 122–66, 170; "Fare Thee Well," 14, 129; *Hours of Idleness*, 43; "Ode from the French," 138, 147; "A Sketch from Private Life," 14; "The Vision of Judgment," 41

Calhoun, Craig, 12n
Cameron, Kenneth, 11, 129n
Canning, George, 69n, 71, 127, 128, 163–64

Canova, Antonio, 185, 188
Carey, William Paulet, 196–97
Carlile, Richard, 20
Carpenter, Humphrey, 133n
Casti, Giambattista, 140
Castlereagh, Robert Stewart Vicount, 123, 127–28, 130, 131n, 153, 156, 158–60
Chambers, E. K., 59n
Champion, 14, 179, 185, 200, 201
Chandler, James, 51n
Chapman, George, 172
Charlotte, Princess, 138, 142
Chatterton, Thomas, 48, 96
Chaucer, Geoffrey, 96, 111–13
Chauntry, Francis, 187
Christensen, Jerome, 43
Christie, James, 178, 204
Cibber, Colley, 131
Cicero, 20, 50, 103
Cobbett, William, 12, 47, 48, 125, 129, 149
Coigley, Rev. James, 73
Coleridge, Rev. George, 78
Coleridge, Samuel Taylor, 16, 34, 48, 51n, 53, 123n, 126, 144–47, 150, 152, 161, 169, 181n; *Biographia Literaria*, 44–45, 65, 88, 108n, 137, 147–49, 157n, 171n; "The British Stripling's War Song," 58; "A Character," 59; "Christabel," 14, 40, 43, 55, 126n; "A Christmas Carol," 58; *Conciones ad Populum*, 51, 82, 86; "Dejection: An Ode," 40, 41; "Destiny of Nations," 41, 70n; "The Dungeon," 109; "The Eolian Harp," 29, 39, 40, 67; *Essays on His Times*, 30, 53, 56, 70, 72–73, 100; "The Fall of Robespierre," 43; "Fears in Solitude," 67, 73–75, 76, 80, 89, 91–92; *Fears in Solitude*, 9, 25, 55, 67–68, 70, 76–77, 85–86, 88, 90–94, 101, 145; "Fire, Famine, and Slaughter," 56; "The Foster Mother's Tale," 109; "France: An Ode," 59, 67, 72, 85, 88–90; *The Friend*, 76; "Frost at Midnight," 9, 40, 67–68, 77–78, 84–94, 109; "Kubla Khan," 40; *A Lay Sermon*, 148; "This Lime-Tree Bower," 9, 25, 40, 46, 53–66, 67, 93; *Lectures on Shakespeare and Milton*, 17; *Lectures 1795 on Politics and Revealed Religion*, 13, 64–66, 70, 74, 82, 86–87; "Letters on the Spaniards," 30; "Lewti," 42; "The Mad Ox," 56, 59, 79–80, 85; "The Nightingale," 110; "Ode on the Departing Year," 46, 63, 88–90; "Ode to Georgiana: Duchess of Devonshire," 58; "Osorio," 102–3; "The Pains of Sleep," 40; "Parliamentary Oscillators," 73; *Poems* (1797), 29, 110; *Poems on Various Subjects* (1796), 29, 108, 110; "The Plot Discovered," 105; "Reflections on Having Left a Place of Retirement," 29, 41, 63; Review of *The Monk*, 44; "The Rime of the Ancient Mariner," 9, 39, 40, 95–103, 108–9, 111, 114–17, 121, 168, 177; *Sibylline Leaves*, 39, 55, 62, 67, 88, 92, 101; "To the Author of 'The Robbers,'" 107–8; "To a Friend," 58; "To the Rev. George Coleridge," 78; "Vision of the Maid of Orleans," 41, 59, 70, 109; *Watchman*, 70, 82
Collins, William, 111
Colmer, J., 16n
Conder, Josiah, 173–76, 177, 189
Cooke, Margaret, 106n
Corinthians, 61
Correggio, 100
Cottle, Joseph, 45, 56, 63, 110, 113
Courier, 100, 131, 144, 146
Critical Review, 44, 84, 100
Croker, John, 128, 139, 162–63, 165, 176, 177
Crompton, Peter, 158n
Cruikshank, Isaac and George, 134
Curry, Kenneth, 56n
Curtis, Jared, 30n, 33

Daniel, Samuel, 139, 140
Dante, 112, 116
Darbishire, Helen, 183n
Darwin, Erasmus, 48
Davies, Scrope, 127, 130, 161
Davis, Richard, 62n
Day, Alexander, 187
Deane, Seamus, 17n
de Man, Paul, 51
Derrida, Jacques, 9, 27–28
Desmoulins, Camille, 115
Dilettanti Society, 177
discourse, public, 11–31, 37–39
Dowden, Wilfred, 165n
Drayton, Michael, 139, 140
Dryden, John, 34, 111, 125, 135, 150, 165, 166
Duff, David, 147n
Dyer, George, 43n

Eagleton, Terry, 12, 169n
Eaton, Daniel Isaac, 12, 124
Eclectic Review, 131, 173–75
Edinburgh Review, 40, 45, 97, 124, 131, 141, 146, 148, 150, 189
Eldon, Lord, 143
Elgin, Lord, 184–89
Elgin Marbles, 168, 177, 179, 181–92, 197, 200, 201, 204, 208
Ellis, George, 69n
Elmes, James, 183, 192–94, 197, 199, 200, 202. See also *Annals of the Fine Arts*
Emmet, Robert, 160
Empson, William, 95
Erdman, David V., 11, 30, 70n, 72–73, 80n, 95, 129n, 156
Erskine, Thomas, 3–4, 17, 52, 86
Estlin, J. P., 46
European Magazine, 44
Evans, B. Ifor, 76n
The Examiner, 41, 124–26, 131–32, 135, 143, 146–50, 162, 163, 179, 185, 188, 194, 208, 209; "The Bellman v. The Laureate," 72, 136–37; "Death and Funeral of the Late Mr. Southey," 146–47, 150; "Heaven Made a Party to Earthly Disputes," 154–56; "The Laureate Laid Double," 139–41, 150; "Parliamentary Profiles," 159; "Young Poets," 170. *See also* Hunt, Lee

Farington, Joseph, 187
Favret, Mary, 37n
Ferry, Anne, 29n, 46, 102
Fischer, Doucet, 29n, 138
Fisher, Philip, 179
Flaxman, John, 169n, 186n, 187, 188
Foakes, Reginald, 17n, 181n
Foot, Michael, 157n
Foucault, Michel, 9, 22–26, 28
Fox, Charles James, 18, 178
Frere, John H., 69n, 71, 127, 140, 142, 161, 163, 165
Fulford, Tim, 59n

Garlitz, Barbara, 183n
Geertz, Clifford, 38n
Genette, Gérard, 4–5, 27
George IV (Prince Regent), 46–47, 51, 136, 141, 156, 161, 164
Gibbon, Edward, 159

Gifford, William, 48, 51, 69n, 71, 133, 162
Gillray, James, 48, 56, 69–70
Gisborne, John, 149
Godwin, William, 12, 21, 58, 60, 61, 82, 107, 124, 164–65; *Life of Chaucer*, 111–13; *Political Justice*, 16, 20, 87
Goethe, Johann Wolfgang, 98
Goslee, Nancy, 169n
Graham, Peter, 128n, 142
Gray, Thomas, 104
Griffin, Dustin, 12n
Grigely, Joseph, 40n
Griggs, E. L., 59

Habbakuk, 65n
Habermas, Jürgen, 8–9, 11–13, 15, 16, 21, 23, 50, 53–54
Hackwood, Frederick, 163n
Hamilton, Paul, 169n, 177n
Hardy, Thomas, 198
Harrington, James, 17, 30, 156
Hartley, David, 58
Haydon, Benjamin Robert, 10, 168, 170, 177, 178, 181, 188, 191, 193, 197; *Annals of the Fine Arts*, 172, 183, 193, 197, 200, 202, 203, 208; *Autobiography*, 132, 184–86, 192
Hazlitt, William, 10, 14, 35, 56, 61, 109, 131, 136, 138, 165, 170, 173, 176, 177, 188n, 202; "An Account of Sir Joshua Reynolds' Discourses," 41, 168, 178, 181, 200–201; "The Elgin Marbles," 179, 188–89, 208; "On the Elgin Marbles," 190; "Fine Arts," 190; *Lectures on the Dramatic Literature of the Reign of Queen Elizabeth*, 98–99; *Lectures on the English Poets*, 97–98, 100, 175–76, 195; "Letter to William Gifford," 47, 48, 51; Review of *Biographia Literaria*, 94; Review of *Christabel*, 40; Review of *Letter to William Smith*, 146, 148–51; Review of Schlegel's *Lectures on Dramatic Literature*, 189–90, 205; *The Spirit of the Age*, 203; *The Round Table*, 194; "On Gusto," 194; "What is the People?" 16
Heath, William, 103
Heinzelman, Kurt, 101n, 135n
"Hey Diddle Diddle," 132–33
Hill, Herbert, 127
Hoagwood, Terrance, 70n
Hobbes, Thomas, 107

Hobhouse, John Cam, 127, 128, 129n, 130, 142n, 160–61, 165
Hogan, Charles Beecher, 13n, 106n
Hogg, James, 135, 139
Holcroft, Thomas, 164
Hollander, John, 52
Hone, William, 124, 143, 163–65
Horsley, Bishop, 65
House, Humphrey, 95, 109
Howe, P. P., 194n, 200n
Hume, David, 181
Hunt, Henry, 126, 129, 143, 173
Hunt, Leigh, 112, 127, 129n, 131, 135–41, 150, 157, 159, 165, 170–74; *Autobiography of Leigh Hunt*, 163; *Foliage*, 149, 172; *The Story of Rimini*, 47, 167, 172. See also *Examiner*; *Indicator*
Hyde, M. H., 158

Illuminati, 76, 99–100, 106
Inchbald, Mrs., 107
Indicator, 174
Isaiah, 34–35

Jack, Ian, 192
Jeffrey, Francis, 98–100, 109, 131, 143, 152, 165, 175–76, 177
Johnson, E.D.H., 161n
Johnson, Joseph, 55, 60, 67–68, 77, 78
Johnson, Samuel, 17, 80, 111, 133, 197
Johnston, Kenneth, 120n
Jonson, Ben, 139, 140
Joseph, M. K., 123n, 149n
Joyce, James, 27, 30

Kandl, John, 41n
Kant, Immanuel, 27–28, 99, 148
Keach, William, 140, 176n
Keane, Patrick, 95n
Keats, John, 53, 188; *Endymion*, 43, 167, 171–73, 174n, 176, 177n, 181, 182n, 194, 201; "On First Looking into Chapman's Homer," 41; "Hyperion," 198–99; *Lamia*, 42, 173, 174, 205; "Ode to a Grecian Urn," 8, 10, 28, 41, 52, 168–70, 192, 194, 202–10; "Ode on a Nightingale," 41, 192; "To one who has been long in city pent," 41; *Poems* (1817), 173; "On Seeing the Elgin Marbles," 190
Kelley, Teresa, 186n
Kelsall, Malcolm, 157n

Kinnaird, Douglas, 127
Kitson, Peter, 62n
Klancher, Jon, 11n, 14–15
Kneale, Douglas, 50n
Knight, Richard Payne, 10, 168, 177, 187, 188, 199, 203; *Analytical Inquiry*, 50, 181–82; *The Progress of Civil Society*, 48, 179–81, 183; *Specimens of Antient Sculpture*, 182–83, 198; *The Worship of Priapus*, 178
Kotzebue, August von, 13, 98, 100, 106

Lamb, Charles, 9, 45, 54, 56–58, 63, 69, 110, 132, 133
Lawrence, Sir Thomas, 187
Leader, Zachary, 40n
Lépeaux, Louis La Révellière, 69–70, 84, 164
Lessing, Gotthold, 98
letter, 37–39, 42–53, 58–62
Levinson, Marjorie, 35n, 177n
Lewis, Matthew, 44
Literary Gazette, 125
Liu, Alan, 5–6
Lloyd, Charles, 45, 54, 56–58, 63, 69, 110
Locke, John, 17
Lockhart, John G., 47, 167–68, 171n, 172n, 173, 174, 177, 193; *A Letter to . . . Lord Byron*, 161–62, 163, 165. See also *Blackwood's*
London Corresponding Society, 16, 73, 198
London Magazine, 190
Luther, Martin, 61, 164

Mackintosh, James, 46
Macpherson, James, 48, 96
Maginn, William, 167
Malthus, Thomas, 47–48
Manning, Peter, 123n
Marchand, Leslie, 142n, 161n
Marshall, William, 41n
Martyn, John, 34–35
Marvel, Andrew, 30
Mathias, T. J., 99
Matthew, 87
McDowell, R. B., 15n
McGann, Jerome, 14, 39n, 40, 95, 123n, 129n, 134n, 157, 169n
mediation, 27, 52
Merivale, John, 140
Messman, Frank, 177n

Michaelanglo, 201
Milman, Henry, 162
Milton, John, 30–31, 52, 61, 81, 109, 111, 124, 130, 132, 135, 166; "Animadversions . . . ," 151; "On Education," 99n; "On the Morning of Christ's Nativity," 34; *Paradise Lost*, 53, 61, 64, 66, 104, 153–58
Mitchell, L. G., 147
Monthly Magazine, 41, 43n, 69, 102, 106, 108
Monthly Mirror, 44
Moore, Thomas, 127, 149, 160, 171, 173
More, Hannah, 106
Morning Chronicle, 105, 138
Morning Post, 41, 42, 55, 56, 59, 60, 67, 69, 70, 72–73, 79, 80n, 90, 100, 108, 131
Moses, Henry, 178
Mother Goose's Melody, 132
motto, 46, 52
Mounier, Jean-Joseph, 99n
Murray, John, 122–24, 127–29, 141, 147, 160–66

Napoleon, 30, 112, 151
Negt, Oskar, and Alexander Kluge, 12n
Newlyn, Lucy, 51n
Newton, Isaac, 132
Nicholson, Andrew, 132n, 134n

O'Connor, Arthur, 73
Ogilby, John, 34
Olney, Clarke, 194n, 200n
Opie, Amelia, 56
Opie, Iona and Peter, 133n
Ovid, 174

Paine, Thomas, 17, 60, 76, 86, 94, 164; *Age of Reason*, 84; *Rights of Man*, 3, 15, 20, 47, 49, 52
Paley, William, 17
paratext, 4–5, 27
Paulson, Ronald, 115
Peacock, Thomas Love, 149, 178
Peck, Louis, 44
Penny, Nicholas, 194n
Perceval, Spencer, 20
Percy, Thomas, 133
Perri, Carmela, 48
Phillips, Richard, 43, 45
Phinney, A. W., 186n
Pitt, William, 22, 71, 74, 124, 158, 164
Plato, 65, 168, 181

Plunket, William, 158, 165
Poetic Mirror, 139
Poetry of the Anti-Jacobin, 41, 42n, 55, 134n, 164
Pollin, Burton, 57
Poole, Thomas, 45, 103
Pope, Alexander, 41, 50, 111, 124, 125, 135, 150, 163, 165, 166
Pope, Willard Bissell, 185n
Pratt, Willis, 131n, 133n
Price, Richard, 13, 81, 83, 84
Prichard, Mari, 133n
Priestley, Joseph, 43n, 58, 62, 65, 84, 93, 164
Pulci, Luigi, 140
Pye, Henry, 131, 133–34, 136

Quarterly Review, 125, 127, 128, 147, 151, 165, 176, 191, 192, 199, 203, 208, 209, 210
Quintilian, 20, 50
Quixote, Don, 146–47, 148, 149

Raphael, 100, 208, 209
Reeves, John, 22
Reiman, Donald, 36n, 39n, 138n
Republican, The, 20
A Review of Blackwood's Edinburgh Magazine for October 1817, 171n
Reynolds, John Hamilton, 170
Reynolds, Sir Joshua, 10, 41, 168, 169, 178, 181, 184, 186, 188, 189, 192, 194, 200–202
Ribeiro, Aileen, 194
Ridenour, George M., 123n
Robbins, Bruce, 12n
Robespierre, Maximilien, 115
Robinson, Crabb, 99
Robinson, Mary, 43n
Robinson, Nicholas, 147n
Robison, John, 99–100
Roe, Nicholas, 73, 208
Rogers, Samuel, 127
Rooke, Barbara, 40n, 76n
Rose, William, 140
Rosenfield, Sybil, 106n
Rousseau, G. S., 178n
Rousseau, J. J., 76, 84
Royal Academy, 168, 172, 178, 193, 195, 202
Ryan, Robert M., 168n

St Clair, William, 130n, 177n, 186n
St. Paul, 61, 128
Sambrook, James, 197n
Samuel, 153, 156, 158
Schiller, Friedrich von, 48, 98, 100, 104–9,
Schlegel, August Wilhelm von, 189
Scott, Grant, 186
Scott, John, 14, 179. See also *The Champion*
Scott, Walter, 14, 102, 154, 161
Scrivener, Michael, 18, 19n, 45
Seward, Anna, 43n
Shakespeare 35, 52, 97n, 99n, 108, 124, 131,
   133, 139–40
Sharp, Ronald, 168n
Shelley, Percy, 17, 36, 41, 148–49, 169n,
   170, 174, 178, 181
Sheridan, Richard B., 13, 102–3, 106
Sibylline Fragments, 34
Sidney, Algernon, 156
signature, 42–46
Siskin, Clifford, 23n
Skinner, Quentin, 25
Smith, Charlotte, 43n
Smith, Olivia, 13n, 163n
Smith, William, 48, 62, 143–48
"A Song of Sixpence," 132–34
Southey, Robert, 10, 17, 43, 51, 57, 63, 100,
   101, 102, 107, 109, 122–66, 167; *The An-
   nual Anthology*, 9, 46, 54–56, 58–59,
   61–64, 110; "Carmen Triumphale," 135;
   "On Evangelical Sects," 151; "Inscription
   for the Apartment . . . Martin," 134; *Joan
   of Arc*, 14, 30, 41, 56, 69, 70, 87; *Lay of the
   Laureate*, 130, 138–42, 149; *Letter to
   William Smith*, 47, 144–50; *Letters from
   England*, 56, 142, 143n; "To My Own
   Miniature Picture," 131–32, 137, 139;
   Poems (1797), 47, 110, 132; "The Poet's
   Pilgrimage to Waterloo," 140; "The Sol-
   dier's Wife," 71, 136; *Thalaba*, 98; "A Vi-
   sion of Judgment," 46, 51; *Wat Tyler*, 47,
   56, 130, 135, 143–47; "The Widow," 134
Spence, Thomas, 12, 18–19, 124
Spenser, Edmund, 116, 135, 139, 140, 155,
   175
Spinoza, Baruch, 93
Steevens, George, 133, 165
Steffan, T. G., 128n, 131n, 133n
Stillinger, Jack, 39–40, 42, 54n, 85
Strout, A. L., 167n
Stuart, Daniel, 60, 72

Sullivan, Alvin, 42n, 192n
Summerfield, Geoffrey, 133
Swift, Jonathan, 81, 125, 163

Taylor, Jeremy, 34
Taylor, John, 176, 181
Taylor, Thomas, 43n
Taylor, William, 55, 56, 102
Thelwall, John, 15, 18–19, 43n, 45, 60, 61,
   82, 105, 124, 164
Thompson, E. P., 73
Thomson, James, 197–98, 199
Thoreau, Henry David, 101n
Thorpe, James, 40
Tillyard, 95, 168
Todd, William, 15n
Tooke, Horne, 69, 111
Townshend, C. H., 127
Tully, James, 25n
Tyson, Gerald, 68n
Tytler, A. F., 104–5

Vane, Henry, 30
Vassallo, Peter, 141
Vendler, Helen, 207
Virgil, 32–36, 52

Wakefield, Gilbert, 68
Warren, Robert Penn, 95
Weishaupt, Adam, 99–100
Wellington, Arthur Wellesley, Duke of, 125
West, Benjamin, 187–88, 191, 196, 203
Westminster Review, 129
Wheatley, Phillis, 7
Whitehead, William, 131
Wickwar, William, 13, 14n, 20n, 62n
Williams, Helen Maria, 17
Willoughby, L. A., 106n
Wilson, John, 148, 165
Winckelmann, 169n, 184, 186n
Wollstonecraft, Mary, 17, 47, 69
Wood, Marcus, 133–34, 163n
Woodring, Carl, 11, 81n, 95, 97, 168
Wordsworth, Dorothy, 54
Wordsworth, William, 14, 39, 50–52, 63,
   66, 67, 102, 124, 126, 132, 150, 161,
   171,181n; "Complaint of the Forsaken
   Indian Woman," 109; "The Convict," 42,
   109, 120; "Elegiac Stanzas . . . Peel Cas-
   tle," 31–33; "Epistle to Sir George Beau-
   mont," 76; *The Excursion*, 152, 155; "The

Female Vagrant," 109, 113–20; "Home at Grasmere," 155; "The Idiot Boy," 100; "The Last of the Flock," 109; "Lines . . . Tintern Abbey," 42, 53, 67, 109, 110; "Lines left upon a Seat," 109; "London 1802," 29, 156–58; *Lyrical Ballads* (1798), 9, 41, 42, 46, 55, 96–97, 100–3, 109–21; "The Mad Mother," 42, 109; "Michael," 34; "Occasioned by the Battle of Waterloo," 154; "Ode" ("Immortality Ode"), 9, 31–36, 53; "Old Man Traveling," 109; "Peter Bell," 113; *Poems in Two Volumes*, 9, 30n, 31, 33, 132, 156; Preface to *Lyrical Ballads*, 106; *The Prelude*, 45, 116; "The Ruined Cottage," 54, 113; "Salisbury Plain" (*see also* "The Female Vagrant," this rubric), 113–14; "The Siege of Vienna Raised," 154; *Sonnets* (1838), 30; "The Thorn," 116; "Vaudracour and Julia," 17; "Written in March . . . Brothers Water," 132
Wu, Duncan, 34
Wynn, C. W. W., 127–28

Young, Edward, 111

Zeller, Hans, 40

Paul Magnuson is Professor of English at New York University and the author of *Coleridge's Nightmare Poetry* (Virginia 1974) and *Coleridge and Wordsworth: A Lyrical Dialogue* (Princeton 1988).